China's Fintech Explosion

CHINA'S FINTECH EXPLOSION

Disruption, Innovation, and Survival

Sara Hsu and Jianjun Li

Columbia University Press
New York

Columbia University Press
Publishers Since 1893
New York   Chichester, West Sussex
cup.columbia.edu
Copyright © 2020 Columbia University Press
All rights reserved
Library of Congress Cataloging-in-Publication Data

Names: Hsu, Sara, author.
Title: China's fintech explosion : disruption, innovation, and survival /
Sara Hsu and Jianjun Li.
Description: New York : Columbia University Press, [2020] |
Includes bibliographical references and index.
Identifiers: LCCN 2019057856 (print) | LCCN 2019057857 (ebook) |
ISBN 9780231196567 (cloth) | ISBN 9780231551717 (ebook)
Subjects: LCSH: Finance—China. | Finance—Technological
innovations—China. | Financial services industry—Technological
innovations—China.
Classification: LCC HG187.C6 H78 2020 (print) |
LCC HG187.C6 (ebook) | DDC 332.0951–dc23
LC record available at https://lccn.loc.gov/2019057856
LC ebook record available at https://lccn.loc.gov/2019057857

Columbia University Press books are printed on permanent
and durable acid-free paper.
Printed in the United States of America

Cover design: Noah Arlow

Contents

Preface

FRESHLY MINTED college graduates starting their own tech companies. An industry awash with venture capital. Disruption of traditional business. Money for new luxuries. These phrases describe aspects of the dot.com boom in New York City's Silicon Alley in the late 1990s, during which time I obtained my first job after graduating from Wellesley College. I worked as a product manager for a financial technology (fintech) company that was eventually acquired by Western Union. The atmosphere was one of exuberance and success. Young people were shaking up the traditional ways of doing business, in an environment of constant invention.

The same feeling is pervasive today in China's innovation hot spots, especially those that house China's rapidly changing fintech industry. The feeling that the potential for invention and profit is limitless permeates the air at China's major fintech firms, such as Alipay and CreditEase. At the Lang Di Fintech Conference in Shanghai, crowds clamor to hear what fintech CEOs and COOs are talking about, because it could change the way they conduct financial transactions in a matter of months, if it hasn't already. After speaking with CEOs at the conference, I feel confident that fintech will help China develop its financial sector far more rapidly than it otherwise would be able to.

When I was in graduate school in the early 2000s, I traveled to China and noticed the many small sellers of goods along the street and in local shops. I wondered how, in a credit-constrained environment, these sellers could obtain funding for their enterprises. I did some preliminary research and found that they were forced to borrow from the curb, or informal, market. When I came back to the United States,

I chose the topic of informal finance in China as my dissertation thesis. I asked Professor Jianjun Li of the Central University of Finance and Economics to help me with the study, and we later collaborated on a book about informal finance, with contributions from the leading U.S. and Chinese scholars on the subject. Since then, I have written a lot on the topic of nontraditional finance, including shadow banking, and now fintech, each of which has striven to serve underserved areas of the economy.

Fintech is the next frontier of inclusive finance and Chinese financial development. Cutting-edge technological and business innovations compete in this space. Although many traditional banks have embraced the use of fintech, the fintech industry still features an element of rapid growth and innovation, an aspect that diverges from the development of mainstream finance. Better use of big data and the widespread use of mobile phones have promoted China's fintech industry, expanding financial knowledge and application ever wider. This fills me with excitement, seeing a new and cutting-edge industry transform the way finance is done. It's personal for me, reinforcing my life experiences that have brought me to this point. I hope that you will enjoy reading this book as much as I have enjoyed researching and writing it.

Sara Hsu
New Paltz, NY
October 2019

Acknowledgments

I WISH to thank Beibei Sun for helping me connect with Chinese fintech firms. Beibei has been a constant source of support for this project and source of insight as an experienced PR executive who knows the ins and outs of the Chinese fintech industry. Thanks to others at Lendit, including Shawn Yu and Bo Brustkern.

Thanks so much to Jiaqian Liu for her tremendous assistance in supplying data. Without her help, we would not have some of the wonderful tables and figures that are included in this book. We are also grateful to Shuyuan Zhou for her assistance in helping conduct Chinese language research. Thanks to Shan He and Xun Han.

Myles Thompson and Brian Smith at Columbia University Press have been encouraging supporters of this book. We appreciate their efforts in making the publishing process easy and fun.

I want to acknowledge my coworkers at Speedpay, a U.S.-based payments firm, where I worked in the late 1990s, for helping me to understand the ins and outs and appreciate the importance of fintech. They are Darren Manelski, Marc Mehl, Albert Lingelbach, Gabriel Nichols, Alexis Blackstead, Sruli Shaffren, and Chaim Drellich. We knew the hardship of working '996' first during the dot.com boom in New York City.

Thanks also to my professors for shaping my thinking and encouraging me: Stephen Reynolds, David Kiefer, E. K. Hunt, Gabriel Lozada, Karl Case, and James Galbraith. And thanks to my colleagues at SUNY New Paltz for their support: Edith Kuiper, Mona Ali, Hamid Azari, Simin Mozayeni, Laura Ebert, Jonathan Schwartz, Kristine Harris, Akira Shimada, Lauren Meeker, Nathen Clerici, Elizabeth Brotherton,

Sunita Bose, David Elstein, Melissa Rock, and Sun Hee Kil. Let us raise a glass to free and open thought, and to exploratory research.

Last but not least, many thanks to my loving family—Joyce Keller, John Hsu, and Asya Hsu—for keeping me sane during the writing of this book.

—Sara Hsu

I want to thank Sicong Wang, the former CEO of Yilong Dai, and Qian Wang, the vice general manager of Yilong Dai, who helped us visit Yilong Dai and revise the case study.

Dean Zhenhua Li of Ant Financial Institute and the fellows Yanyan and Chengcheng Feng at Ant Financial Institute gave us assistance in investigating the Ant Financial operations and helped us perfect the Ant Financial case study.

—Jianjun Li

China's Fintech Explosion

CHAPTER ONE

Overview of China's Fintech Industry

FINANCIAL TECHNOLOGY, or fintech, increasingly boasts innovations that incorporate big data analysis, blockchain, and cloud computing, all of which have amplified the performance of traditional internet transactions, into financial services. These innovations have much transformative potential, especially in China.

China's fintech industry has grown massively in recent years, taking shape from an industry providing electronic payment and risky loan services to a more integrated system with major banks and better regulation to control risks. Fintech has grown not only to complement traditional banking services in China but also to fill the gaps that the mainly state-owned banking sector could not fill. The state-owned banking sector has preferred to cater to larger and state-owned firms, carrying out government policy directives as needed. State-owned banks have not been able to provide loans consistently to smaller firms and poorer individuals, and fintech has stepped in to address these needs.

The growth of fintech has supported China's structural change process as the nation has become more consumption oriented. The Asian nation has moved away from its focus on production of low-value-added goods as a source of growth to a focus on consumption. As it has done so, incomes and standards of living have risen. As such, people are demanding better access to funding and financial tools.

Fintech began in the West, with the online checking account offered by Wells Fargo in 1995; the first virtual bank, ING Direct in Canada, in 1997; the launch of PayPal in 1998; and the launch of Prosper and Lending Club in 2006 and 2007, respectively. The global financial crisis of 2008 has been widely viewed as a financial industry disruptor that changed the way consumers viewed banks. Banks lost their footing and were forced to comply with new regulations, and simultaneously, consumers lost their faith in banks. This loss of faith, coupled with the advent of new internet financial firms without the same regulatory and capital constraints, paved the way for the rise of fintech.

Millennials have been quick to embrace the new technologies, using fintech apps such as Venmo and Apple Pay in the United States, and obtaining lower interest rate personal loans from lending platforms like Lending Club and Prosper. Traditional banks have been forced to add online components to compete with fintech companies. For example, in October 2017 TD Group set aside $3.5 million to finance fintech endeavors, and other banks are doing the same. Banking has increasingly become a non-physical-consumer experience.

All of this is happening in China as well. Fintech has exploded in the Asian nation and has received an increasing amount of attention and funding. By 2016, China represented 47 percent of global fintech investments. One aspect of Chinese fintech, peer-to-peer (P2P) lending, has grown from 31 billion renminbi (RMB) in January 2014 to 856 billion RMB in January 2017.[1] In three years, P2P lending increased twenty-seven-fold. By 2017, the total amount of P2P loans hit 1.2 trillion RMB.

Notably, fintech in China has helped to make up for an underdeveloped financial sector that has been unable to accommodate all consumers and firms that demand financing. Individuals and small and medium-size enterprises (SMEs), for example, frequently were unable to obtain sufficient loans to carry out business or personal activities. Additionally, unlike nations in the Western hemisphere, China did not experience a diffusion of credit card usage. Most people had to rely on cash or debit cards and were not privy to lines of credit. Individuals could not easily access credit for consumption or emergency purposes. Finally, some elements of finance are lacking in China, particularly profitable financial investments. Even China's stock market is dominated by state-owned or -related institutions, and both government intervention and a lack of institutional investors have kept a lid on real profits. Firms and consumers have needed alternative investment products that can earn them a better rate of return than a bank deposit account.

For these reasons, fintech has been wildly popular in China. Fintech firms have rushed to assist a swathe of consumers and small firms with little to no bank credit history and high levels of demand. Fintech firms generally strive to stay out of the deposit-taking business and to offer customers better returns on investment than other outlets. Customers have flocked to these firms, seeking loans, ease of payment, and investment profits.

This book focuses mainly on mainland China and its experiences with fintech, although some information is included on the Hong Kong fintech industry as well, which is also booming. In terms of location, the types and performance of the firms sharply contrast, and this provides us with somewhat of an alternative paradigm.

The sector is quite new and has undergone massive changes. It's hot right now, attracting lots of private investment as well as public support. There is much to chronicle, and, as such, this book provides a story of China's fintech industry based on several primary and secondary sources. Primary sources include interviews with fintech industry insiders, including firm CEOs, and newspaper articles. Secondary sources include government and private sector research reports and academic articles written about the industry, written in both Chinese and English.

In the book, we will cover the topics of digital payment systems, P2P lending and crowdfunding, credit card issuance and internet banks, blockchain finance and virtual currencies, online investment and insurance, disruption of traditional banking, and risks of fintech and regulatory technology. We find the subject massively interesting, and hope that this passion is reflected in this work, one of the first publications on the industry as a whole.

Stages of Growth in Chinese Fintech

A clear guide to China's fintech industry's stages of growth does not exist, but we can make some generalizations. We can classify the periods of development into three stages: early growth stage (pre-2013), the diversification stage (2013–2016), and the legitimization stage (2017–the present).

In the early growth stage before 2013, internet-based finance was in its nascent development, arising in the 2000s with the advent of companies like Ant Financial/Alipay and PPDAI Group. The success of these early entrants was key in gaining support from customers and investors, as people were able to witness the benefits of using fintech in their everyday lives. Also, during this time, massive upward growth in e-commerce began around 2010, multiplying the number of internet users and the potential market for fintech. Using the internet to pay for goods and services gradually became second nature for many consumers, and extending this habit to loans and other fintech services was a natural next step.[2]

Over this period, shadow banking, of which P2P lending was a part, was not subject to extensive regulation. Shadow banking encompassed a number of nonbank financial activities, and even some nontraditional activities within banks themselves. For these shadow-banking institutions, credit risks were hard to manage for firms that lacked access to proprietary consumer data, and technology was not yet sufficiently advanced to allow firms to make use of noncustomary data, such as social media data. Therefore, the industry was underdeveloped in terms of both risk management and regulation, which made it difficult for many firms to survive. Regulators allowed the industry to grow to expand the reach of inclusive finance, until fintech, and particularly the P2P industry with it, became overly risky and systemically important years later.

The diversification stage was ushered in in 2013 and lasted through 2016. Some regulation was implemented in that year, and seventy-five P2P lending platforms defaulted. Despite this initial regulation, sufficient risk-based modeling was not in common use yet, and many smaller fintech companies continued to have poor control over their customers' credit risks. Over this period of time, firms gradually improved their credit risk models by accessing big data through mobile phones and creating innovative risk modeling applications. The problem of customer credit risk was, by the end of this period, greatly resolved for the larger fintech companies.

During the diversification period, a number of new types of fintech firms arose. These included online credit card firms, insuretech, and blockchain fintech firms. Some of these companies were funded by the larger e-commerce firms like Alibaba Group Holding Limited (Alibaba) and Tencent Holdings Limited (Tencent), as well as by private investors. The fintech sector diversified over this period, as regulation continued to be somewhat light. Newer types of firms, many times started by former banking executives, often had more sophisticated business models and used technology to create credit profiles for underbanked customers.

Notably, the rest of China's financial sector was undergoing rising risks and volatility over this period, which contributed to an understanding within the fintech sector that meeting customer demand while controlling for risks should be a main focus. The trust industry, a large component of shadow banking, went through a period of defaults in 2013. By 2014, the Chinese government had set up a fund to bail out failing trust companies. In 2015, China's stock market experienced a meltdown that required government intervention to put a floor on the losses. Needless to say, regulators had their hands full administering to the financial sector outside of the fintech industry. Fintech regulation, however, would be a key focus in the next period, starting in 2017.

The legitimization stage began in 2017 and brought China to a new level of maturity in the fintech industry, as this interval introduced different dynamics. In 2017, the fintech sector was rocked when a new set of regulations was imposed on the P2P lending sector, forcing the companies to come into compliance by the following year. This set of regulations made it compulsory for P2P lending firms to register with local authorities the following year, bringing these shadowy entities into the light.

Although P2P regulations had been imposed in 2016 as well, the 2017 rules would bring existing P2P firms into legitimacy; in addition, the government warned at the outset of 2017 that the P2P regulations would be so strict that 90 percent could fail that year.[3] Many of these firms did fail because they could not comply with the regulations, and such failures created, to some extent, a drag on the growth of other fintech firms that were connected to P2P lending firms through funding or reputation. Many P2P lending insiders believed that the industry would emerge healthier and stronger, and that controlling for risks had become a basic minimum requirement for Chinese fintech firms. A threat hung over the industry, however, that the government would shut down all P2P lending firms. By the end of 2018, there .were rumors that the government would wind down small and midsize P2P lending platforms and force larger platforms to cap outstanding loans and reduce them over time.[4]

By mid-2018, according to the China Financial Technology Enterprise Database, the number of companies in Beijing, Shanghai, and Shenzhen amounted to more than 2,500.[5] Looking at the concentration of fintech firms, the top five cities included those three as well as Hangzhou and Guangzhou. These top five cities have extensive financial infrastructure as well. The cities ranked six to twenty are as follows: Chengdu, Wuhan, Nanjing, Xiamen, Tianjin, Chongqing, Hefei, Qingdao, Ningbo, Changsha, Suzhou, Jinan, Xi'an, Zhengzhou, and Shijiazhuang.

In addition, different types of fintech sectors favor particular industries, as can be seen in table 1.1. The table shows the top-funded industry sectors by fintech model in China.

TABLE 1.1
Top Funded Industry Sectors by Model in China

Model	Industry Sector
Peer-to-Peer Consumer Lending	Retail and wholesale Manufacturing and engineering Finance, business, and professional services
Peer-to-Peer Business Lending	Manufacturing and engineering Retail and wholesale Real estate
Reward-Based Crowdfunding	Film and television Arts, Music, and Design High-tech industry
Balance Sheet Consumer Lending	Agriculture, forestry, and animal husbandry Internet and electricity providers Real estate
Balance Sheet Business Lending	Manufacturing and engineering Transport and utilities Agriculture, forestry, and animal husbandry

Source: Kieran Garvey et al., *Cultivating Growth: The Second Asia Pacific Region Alternative Finance Industry Report* (Cambridge Centre for Alternative Finance at University of Cambridge and Australian Centre for Financial Studies at Monash University, 2017), https:// australiancentre.com.au/wp-content/uploads/2017/09/Cutivating-growth.pdf.

Factors Prompting Growth in the Chinese Fintech Industry

Several elements came together to allow for the explosion of Chinese fintech. Without these key elements, it could be argued that the industry would not have grown nearly as rapidly.

The first element was the enormous spread of internet use across China, with many people using mobile phones to access the internet. Only 10.5 percent of Chinese people had access to the internet in 2006, whereas 53.2 percent had access in 2016.[6] The Chinese government strove to expand internet infrastructure to both urban and rural areas of the country to provide a foundation for this growth. Accessing financial services online became a critical part of carrying out everyday business. In 2016, Chinese customers spent 157.55 trillion RMB ($22.8 trillion) using mobile payments.[7] The rapid uptake in the use of the internet for financial services reflects the greater comfort the Chinese have inputting personal data online. Chinese consumers are more amenable to sharing information over the internet, in contrast to Western consumers, who have been more concerned with data safety.

Figure 1.1 illustrates the incredible expansion of the internet between 2007 and 2017 in terms of both scale and internet penetration rate. Between these years, the number of netizens grew by 562 million users.[8]

The second element prompting growth of the Chinese fintech industry was the expanded use of e-commerce. Certainly, this accompanied the expansion of the internet, but it also involved increased demand for online products. Alibaba was the first e-commerce company in China, originating in 1999 and growing rapidly over the 2000s and 2010s. Alibaba's use of Alipay for online payments and the company's expansion into wealth management products were pivotal moments. Customers used Alipay to pay for the goods online. Alipay was a subsidiary launched in 2004, which had more than fifty million users by 2007, which was more than the existing number of credit card users.[9] Alipay (along with WeChat Pay, a later rival) began to use QR codes in 2011, and this has since become a ubiquitous method of payment.

In addition, Alipay's growth into the wealth management product industry in June 2013 provided customers with a much-needed investment outlet from a trusted company. Customers who were receiving little in interest through their bank deposits were suddenly able to

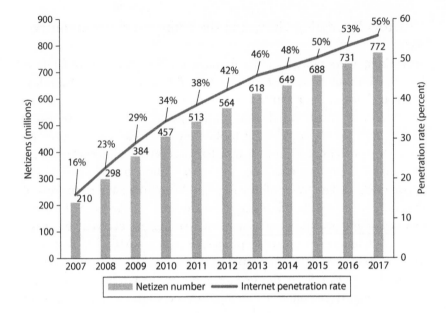

Figure 1.1 China's Netizen number and Internet penetration rate. *Source:* China Internet Information Center, China.org.cn.

easily invest funds without a large sum of money. This provided them with the ability to invest, a newfound financial capability. These events spurred by Alibaba's Alipay have brought to the fore the ubiquity of fintech in China, making it possible for myriad other businesses to gain the confidence of using internet applications for all of their financial needs.

The third element promoting use of fintech in China was the increasing use of social media and the interaction of fintech with social media apps. This factor acted as a kind of steroid that amplified e-commerce and financial technology. Social media, such as WeChat, could reach new consumers through advertising and person-to-person communication. This type of customer acquisition model has created an atmosphere in which fintech is deeply intertwined with individuals' everyday lives. The relationship has been self-reinforcing, as fintech firms have been able to access users' online history to determine which products consumers prefer and market directly to them via social media.

Leading fintech firms benefit from the use of social media by having lower costs in acquiring new customers, being able to obtain safer customers, and facing lower funding costs. Top fintech firms face lower advertising costs, and safer customers may be acquired due to existing information provided by data from online purchases and social media. As information is more available to investors, this has lowered funding costs and increased the number of investors interested in making their funds available for lending, particularly in the case of the P2P lending sector.

These days, fintech in China has transformed from a service used to complement e-commerce to a service that has, to a large degree, replaced regular traditional banking services, especially for SMEs and individuals. SMEs provide 60 percent of gross domestic product (GDP) but obtain only 20 percent of traditional bank loans. Locked outside of traditional credit channels, SMEs have been forced to find funding from the informal sector. Now, however, thanks to the availability of big data analytics, SMEs have been able to access loans at better interest rates. Consumers who previously had little credit history have been able to build up a credit history based on their activities, making use of financial technology.

Shadow Banking

In the early days of fintech, P2P lending and other aspects of fintech were classified by some experts, including the authors, as shadow banking. Shadow banking grew out of the need to access liquidity that banks could not, or would not, provide—could not, because of a lack of funding, and would not, because of high risks. As a result, firms like trust companies were providing financing to overleveraged and riskier sectors. The funds came from investors who were interested in obtaining a higher rate of return than they otherwise could receive in China's financial sector—hence, supply of and demand for funds both were large.

In the early days of development of the P2P sector, most P2P lending firms were truly shadowy. Although P2P lending firms were less involved in lending to real estate or mining sectors, both of which held excessive debt, they were as sloppy as other shadow-banking entities in terms of reducing risks. P2P firms lent to risky customers—some lending to pretty much anyone—and frequently failed to carry out due diligence to know their customer. To some extent, this was due to an absence of customer data, firm know-how, and firm capacity to meet their customers, especially if the client was far away. Some P2P firms even deliberately defrauded customers, using a business model that turned out to be no more than a Ponzi scheme. These firms cast a shadow over the legitimacy of the sector as a whole.

The P2P lending sector was lacking in information and skills for some time. Entrepreneurs were lured by the potential to make a profit off of other people's lending activity, often without sufficient financial or technical background. According to Joe Zhang, "when the online lending industry got started in China around 2011 to 2013, credit data was scarce and analytical skills even scarcer. One pioneer in the industry told me that most operators were 'simply shooting in the dark,' putting all their faith in their lending model and the magic in their financial machine."[10] These P2P lending firms generated a lot of risk under insufficient regulation and poor business models.

P2P lending platforms came under increased scrutiny in 2017 and 2018, and regulators required that these firms comply with more than one hundred requirements and register with the government to remain in business. The year 2018 was marked by a large number of P2P firm failures as a result, but the remaining companies were viewed as stronger and more legitimate.

Other shadowy risks came from the sale of products that were not based on sound underlying assets. These wealth management products, some of which have been viewed as excessively risky, were sold online as well as in person. As of 2018, about 13 percent of internet wealth management customers were purchasing bank wealth management products online.[11] These products were strenuously regulated several years after their introduction, as they were a core part of the shadow-banking sector and brought about the potential for systemic risk, because of inter-relatedness, ubiquity, and composition of risky products.

One major risk associated with such products is that investors expected that the wealth management products would carry an implicit guarantee of repayment, which was not the case, as regulators had signaled that they were willing to let such products fail if they encountered repayment issues. The widespread purchase of such risky products both online and offline created a problem before regulations were implemented wholesale, posing a danger to consumers and financial institutions regarding how potential product failures would be dealt with and how this might result in a run on all of these asset types.

This period of high systemic risk may be viewed as diminishing, as wealth management products have faced greater regulation. Several new rules have been released. For example, in July 2018, the China Banking and Insurance Regulatory Commission (CBIRC) released draft rules on how commercial banks' wealth management products should be regulated. The rules specifically targeted the elimination of banks' practice of providing investors with implicit guarantees. Rules on asset management products, including wealth management products, had been laid out previously in November 2017. The rules placed limits on leverage for asset management products and prevented investors from using their asset management products as collateral. They also stopped financial institutions from creating a cash pool with income from asset management products, used to pay off existing products.

Now that the P2P and internet financial sectors have been better regulated, they are moving out of the shadows and into the mainstream digital finance sector. This is essential, as internet finance has a growing number of users and is becoming increasingly important to China's economy. This is in line with the government's attempts to promote internet finance while simultaneously reducing financial risks.

Major Firm Disruptors

Many disruptors have positively shaped the fintech sector; China is home to several major firm disruptors that have changed the way in which banking and finance are carried out on a day-to-day basis. These firms have forced the traditional banking sector to cater to a growing online customer base and to innovate outside of its comfort zone. They also have reached underserved populations and created new products that serve some of China's most pressing financial demands.

Alibaba's Ant Financial is the oldest one of these disruptors, and its competitors constantly challenge it to remake its business model. Ant Financial's focus has been its customers, and the company has developed metrics to measure customer satisfaction. This is a major reason for its success. Alipay plays a major role in the electronic payments sector in China. The scale of digital payments is massive and continuing to grow, as customers use the service to purchase goods online as well as offline. Ant Financial also specializes in wealth management, housing the world's largest money market fund to help its clients easily invest their savings and earn higher returns than bank accounts provide. In these ways, the firm has changed the way people think about commerce and investment, creating savvier customers by the day.

Tencent has remained a strong competitor of Alibaba, and this competition has given rise to enormous innovation. According to economic theory, competition among a few large firms with lots of market share (an oligopoly) can lead to major strides in innovation. This is certainly true of Tencent, which has developed WeChat Pay and a wealth management business, both of which compete heavily with Ant Financial. Tencent's Licaitong, its wealth management business, has seen its money market fund triple within the three years leading up to January 2018.[12] Tencent has set up a digital trading platform for Chinese bonds called Qtrade.[13] Traders use Tencent's QQ messaging app to communicate before they make a trade, and the new app allows traders to complete trades using a streamlined application. The heavy competition has given rise to constant innovations in the digital payments and online investment space.

ZhongAn Online P&C Insurance (ZhongAn) was China's first online-only insurance company, creating a new industry called insuretech. The company was founded by Alibaba's Jack Ma and Tencent's Pony Ma. ZhongAn has built a strong customer base using big data and artificial intelligence, capturing much of the auto insurance segment. ZhongAn has changed the way that Chinese consumers think about insurance, as it offers innovative products such as travel insurance and product return insurance. The firm has forced traditional Chinese insurers to change their marketing strategy to selling goods online to reach younger and tech-wise consumers. Its approach also helps to reach more customers, as China's insurance industry is still underdeveloped.

Qudian is a microlender backed by Alibaba. The company uses big data to model risk so that it can extend credit products like small cash and merchandise credit to underserved customers. Qudian uses both internal data from previous transactions and external data, such as consumption and delinquency history. Business is carried out fully online, and often mainly through mobile phones. Qudian's partnership with Ant Financial, until its demise in 2018, allowed it to obtain data about consumer credit and, in turn, to provide credit to Alipay customers in need of loans.[14] The company has boosted China's policy to ensure that more individuals have access to financial services. In turn, providing smaller clients with loans has helped to pull many Chinese households out of poverty.

Lufax (the Shanghai Lujiazui International Financial Asset Exchange) is one of the largest P2P lenders in China, matching borrowers to lenders. The company was founded in 2011 by Ping An Insurance, China's largest insurance firm, and has become a leader in the P2P lending industry because of its capacity to manage risk. Lufax also engages in a secondary trading business and sells securities to provide corporate finance. The business employs numerous technology specialists; more than half of its employees are engineers and coders. P2P lending companies have allowed smaller businesses and customers to gain access to loans. Its borrowers are individuals who otherwise would have to turn to the curb market to obtain most of their finance. For these customers, being able to access loans through Lufax's P2P lending platform has allowed them to improve their cash flow.

Technology Disruptors

If companies can act as major disruptors in the fintech industry, so, too, can technologies. Several technology disruptors have changed the way Chinese fintech firms do business. These include artificial intelligence (AI), blockchain, cloud computing, and big data (referred to as ABCD).

Artificial Intelligence

Coupled with large amounts of big data and the adaptability and speed of cloud computing, AI has changed the way that financial firms think about customer acquisition and retention and risk management. AI can allow firms to understand customer risks and potential fraud cases, better match customers with products, and interact with customers.

The scope of application of AI to China's financial field includes intelligent customer service, smart investment, intelligent risk control, intelligent investment research, and intelligent marketing. AI has been particularly useful in China, where consumer data are easy to obtain.

Consumer consent allows firms to access vast amounts of data transactions. In China's nonuniform world of credit-related data, including social media data, understanding credit risks is difficult without the use of AI. AI allows firms to analyze consumer relationships to predict potentially poor credit risks, and to do so in a way that is faster and more accurate than traditional means of inquiry. Some of these relationships are discernible only to machines and are not immediately recognizable to humans. This discernment greatly improves the usefulness of data while significantly lowering transaction costs for firms, allowing machines to carry out the most challenging part of finance's core business function, know your customer (KYC).

AI has come to the forefront in assisting investors and customers as well. Robo-advisors are automated investment advisors that can assist individuals in determining which investments are right for them. These assistants can continue to monitor asset prices in order to help customers meet their financial goals. Robo-advisors are also more cost effective for middle-class investors than personal financial advisors. Chatbots can face a wide range of customers to answer simple questions, and the use of this form of AI is becoming increasingly widespread in the financial industry around the world.

AI has been proven to help financial firms comply with regulation. AI also can help fintech firms gather and analyze information rapidly to ensure compliance. Investigation of potential fraudulent cases can be hastened and improved by the use of AI.

Blockchain

Blockchain is a technology with the potential to seriously disrupt the fintech industry. Although still in its early stages, the technology can greatly reduce the need for intermediaries, changing the way in which demand for and use of financial firms are shaped. In fact, blockchain technology can even remove the need for banks and fintech companies.

The blockchain is a distributed ledger (distributed across a network) made up of blocks that can be verified by anyone, whose transaction records are irreversible. The use of cryptography renders the exchanges secure. Trade and loan transactions as well as contracts can be included in the blockchain, eliminating the need for trusted third parties. The transparency and indelibility of the blockchain can remove the threat of fraud or money laundering.

Cloud Computing

Cloud computing has made fintech businesses lighter and more easily adaptable to different business scales. It allows businesses to use third-party technology and services as needed, thereby reducing the costs of technology. The business model of most cloud-computing firms is pay per use, so that clients can pay for the extent of services by transaction. The advantages to client firms of using cloud computing include reliability and scalability of services. This type of computing structure also can reduce the isolation of information in the financial industry and link technology components across institutional departments on a unified platform.

Within the cloud-computing technology architecture is the infrastructure and operating system. This infrastructure contains the data center infrastructure, physical resources, and virtual resources and refers to such things as computing, storage, and network. The cloud-computing operating system is a software system that allocates information technology (IT) resources. Cloud computing is growing in China. Sales in this sector accounted for 5 percent of China's IT market in 2014, but this is expected to rise to 20 percent by 2020.[15] Cloud computing is another priority technology sector for the government. Compared with the traditional banking computation model, which makes use of a mainframe and computers, cloud computing is far more cost effective.

As an example of a Chinese cloud-computing company, Alibaba uses cloud computing in Alibaba Cloud, which has six data centers throughout China. The subsidiary was deployed in 2009 and accounted for about a third of the cloud market in 2015. Larger financial institutions tend to use their own systems, coupled with cloud computing, whereas smaller institutions, including fintech companies, have gravitated toward a cloud-only model.

Big Data

Big data is comprised of large data sets that can be analyzed to reveal patterns and associations. Big data possesses the three qualities of high volume, high velocity, and high variety.[16] High volume means that there is a lot of data. High velocity means that data are created at a fast rate. High variety indicates that there are a lot of different types of data. The data can come from several sources, such as social media, machines like smart meters, and Global Positioning Satellite maps. Therefore, big data technology relies on a large amount of data in a wide range of formats, including text, photos, and videos.

The aim of big data analysis is to extract valuable information from the data, providing accurate evaluation, prediction, and improving operational efficiency. This technology helps financial institutions create dynamic decision-making scenarios, identify fraud, strengthen risk control and prediction, and understand customer needs to target marketing activities. Big data analysis is becoming increasingly important for firms that wish to remain competitive in an information-rich world.

Fintech firms can use big data to understand customers' risk profiles, minimize fraud, closely assess customer repayment capacity, personalize the application process, and speed up the credit decision. Big data can improve internal accountability and show auditors and regulators that a firm is compliant with existing rules.

Financial and Policy Support

Government officials have seen the success of firm disruptors and have gotten behind the industry as a whole both politically and financially. China's fintech sector has been lucky to have access to public funds to boost early and late-stage business development. For example, the central government raised $231 billion for start-up funding in 2015. China's government also provides incentives for high-tech firms, which pay only 60 percent of the normal enterprise tax rate and can earn a tax exemption on certain applications.

China's government has identified AI as a key policy priority and AI innovation hubs in Shanghai, Beijing, and Shenzhen have arisen. These include a state-owned venture capital firm in Shenzhen, which has raised $30 billion to fund new AI companies. In addition, Beijing will invest $2 billion in its AI industrial park, and Tianjin will invest $16 billion in the industry.[17]

The fintech sector has enjoyed the policy support of the Chinese government through a series of actions and plans promoting development of the industry. In 2015, the State Council released Internet

Plus and the *Guiding Opinions on Advancing the Healthy Development of Internet Finance* to integrate internet innovations into every industry, including finance.[18] In 2016, the National Development and Reform Commission laid out a plan to promote Internet Plus and AI. AI is to be developed in the areas of funding, system standardization, human resources, international cooperation, and intellectual property protection.

Policies include also the 13th Five-Year Development Plan for China's Financial Industry Information Technology, New Generation Artificial Intelligence Development Plan, and Three-Year Action Plan for the Development of Smart Industry (2018–2020). The 13th Five-Year Development Plan for China's Financial Industry Information Technology discussed the infrastructure that would allow China to reach global stature. The New Generation AI Development Plan contains plans and targets for research and development, industrialization, talent development, regulations, and security, aimed at making China the leading center of AI development by 2030. This plan also laid out requirements for smart finance, particularly the need to create a financial big data system and implement smart customer service and risk monitoring. The Smart Industry plan outlines the development of smart products and intelligent manufacturing.

China's National Internet Finance Association has launched its digital Credit Information Sharing platform. The platform helps member companies capture and share customer data. Member companies have encouraged more internet finance companies to join the platform. The first group of members included Ant Finance, JD Finance, and Lufax. Members do not share individual customer information, but rather they are able to obtain specific information on request.

Many of the large and emerging fintech firms have received funding from private sources. China is home to many of the world's fintech unicorns—that is, fintech start-ups with valuations of over $1 billion. These include Ant Financial, valued at $150 billion; Lufax, valued at $18.5 billion; Qufenqi, valued at $5.9 billion; and ZhongAn Insurance, valued at $2.7 billion. Other unicorns include Du Xiaoman Financial, Baidu's financial arm; and JD Finance, which offers online financial services.

The largest firms have raised several series of mega-funding rounds. For example, Ant Financial raised $4.5 billion in Series B funding in 2016 and $14 billion in its Series C round of funding in June 2018

TABLE 1.2

Top Fintech Investment and Financing Cases Exceeding 100 Million, U.S. Dollars 2018

Firm	Funding Round	Amount (in US$100 million)	Investor
Ant Financial Service	Series C	140	Alibaba Group
Grassroots Investment Internet Finance	Unknown	3.59	Intercontinental Oil and Gas Group
Immediate Finance	Unknown	3.02	Undisclosed
Ant Financial Service	Minority Shares—II	2.45	Pacific Insurance
Bairongjinfu	Series C	1.59	China Reform Fund
Extreme Trust Blockchain	Seed money	1	Xiong'an Fund

Source: China Institute of Information and Communications (CAICT), *Internet Investment and Financing in the Second Quarter of 2018* (in Chinese) (China Institute of Information and Communications, 2018), 7, http://www.caict.ac.cn/kxyj/qwfb/qwsj/201807/P020180720343745695019.pdf.

(table 1.2).[19] Funds were raised in two tranches, gleaning $3 billion in RMB and the balance in U.S. dollars. Funds were earmarked for global expansion and improvement in technology and innovation.

The number of fintech financing deals tripled from 54 in 2016 to 146 in 2017.[20] Wecash, a Chinese credit assessment and reporting company, obtained $160 million in its Series D funding round in March 2018.[21] The company has been expanding into South America and Southeast Asia. PINTEC, a technology platform that supports Chinese financial services, raised $103 million in financing in June 2018.[22] Some of the funds came from Sina Corp, which established a relationship with PINTECH to cooperate in obtaining user data from online traffic and to improve product development. 100Credit, a Chinese fintech start-up specializing in AI, received $159 million in a Series C funding round in April 2018.

The private sector raised millions of renminbi for angel investment in the first fintech angel fund, Finplus, backed by the Fugel Group in 2016.[23] Finplus focuses on investing in core technology worldwide.

Inclusive Finance

China has focused on expanding inclusive finance as a major policy directive. Few individuals can obtain sufficient financing. According to one survey, about a third of adults reported borrowing money in the past year, whereas only a third of those were able to obtain loans from formal financial institutions.[24] Although the nation has been attempting to improve financial access since 2005, with a pilot program to set up microloan companies in several provinces, it has struggled to address financing gaps using traditional institutions because of lack of profitability in the sector. Fintech has sought to fill this gap, and, through better credit risk modeling and ease of access, it has improved the outlook of inclusive finance.

China's inclusive finance directive, issued on January 15, 2016, set up a five-year plan to increase the reach of inclusive finance by 2020. The aim is to reach farmers, disabled and poor individuals, microbusinesses, and seniors.[25] Inclusive finance would incorporate both banking and insurance services. Furthermore, in 2017, the CBIRC and eleven other ministries and commissions issued the "Implementation Plan for the Establishment of Inclusive Financial Business Units for Large and Medium-Sized Commercial Banks." The plan requires that bank headquarters set up a unit for inclusive finance, which should have separate responsibilities from those of other units. The unit should focus on small, medium, and micro-enterprises, with special risk control practices in place for those entities.

To monitor the progress of inclusive finance, the Digital Finance Research Center of Peking University (PKU) and Ant Financial created the PKU Digital Inclusive Financial Index, which covers 31 provinces, 337 cities and 1,754 counties in China.[26] The research covers the breadth and depth of digital inclusive finance in the areas of payment, insurance, money funds, credit reporting, investment, and credit. The PKU Digital Inclusive Finance Index rose from 40 in 2011 to 220 in 2015, with the digital support index growing fastest. Regional differences emerged, but this regional disparity is rapidly shrinking, reflecting the fact that finance is becoming increasingly available through digital means.

The growth rate of less developed provinces has been high—internet finance in Tibet, Heilongjiang, Guizhou, and other underdeveloped provinces has grown quickly. Internet freight insurance growth has been high in remote areas, such as Ningxia, Xinjiang, Tibet, Qinghai, and Hainan, as the cost of freight transportation in remote areas is much higher than in other locations.

The situation of inclusive finance is improving. The China Banking Industry Service Report released by the China Banking Association showed that as of the end of 2017, the balance of agricultural loans extended by banks amounted to 30.95 trillion RMB, a year-on-year increase of 9.64 percent. Loan support for small and micro-enterprises and farmers rose over this period. The number of small and micro-enterprise loans in the country reached 15.29 million in 2017, a year-on-year increase of 11.1 percent.[27]

Still, however, rural areas have been particularly hard to reach in terms of financial penetration. The areas can be isolated from information systems, with no unified information database available. Many rural financial institutions have not yet developed online banking and online lending. In some villages, many of the younger people have left to work in urban areas, so those who continue to dwell in the villages are elderly or less educated, with low levels of technology use. Indeed, He et al. used survey data to analyze farmers' Internet finance demand characteristics.[28] The results show that income and education level affect the use of internet finance by farmers, reducing the likelihood that the poorer and less educated will use online financial services.

Chao Xu points out that rural areas often lack internet-accessible terminal equipment and that the fragmentation of big data in rural areas is not conducive to internet financial institutions' use of big data analysis technology to achieve precise operations.[29] The credit information system in rural areas is lacking, and rural residents' awareness of credit is weak, which makes it difficult to meet the existing loan demand. To make matters worse, fintech expertise is lacking, and few researchers are working on rural network financial products.

A major reason for the remaining underfinanced populations in China is due to a lack of physical access to an automatic teller machine (ATM) or branch bank. Fintech can bridge this gap, particularly for customers with a bank account who wish to obtain more frequent and additional financial services, as the costs of providing digital services are much lower than building up brick-and-mortar services. Fintech providers who have the capacity to reach underserved populations include internet banks, online microcredit companies, and P2P platforms. Many of these providers have access to big data and new types of credit risk modeling that make use of alternative data such as mobile phone payment records.

Furthermore, agricultural loans are in their own category, as farmers often operate in an environment characterized by market failures. In the most extreme cases, the market may not exist. Other market failures may be due to limited access to working capital credit arising from seasonal differences in agricultural spending and income. If farmers must purchase many inputs in the face of having a low income, rural households need to obtain loans.[30]

Fintech can bridge the gaps in the formal financial system, particularly for customers with a bank account who wish to obtain more frequent and additional financial services, as the costs of providing digital services are much lower than building up physical services. Fintech providers who have the capacity to reach underserved populations include internet banks, online microcredit companies, and P2P platforms. Many of these providers have access to big data and new types of credit risk modeling that make use of alternative data such as mobile phone payment records.

Some regions have attempted to promote digital finance to resolve some of these issues. Liu and Wei show that the "Tiandong Model" can overcome some of these barriers.[31] A pilot carried out in Tiandong County aimed to solve the difficult stage of rural financial services. In October 2008, Wu Bangguo, member of the Standing Committee of the Political Bureau of the CPC Central Committee, conducted an in-depth investigation in Baise City, Guangxi Province, to lay the foundation for the selection of Baise City as a pilot for rural financial service reform. The pilot was later expanded to Tiandong County.

Among both online and offline activities, Tiandong County strove to build a property rights trading platform. On December 18, 2012, Tiandong County officially established the Rural Property Rights Trading Center, which is the only rural property rights trading platform in Guangxi province. Tiandong County uses this platform to administer services such as forest rights, land management rights, housing ownership, asset ownership, investment, financing, mortgage loans, and collective equity. The Tiandong County Rural Property Rights Trading Center helps to transfer Tiandong rural property rights—the trading center is free to list for farmers, reducing information asymmetry. The system also has improved the monitoring of Tiandong rural property rights, and the trading center has collected a large amount of property rights information for the county.

Other governmental institutions have attempted to reach the rural population as well. For example, China's central bank in Ningbo has built a mobile platform to provide loans to rural residents living in remote areas. The program has been quite successful, with lending rising by 302 percent in a short time. The platform uses credit information from local banks, government, telecommunication companies, and public service agencies.[32]

Businesses like Ant Financial and JD Finance have worked to achieve a more inclusive financial system. Ant Financial provides loans for e-commerce stores on Taobao and extends loans to farmers who sell their agricultural products online. Jingdong Finance has helped peasants from more than three hundred thousand villages improve their financial situation. Wang and Wu describe how, in 2015, Jingdong Group first proposed the 3F Strategy for the development of rural e-commerce, including introducing industrial products into rural areas, creating a rural financial strategy, and promoting new internet financial strategies.[33] JD.com has helped reduce the borrowing difficulties faced by farmers. In 2016, Jingdong and the State Council Poverty Alleviation Office signed the Electronic Business Accurate Poverty Alleviation Strategy Cooperation Agreement to implement the four strategies of industrial poverty alleviation, recruitment and poverty alleviation, entrepreneurship poverty alleviation, and financial poverty alleviation nationwide. Jingdong Group cooperates with poor local governments and local agricultural firms to provide services related to e-commerce. Jingdong electronic business service points have been implemented to realize the sales of agricultural products and promote industrial development in poverty-stricken areas. Big data is used to improve credit access in poor areas to boost the use of e-commerce. JD.com can thereby prevent credit risk and provide financial services to rural residents and firms.

Rural financial services, such as Jingnong Loan, have been introduced. Jingnong Loan is a core credit product launched by Jingdong to provide rural financial services. The product features low interest rates and no collateral requirements, and the approval process is quick. When agricultural products are put on the market, they are packaged and branded. Then they are sold to all parts of the country through e-commerce platforms, and the previous loans are returned with sales proceeds so that poor households can earn income. For poor areas with low transaction volume and counties that have not developed e-commerce, however, it remains difficult for e-commerce platforms to carry out credit ratings for farmers. The ability to provide these financial services continues to pose significant risks.

Traditional banks also have tried to improve the outreach of inclusive finance. As of the end of 2016, the number of mobile banking users of Anhui Rural Commercial Bank exceeded six million.[34] This means that almost one in ten people is using Anhui Rural Commercial Bank mobile banking. An information asymmetry between banks and customers persists, however, resulting in mismatches in bank credit resources and in high transaction costs between banks and customers. In some relatively underdeveloped areas of Anhui Province, write-off loans to rural commercial banks accounted for 17.4 percent of total loans. To combat this, the Anhui government released the Outline of Anhui Social Credit System Construction Plan (2015–2020) in September 2015, and the Hefei Central Branch of the People's Bank of China stated that it would work on the development of SMEs and the rural credit system.

The Agricultural Bank of China (ABC) has attempted to improve inclusive finance but has encountered difficulties along the way. ABC has faced large inefficiencies in providing banking services, forcing customers to wait for long periods.[35] Outlets need to be improved to provide better service, including providing intelligent self-service and VIP services. Super counters, self-service card-issuing machines, and business preprocessing services should be provided in physical outlets. Internet finance is especially effective because it can be customized for each customer. Traditional outlets of ABC face higher thresholds for investment than online investments do—for example, personal wealth management products sold through the bank branch have a threshold of more than 50,000 RMB. Purchasing such products online, however, requires a minimum of only 1 yuan. The emergence of internet virtual credit cards, such as Jingdong, Ant, and Tmall installments, for online consumption compete with ABC credit cards and are increasingly popular.

Zhenggen He finds that financial inclusion at the village level can occur by issuing bank debit and credit cards, encouraging small and micro-enterprises to open settlement accounts, and implementing online approval methods in remote villages.[36] Implementation of multimedia terminals that can accept payment services and point-of-sale (POS) transfer telephones for village development merchants would further expand financial inclusion. Banks increasingly have deployed ATMs in villages, and villages increasingly are using mobile banking and e-wallets.

Some villages have launched mobile phone SMS payment services and promoted mobile payment service stations, at which village residents can carry out water, electricity, and coal fee payments. Electronic payment systems have assisted the payment for the purchase of agricultural products. For example, some locales have successfully launched what are called "Fu Nong Tong" and "Lianyin Express" products to purchase goods. Farmers also can obtain subsidies electronically. The "Yinxuntong" business is an example of this; it uses a mobile phone app client with an MPB device (an external card swipe box) for mobile payment. The "Yinxuntong" platform can not only handle financial services such as subsidies for donations, withdrawals, balance inquiries, and transfer losses, but can also provide rural insurance; rural cooperative medical insurance and agricultural subsidy funds for rural residents; water, electricity, communications, public utilities, redemption of sericulture, and other industrial chain funds; and even financial services, such as provision of funds, insurance, wealth management, precious metals, loan collection, and financial knowledge.

Digital payments have been used for the collection and payment of village collective funds. For example, some local governments provide an account for the village committee with access to online banking, deploying POS terminals and installing computers for ease of access. This improves the fundraising function (such as collecting rent) of the collective village committee, helping farmers to withdraw money and remittances. Income and expenditures of the village committee account can be easily made available to the village committee to improve payments as well as village-level management.

The following stories from Yilongdai, a P2P lending company, illustrate how fintech has helped improve the lot of farmers. With the implementation of the rural revitalization strategy, increasing numbers of migrant workers have returned to their hometowns to start their own businesses and assist with rural revitalization and innovation. Invisible barriers, such as shortage of funds, lack of experience, and lack of contacts, make this a major challenge, however, and the road to alleviate peasants' entrepreneurial poverty is full of ups and downs. The development of inclusive internet finance by companies such as

Yilongdai have effectively filled the gap in the provision of rural entrepreneurial funds and have helped peasants clear the first roadblock on the path to entrepreneurship. The following true story illustrates the importance of fintech in rural finance.

> Today, the pet economy is booming, and fintech loans have pulled one dog breeder out of poverty. Li Qiang, a 36-year-old borrower, has stood at the forefront of the industry by setting up a pet dog farm.
>
> Li Qiang's hometown is located in Zhangzhou City, Shanxi Province. It is the only poverty-stricken city that spans both the Taihang Mountains-Yanshan and the Luliangshan concentrated contiguous poverty-stricken areas. Under the leadership of the local government, poverty alleviation has become the goal of the villagers.
>
> Growing up in poor rural areas, Li Qiang made a living by planting corn in the early years, relying on this for food because family income was unsatisfactory. The turning point occurred in 2013. Through media channels such as TV and internet, the husband and wife saw that more and more families were adopting pet dogs, and they thought of setting up a special pet breeding business. They took out all their savings and bought a pair of dogs in order to set up a dog farm. However, the road to entrepreneurship was not so easy. After two years of operation, not only was there no profit, but the couple divorced.
>
> Yet Li Qiang persisted. He did not want to give up his career and his newfound love of pet breeding. The upward expectations of the pet economy and Li Qiang's firm belief in entrepreneurship supported his determination to overcome difficulties. He decided to introduce a better breed of dogs and bring new hope to the farm in the future, if he could obtain a loan.
>
> The process of raising funds, however, was not smooth. "We are all old farmers, and few workers are willing to give us guarantees," Li Qiang said. Traditional financial institutions require collateral guarantees, and as expected, he was turned away. Mr. Li decided to apply for a loan through the Wing Nong Loan app of Yilongdai.
>
> Soon, the staff of the Yilongdai company cooperated with Li Qiang in accordance with the prescribed risk control process. Li Qiang submitted complete materials such as his account book, ID card, and call details. After a few days, he received a loan of 60,000 yuan through Yilongdai.

After obtaining this working capital, Li Qiang first re-organized the dog farm and bought 10 dogs, enriching the variety of dog breeds. With years of farming experience, after more than a year of careful care, Mr. Li brought pet puppies to the market, and some were even sent to Guangxi province thousands of miles away. As his invested funds returned, Mr. Li's kennel business was booming. Li Qiang not only paid off the loan, but also saved more than 100,000 yuan and built his own house.

According to statistics, the annual transaction volume of Chinese pets and supplies has exceeded 10 billion yuan. As people's living standards improve, pet dogs become part of families and this trend is growing year by year. Li Qiang's pet farm holds great promise for the future.[37]

Li's story is representative of numerous individuals living in rural areas who have struggled to obtain funding for their own small businesses. Fintech has given them access to funds that they previously lacked, allowing many rural residents to improve their businesses and foster growth in their local economies.

Profitability and Risks

China's fintech sector has much room for growth. This is because 753 million people in China use mobile phones to access the internet. More than half of these users are between the ages of twenty and thirty-nine years old, and more than half of them have a monthly income of about 2,000 to 8,000 RMB.[38] Market potential exists not only in the number of additional users who have yet to come online but also in selling new types of financial products to existing customers. Chinese households have a huge pent-up demand for sound investment products that will provide them with basic returns. They also increasingly favor the convenience of new technologies, such as AI and biometrics, as well as the ongoing integration of fintech into their daily lives. Many of these prospects have yet to be fully realized.

The sector is looking increasingly attractive not only because of its increasing potential for profit but also because of falling risks. Risks have declined in recent months as a result of increased regulation throughout the fintech sector. The P2P lending sector, which had been one of the riskiest areas of finance for several years, was forced to impose new restrictions that may reduce profits in the short run, but that will have a stabilizing impact in the long run. In addition, P2P lending platforms increasingly focus on prime or near-prime, rather than subprime, borrowers. After a grueling shakeout of poorly managed firms, the sector will stand stronger than ever.

Fintech firms are increasingly learning to cope with several risks, however. These include liquidity risk, operational risk, credit risk, legal compliance risk, and technology and security risk. Liquidity risk occurs when a firm is unable to meet obligations as a result of lack of sufficient cash flow at the time. This can occur because of maturity mismatch in assets and liabilities. Operational risks may arise due to human error or failed internal processes. Credit risk results from the potential default risk of customers. Legal compliance risk occurs when firms fail to comply with existing regulations. To address this issue, firms require effective supervision and investor risk awareness. Technical and security risks stem from hidden dangers of data transmission and storage. Information may be used for criminal purposes, for example, if it is leaked. To combat these risks requires additional money and effort, and these risks can present major challenges to running a successful fintech enterprise.

Fraud is another issue that may be related to security or operational risk. In one type of criminal scheme, the internet finance firm may seek to defraud the public through illegal fundraising, offering high interest rates to attract investment. Such companies may illegally absorb public deposits and generate Ponzi schemes. In another scheme, hackers attempt to steal information and funds from internet financial firms. Phishing schemes are commonly used to attract customers to enter private information into a false website. Internet finance also may be used to launder criminal proceeds.

Fintech firms continue to address these issues. In general, risk management has improved over time, as fintech firms improve their credit risk modeling processes, make use of alternative and big data, and ensure their operations and security processes. The strides that P2P lending companies have made are evident in firms that offer credit cards online, insuretech, investment products, and other types of fintech services. Technology is catching up with entrepreneurs' aspirations.

Much of this progress is due to regulation. The most general regulation, the Guidelines on Promoting Sound Development of Internet

Finance, was issued by government departments in July 2015 to define internet finance and state valid objectives, including the promotion of innovation, encouragement of cooperation among firms, improvement in internet finance firms' access to funds, streamlining administrative approvals, implementation of beneficial fiscal and tax policies, and promotion of credit intermediation services. The rules also assign certain areas of supervision to the regulatory bodies and describe areas that need more regulatory intervention. Money laundering has been addressed by the Administrative Measures for Anti-Money Laundering and Anti-Terrorism Financing of Payment Agencies, released in 2010. (Regulations created for specific fintech industries are discussed in the chapters to come.)

Another reason for increased profitability and reduced risks stems from improvements in technology and better availability of data. The major technology disruptors mentioned earlier in this chapter, ABCD, or AI, blockchain, cloud computing, and big data, have created a more secure environment for the industry in a relatively short period of time. This security has allowed firms to construct better credit histories, protect sensitive information, lower the costs of operation, and improve the management process.

Fintech Theories

Several theories can be used to explain the rise of fintech in China. These include Schumpeterian theory on "creative destruction," the synergy effect theory, long-tail theory, financial supervision and financial innovation, disruptive technology, and financial deepening.

Schumpeter and Innovation

Innovation is the key to success in China's fintech sector. One of the most prominent scholars in the field of innovation was Joseph Schumpeter, who originated the concept of "creative destruction," which referred to the necessary breakdown of old systems as new systems are brought into force. The process is also referred to as restructuring and is composed of numerous decisions leading to innovations. Innovators inspire competitors, who create a boom. As profits decline as a result of increased competition, investment moves elsewhere until the next innovation is born. In 1950, Schumpeter stated that the innovation process "incessantly revolutionizes the economic structure from within, incessantly destroying the old one, incessantly creating a new one. This process of Creative Destruction is the essential fact about capitalism."[39]

The fintech sector features constant creative destruction, as companies compete with one another to maintain and grow their market share. For example, in the P2P lending sector, many companies have arisen, and many have gone out of business. The surviving businesses usually have better, more innovative credit risk models. Over time, this has shaped the industry so that making use of big data and better risk analysis software programs has become the norm rather than the exception.

As early as 1934, Schumpeter believed that financial institutions could foster innovation, stating, "[The banker] stands between those who wish to form new combinations and the possessors of productive means. . . . He makes possible the carrying out of new combinations, authorizes people, in the name of the society as it were, to form them."[40] Therefore, it is the financial firm that provides the tools to better, more innovative companies.

China's fintech sector is certainly one aspect of its financial sector. In China's fintech sector, traditional means of banking are being destroyed to give way to digital means of finance. Traditional means of banking includes both formal and informal banks. Fintech firms have, to some extent, replaced loans through formal banks. These firms also have replaced loans from formal banks. Many SMEs and individuals have not been able to obtain sufficient bank loans from formal banks and have relied on the informal sector since reform and opening up began. According to the World Bank in 2014, only 9.6 percent of Chinese individuals had access to loans from any type of formal financial system.[41] Digital means of finance have allowed underserved populations, particularly SMEs, as well as the poor and middle class, to create a credit history and access loans.

Synergy Effect Theory

The synergy effect theory was proposed by J. Fred Weston in 1998.[42] This theory posits that corporate mergers and acquisitions are beneficial to the whole society. This societal benefit is reflected primarily in the improvement of efficiency achieved through synergies, which break the uneconomical scale of traditional management and carry out more effective cooperation on a larger scale.

China's financial technology companies present a distinctive feature that is different from those of other countries, namely, an "ecological" business model through the establishment of a highly integrated business model. The model, ranging from payment, lending, and wealth management to credit scoring, from online business to offline business, seeks to build a closed loop of its own financial ecosystem. A few large-scale hybrid tech–finance institutions have begun to dominate the market. In contrast, companies in Western hemisphere countries tend to focus on one or a few core businesses. Such companies are represented by Visa and MasterCard, or PayPal and Lending Club.

In its 2016 annual report, Alibaba mentioned the word "ecosystem" ninety-five times.[43] Other leading fintech players from Ping An and Tencent to JD and Baidu also have mentioned the word numerous times in their annual reports. Goldman Sachs believes that this "integration" mind-set defines how Chinese entrepreneurs view their strategy, competition, and profitability.[44] The "ecosystem" business model can form a variety of synergy effects, including portfolio effects, financial synergy, marketing synergy, and management synergy, which ultimately achieve value aggregation and complementary advantages. These synergy effects occur through interaction, connection, and communication.

China's fintech giants as well as some of the leading financial institutions have begun to implement technology exports by providing shared services, such as technology cloud and API (application programming interface) services. This technology will promote resource sharing and capacity output within financial institutions, as well as between customers and partners; enhance the synergy of the entire financial market; and build the financial services ecosystem. For example, many banks have begun to cooperate with financial technology companies to achieve win-win cooperation through investment and strategic collaboration. Fintech companies have expanded their capabilities in banking, including technology and data, to drive innovation in banking products and services.

Long-Tail Theory

The concept of long-tail theory was first proposed by Chris Anderson in 2004.[45] The "long tail" is actually a colloquial expression of the characteristics of power laws and Pareto distributions in statistics.

Anderson pointed out that our cultural and economic focus is accelerating, shifting from a few big favorites (mainstream products and markets) at the head of the demand curve to a large number of niche products and markets at the end of the demand curve.

In lay terms, long-tail theory refers to the fact that when the cost of goods storage, circulation, and display is extremely low, the small market share of products that includes those with poor demand or poor sales can transform into a market share that rivals a few hot products. That is, in an era in which shelf space constraints and other supply bottlenecks are nonexistent, products and services for specific small groups can have the same economic appeal as mainstream hot spots. This approach is a complete rebellion against the 80/20 rule, which is well known in today's management sciences. The 80/20 rule, also called Pareto's principle, was proposed by the Italian statistician and economist Wilfredo Pareto in the early twentieth century. He pointed out that in any particular group, important factors are usually only a minority, whereas unimportant factors are dominant. Thus, one can control the global marketplace as long as these few factors of importance are controlled. After many years of evolution, this principle became known as the 80/20 rule—that is, 80 percent of corporate profits come from the largest 20 percent of customers, and the remaining 20 percent are from the 80 percent that are ordinary customers. According to the long-tail theory, a company's profits no longer depend on the traditional 20 percent of quality customers, but on the original neglected, large number of customers.

The same logic applies to the development of China's financial technology industry. China's financial market is bank led. Information asymmetry, transaction costs, and risk control constraints lead to differences in the quality and efficiency of financial services between social groups of different incomes, companies of different sizes, and ownership. The traditional banking sector focuses on serving large enterprises and rejects SMEs and low-income people. These factors make China's financial services coverage seriously inadequate, and it is difficult to fully meet the potential demand of China's financial market. The financing of SMEs is difficult, and the supply of financial services for "agriculture, rural areas and farmers" is weak, which has spawned the long-tail market of internet finance.

Traditional banks have higher profit margins (the average return on equity of China's banking industry has been as high as 15 percent or more in the past ten years) that far exceed the level of banking in the Western hemisphere. This aspect has greatly attracted financial technology companies to intervene in China's banking business. In contrast, it has forced bank reform to allow banks to compete with new fintech firms. The traditional banking sector has begun to actively explore the path of financial technology transformation, which has further promoted the development of financial technology.

The application of financial technology has lowered the threshold of financial services and included long-tailed individuals who have been excluded from financial services in the past, thus inducing financial services to break through the limits of physical business outlets and business hours; reducing transaction costs; and increasing the depth, breadth, and precision of financial services. This emergence of technology has provided accessibility to a wide range of fintech vendors and their products.

Financial Supervision and Financial Innovation

The Bubble Act promulgated by the United Kingdom in 1720 to prevent excessive securities speculation was triggered by the seventeenth-century British "South China Sea Bubble" case, which marked the official start of financial regulation by the government in the history of world finance. The Great Depression of the 1930s underscored the incompleteness of financial markets, and individuals began to petition the government to actively intervene in financial institutions. At this point, the need for financial regulation has been established both empirically and theoretically. Theories of the necessity of financial regulation include the following: those based on the idea of imperfect competition, information asymmetry theory,[46] those that reference systemically important financial institutions,[47] and the financial vulnerability theory.[48]

Financial supervision brings indirect efficiency losses, potentially hindering financial innovation and thereby delaying financial development; weakening competition, resulting in inefficiency; and leading to excessive supervision, which contributes to the loss of financial resources. To circumvent financial supervision and seek development, financial institutions will attempt to create more new financial products and financial instruments, thereby generating new risks. Therefore, financial innovation has challenged traditional financial regulation and increased the difficulty of financial supervision. To maintain the security and stability of the financial system, the financial regulatory structure of various countries has been adjusted—that is, financial innovation has promoted the evolution and innovation of financial supervision. The result of mutual influence and mutual promotion constitutes a dialectical relationship between financial innovation and financial supervision.

The rapid development of China's financial technology is closely related to China's relatively loose regulatory environment. Compared with the United States, which represents the frontlines of financial technology, China's financial technology innovation has been virtually unconstrained in the early stage of development. No regulatory agencies have claimed jurisdiction over fintech firms per se, whereas companies such as Lending Club in the United States have begun to be supervised by the U.S. Securities and Futures Commission.

As one example of this, in May 2018, the EU General Data Protection Regulation (GDPR) came into effect. The GDPR stipulates that internet platforms providing services in the European region need to obtain the consent of each user when utilizing their data, and the user may revoke this consent at any time. Offending companies will face a maximum fine of €20 million euros ($22 million) or 4 percent of their annual global turnover. Data belong to users, and this premise is the core and foundation of the development of financial technology enterprises. Financial supervision policies will naturally inhibit the development of financial technology while protecting the interests of consumers.

Compared with Europe and the United States, the importance of personal information security is not as high in China, no matter whether the user is a regulatory agency, a consumer, or a business. To a certain extent, this is one of the reasons why features such as big data portraits and algorithm recommendations have been rapidly popularized in China.

In the past two years, however, with the deepening of China's financial regulatory system reform, this situation is changing, and the supervision of financial technology is gradually improving. For example, in August 2016, the China Banking Regulatory Commission officially released its most stringent measures, the Interim Measures for the Management of Business Activities of Internet Lending Information Intermediaries, which clearly define the legal status of online lending institutions as information intermediaries, adopt a record-keeping management approach, and define the business boundary. Under these measures, the funds are subject to bank deposit, and the upper limit of the borrowing balance for a single borrower is clearly defined. The P2P industry has ended its barbaric growth and gradually will enter a legal and regulated track. As a result, effective regulation can lead to long-term prosperity.

Disruptive Technology

Disruptive technology (also known as "destructive technology") was first proposed by Joseph Bower and Clayton Christensen in 1995.[49] Since then, this concept has been widely used, from the commercial field to the defense, military, engineering applications, aviation, and other fields, in multiple units, with different experts to explain the characteristics of disruptive technology from different angles according to their respective business needs. Thus far, the academic community has not formed a unified understanding of disruptive technology. According to Bower and Christensen's definition, disruptive technology replaces the technology of existing mainstream technologies in an unexpected way. Bower and Christensen state, "they tend to cut in from the low-end or edge markets, with simple, convenient, and cheap as the initial stage features, along with performance. With the continuous improvement and improvement of functions, it will eventually replace the existing technology, open up new markets and form a new value system."[50]

Disruptive technology has at least three salient features: one is that it is an alternative. Once disruptive technologies penetrate an industry, current products in the industry gradually will be replaced by products that completely or largely contain new technologies. For example, a digital camera replaces a film camera, and a smartphone partially replaces a digital camera. The second feature of disruptive technology is that it is destructive. The emergence and application of disruptive technology will significantly change the status of leading enterprises in the industry. Some innovative SMEs have sprung up, and some leading enterprises that have not adopted disruptive technologies in time have been eliminated. For example, Nikon and Canon replaced the film camera giant Kodak with a digital camera, Apple replaced Nokia with a smartphone, online shopping and unmanned supermarkets replaced brick-and-mortar stores, resulting in the disappearance of many retail giants in the United States. The third feature of disruptive technology is uncertainty. The emergence of disruptive technologies from emergence to maturity has shown that subversive effects require a long-term cultivation process.

In recent years, new breakthroughs in science and technology have emerged, but which have the potential to "subvert"? Think tanks and media, such as McKinsey Global Institute, RAND Corporation, and MIT Technology Review, have been generally optimistic about the prospects, including AI, the Internet of Things, cloud computing, virtual reality, and other fields.

At present, a new round of technological revolution and industrial transformation has emerged. Major disruptive technological innovations such as IT, biotechnology, AI, blockchain, cloud computing, big data, virtual reality, and augmented reality are creating new industries and new formats. Financial technology companies have strong subversive genes within them, and they constantly are trying to use technology to dismantle large financial institutions or systems that are not technologically advanced at present. Subversive technology not only will release huge energy but also will overlap with other technological innovations, bringing more disruptive technological changes. Subversive innovation driven by technological change will become the new engine of economic development. With changes in the productivity of financial technology, the production relationship needs to be adjusted accordingly.

Financial Deepening

Fintech can be viewed as a way to further the process of financial deepening. Financial deepening is the process of expanding the provision of financial services. The concept arose in the 1970s. Both Ronald I. McKinnon and Edward S. Shaw separately emphasized the necessity of finance in the development process.[51] They found that the lack of financial development could hinder growth by maintaining segmented industries, in which some have artificially high rates of return and some have artificially low rates of return because of restrictions on financing availability. This means that capital is not able to reach its competitive equilibrium interest rate, and a disparity in rates of return results from the dysfunction in the lending market.

Although China continues to suffer from financial repression in interest rates to some extent, as a result of state influence in the banking sector, the rise of the fintech sector has helped to lower interest rates in lending to small businesses and individuals. The level of market segmentation has declined, as access to financial services has increased for underserved populations. This is particularly important, because smaller firms and individuals have lacked access to finance for many years.

This means that excessively high returns on risky loans are starting to decline, as risk assessment abilities improve through the use of technology. Loans are more accessible for smaller firms and individuals lacking a formal credit history because online finance has made use of alternative data sources, and the segmentation of risky and underserved borrowers versus less risky and overserved borrowers has been reduced significantly.

Research in China

Several universities are researching internet finance. These include PKU's Institute of Internet Finance, Tsinghua University's Fintech Laboratory, Southwestern University of Finance and Economics' China Microfinance and Internet Finance Innovation Research Center, Shanghai Jiaotong University Internet Finance Rule of Law Innovation Research Center, Southwest University of Communications Financial Big Data Research Institute, Zhejiang University Internet Finance Research Institute, Renmin University of China Financial Technology and Internet Security Research Center, and China University of Political Science and Law's Internet Finance Law Research Institute.[52] We examine three of research centers in the following sections.

Tsinghua University's Fintech Laboratory

Tsinghua University's Fintech Lab was founded by the PBC School of Finance in 2012. The Lab has forty full-time researchers and has completed more than a hundred industry research reports. The lab contains various centers, including the Internet Finance Lab, Sunshine Internet Finance Innovation Research Center, Xinyuan Financial Technology Research Center, Runbo Digital Finance Research Center, Smart Finance Research Center, Blockchain Research Center,

Financial Big Data Research Center, and Tsinghua Financial Technology 100 Forum.

As a specific division within the Fintech Lab, the Internet Finance Lab uses a variety of data, including P2P lending platform data and rating company data, to determine fintech user behavior and risks. Some of the research has focused on carrying out experiments on specific P2P platforms. The Fintech Lab produces both academic and public works.

Fudan University's Fintech Research Center

Fudan University's Fintech Research Center at the Fanhai International School of Finance is a national-level research center that is affiliated with the China Institute of Economics and Finance. The center is also associated with the Fudan-Stanford Institute for China Financial Technology and Risk Analytics, which is focused on finance research and innovation.

The Fintech Research Center is engaged in applied research in the areas of fintech regulation, blockchain and distributed ledger use cases, tokenomics design and theory, business model innovation, cryptoeconomics, e-governance, consensus policy, and financing innovation. The center partners with finance, real estate, and insurance companies.

Peking University's Institute of Internet Finance

PKU's Institute of Internet Finance was established in October 2015 and is affiliated with the National School of Development at PKU. The institute carries out research in the areas of digital finance, inclusive finance, and financial reforms and regularly publishes the "Internet Finance Development Index," which researchers have jointly developed.

The center has published dozens of articles and several books, including *Ant Financial: From Alipay to New Finance Ecology.* The center regularly holds lectures and conferences on related topics.

Chinese Fintech Books

Several books have been recently published on China's fintech sector. *The Chinese Era of Financial Technology: 12 Lectures on Digital Finance* is a collection of twelve lectures of experts, regulatory officials, and relevant corporate executives' speeches, which are from the 2016 PKU "Internet Finance Lectures" and Tsinghua University's "China Financial Practice Class 3—Internet Finance."[53]

This book analyzes such topics as the development and supervision of Internet finance, innovation and challenges, big data credit, online lending, and the development status and future trends of China's digital financial industry from multiple perspectives. The book also explores possible future development opportunities, risks, and challenges in hot areas, such as digital currency, blockchain, and AI.

Chapter One, written by Wang Jianhua of PKU, describes the definition of internet finance according to the "Guiding Opinions on Promoting the Healthy Development of Internet Finance." According to this rule, "communication technology realizes new financial services for financing, payment, investment, and information intermediary services."[54]

Chapter Four, written by Huang Quan Lao of Suning Financial, first questions whether internet financial will subvert traditional finance. The author notes that internet finance has tended to focus on retail rather than enterprise finance. This new industry has promoted a consumption upgrade. Internet finance can address areas that have lacked access to traditional finance, so these two areas may be complementary. These two types of finance, however, are also somewhat different. Internet finance focuses more on technology and on interactive marketing. Products are delivered quickly.

Another recent volume on Chinese fintech is *Financial Technology: The Application and Future of Big Data, Blockchain, and Artificial Intelligence*. After the development of internet finance, financial technology is emerging as a new force to promote economic development and inclusive finance. This book asserts that financial technology intensifies the subversion of the traditional financial industry, but that these turbulent technological changes also have brought new enthusiasm as well as an investment boom to the financial industry.

The first two chapters of this book describe the subversion of financial technology to the financial market, and demonstrate the application of cloud computing, big data, blockchain, AI, and other technological innovations in many fields, such as payment and settlement, loan financing, and wealth management. It analyzes the relationship between financial technology and internet finance and people's daily lives.

The rest of this book systematically details the current hot topics in the field of financial technology, including digital currency, financial technology challenges to traditional banks, third-party payments, wealth management, and innovation and regulation of financial technology. The author states that financial technology needs supervision but cannot be supervised to death. The book also discusses several fintech companies and case studies in China.

Hong Kong Fintech

Hong Kong wants to become a fintech hub, and it has been emphasized that Hong Kong is quite strong in the financial industry. Although this industry contributes about 18 percent of Hong Kong's GDP, it is not as strong in technology, of which Hong Kong tends to be a consumer rather than a producer. Hong Kong also struggles with the use of legacy systems in the banking sector that make it more difficult to change.

To address Hong Kong's slow development of fintech, the government created a FinTech Steering Committee.[55] The government also called for incubator support for fintechs at Cyberport, dedicated platforms with financial regulators to improve communication between regulators and the fintech industry, and a cybersecurity program. The Hong Kong Monetary Authority also set up a Fintech Facilitation Office in March 2016 and laid out a Fintech Supervisory Sandbox for banks in September 2016. In addition, Hong Kong set up the HKMA-ASTRI FinTech Innovation Hub in November 2016.

Hong Kong has a sophisticated regulatory regime, and it is perhaps for this reason that fintech has not grown as rapidly as it has in mainland China. The regulatory regime includes restrictions regarding securities and asset management, banking, currency exchange and remittance, and payment systems.

Hong Kong is moving forward on the payments and asset management front. In terms of payments, Hong Kong takes two approaches. The city first used device-based stored value facilities (SVFs), which allow customers to store money on their devices. Hong Kong had granted thirteen SVF licenses to firms by 2018.[56] The city can continue to use this technology in its retail sector. Hong Kong is also developing a Faster Payments System, a real-time payment system that will allow phone numbers and email addresses to receive funds in Hong Kong dollars or renminbi. Hong Kong has been focusing on developing wealthtech and insuretech, incorporating big data, automation, and AI.

Hong Kong has followed its own path. Rather than attempting to foster companies that are major disruptors to the way the world does business, Hong Kong is focusing on partnering with other successful firms. According to the PwC Hong Kong Fintech Survey 2017, 82 percent of Hong Kong's financial institutions plan to partner with a fintech business in the next three to five years.[57] Hong Kong views its economy as an international financial hub, which, for mainland China, can enable fintech companies to go global. Hong Kong is also geographically within close reach of other Asia Pacific markets.

Comparison with the United States and Europe

Investment in fintech companies reached $26 billion in Europe in the first half of 2018.[58] Much of the fintech activity is concentrated in the United Kingdom. Fintech in the European Union is dominated by P2P consumer lending and crowdfunding. After the United Kingdom, the leading countries for P2P consumer lending are Germany, France, and Finland. In 2016, France was the largest crowdfunding market in the European Union and was followed by the Netherlands, Italy, and Germany. Payment systems and digital currencies are important in the European Union. Payment and settlement systems based on blockchain technology are on the rise. Investment firms have taken advantage of robo-advisors to provide clients with inexpensive investment advice.[59]

Although Europe does not have an overarching fintech regulatory framework, some rules have been passed to facilitate specific aspects of fintech. One example of this is the Payment Services Directive (PSD I) (Directive 2007/64/EC), which established the single European payments area in 2007. In July 2013, the updated Payment Services Directive (Directive (EU) 2015/2366; PSD II) was passed, along with a proposal for a regulation on interchange fees for card-based payment transactions. PSD II expands the definition of payment services and reclassifies providers, which are subject to the same rules as other payment institutions. Regulatory technical standards (RTS) have streamlined the processes and data structures of communication between parties and are essential to achieving the PSD II objectives. The RTS require banks to set up a communication channel that allows third-party service providers to access data.

To promote the use of fintech, the European Commission presented a fintech action plan in March 2018. The plan includes nineteen steps to promote new business models, technologies, cybersecurity, and data protection. The plan also promotes the use of regulatory sandboxes in which supervisors can apply rules to fintech firms in a limited, testable fashion.

Turning to the United States, between 2010 and third quarter 2017, more than 3,330 new fintech firms were established in the United States. Lending by fintech firms now accounts for more than 36 percent of all U.S. personal loans.[60] Some fintech services now reach eighty million members.

According to Gerald Tsai, the United States has three general fintech business models: one in which technology firms provide financial services to customers through mobile platforms or other means, a second in which banks use fintech to improve their contact with customers, and a third in which fintech firms and banks combine to deliver better risk management and customer service.[61] Financial services such as payments, loans, financial education, financial advisory, and digital currency services are provided.

These models operate within a broad regulatory structure at the state and federal levels. The major regulatory authorities include the Federal Reserve, the Office of the Comptroller of the Currency, the Federal Deposit Insurance Corporation, the Consumer Financial Protection Bureau, the Financial Stability Oversight Council, the U.S. Securities and Exchange Commission, the Commodity Futures Trading Commission, and the Financial Crimes Enforcement Network. Many nonbank financial activities are regulated by the states, and the securities and banking industries are regulated by several federal agencies as well as state agencies.

Competition with the Rest of the World

Chinese fintech firms are consistently among the top fintech companies in the world. They not only have funding but also are leading innovation, such as in digital payments and AI. As a result, the demand for Chinese fintech services is large. In China, fintech firms have leapfrogged common steps in the financial development process. For example, before credit card use became widespread, China developed online P2P lending and lines of credit for e-commerce transactions. Before a commonly used credit scoring mechanism could be created, fintech companies used their own credit scoring systems based on big data. In this way, fintech firms have brought China to the next level of financial development through the process of innovation. Lists of the most innovative global fintech firms almost always include Ant Financial, Lufax, ZhongAn Insurance, JD Finance, and Qudian.

Within China, the most globally competitive fintech regions include the Yangtze River Delta, Greater Beijing, and the Guangdong-Hong Kong-Macau region. These areas compete with top global locations, such as Silicon Valley and Greater London. These areas have both financial and human resources as well as access to supporting institutions that can incubate new technologies.

In addition, many traditional banks have developed or are developing a fintech component to compete with pure fintech firms. As a result, traditional banks have developed a number of new capabilities, such as mobile banking, big data analysis, and better marketing models. This innovation has helped such banks remain globally competitive, as the largest global banks have developed online interfaces and other fintech capabilities that have made them widely accessible and more attractive.

China's user base for third-party payment accounts is huge, hitting at more than 3.4 billion in number and far surpassing the United States.[62] China is also a big player in online lending, accounting for about 75 percent of the global market. This intensive use of basic aspects of fintech sets the stage for further development of the industry, which reinforces China's place in the world as a fintech leader.

Going forward, we can expect China to remain at the forefront of the fintech industry. Why this is so will become increasingly apparent in the chapters that follow. We cover a number of topics in this book, including digital payment systems, P2P lending and crowdfunding, credit card issuance and internet banks, blockchain finance and virtual currencies, online investment and insurance, the disruption of traditional banking, and risks of fintech and regulatory technology (regtech).

CHAPTER TWO

Digital Payment Systems

CHINA'S DIGITAL PAYMENT services have become ubiquitous throughout the nation. According to the China Internet Network Information Center (CNNIC), China has 502 million unique mobile payment users.[1] Digital payments allow customers to make payments over the internet, and in China, most of this business is conducted using mobile phones. The two major competitors, Alipay and WeChat Pay, hold 92 percent of this industry's market share. These two companies compete in both online and offline payments, and customers can purchase a wide range of goods and services using these payment apps.

Constumers can make payments in several ways. Customers scan a QR code to transfer funds from their Alipay or WeChat Pay account, which is linked to their Chinese bank account. Users can also take advantage of point-of-service (POS) machines, which have been deployed to many merchants. In addition, they can use the app to make the online payment directly. These payment methods are pervasive, as Alipay and WeChat Pay are present everywhere from shopping malls to street stalls.

Background

Given the widespread popularity of Alipay and WeChat Pay, one might believe these are the only two payment platforms in existence. Far more than that exist, however—more than two hundred. The current 247 third-party payment platforms with licenses can be divided into three tiers according to their market share: Alipay and Tenpay, the first-tier platforms, are the most commonly used payment methods. According to data released by Analysys International at the end of 2017, Alipay accounted for half of the industry, with a market share of 54 percent, and Tenpay held a market share of nearly 38 percent. In the second tier are Lacara, Epro, Baidu wallet, fast money, and other midsize payment platforms. Myriad smaller firms occupy the third tier. Most of the two hundred–plus companies in this tier have significantly fewer customers.

These systems have arisen in just ten years, as digital payments have emerged, expanded, and become commonly used. In this short period of time, the third-party payment industry has experienced the following three stages.[2] The first stage was from 2008 to 2011, when the third-party payment industry emerged. The total transaction volume of the market nearly doubled over this period. The second phase was from 2012 to 2015, when the third-party payment industry's transaction volume continued to grow at a rate of nearly 100 percent. The third stage was from 2016 to 2018. From the beginning of 2016, the growth momentum of the third-party payment industry gradually slowed down, and the annual growth rate dropped from the previous 100 percent to 40 percent to 50 percent. According to iResearch's forecast, the industry's annual growth rate will continue to fall to around 30 percent from 2018 to 2020 as the market becomes increasingly saturated.

Two major factors have contributed to this rapid growth of digital payment systems in China.

The first contributing factor is the expansion of bank account ownership to rural areas. Because of the government's campaign to increase financial inclusion, more citizens now have bank accounts than ever before. Bank account ownership dramatically increased among rural residents from 53.7 percent to 74.3 percent between 2011 and 2014. According to the World Bank Findex, which was last updated in 2014, 66 percent of the poorest quintile in China now have a formal bank account, and women have benefited from this process significantly.[3] This ownership has enabled rural residents to take advantage of digital payment services, which require users to have a Chinese bank account. In fact, 19 percent of adults with a bank account were using the accounts to make mobile payments by 2014, and the percentage has only increased since that period.

The second contributing factor leading to the rapid uptake of digital payments is that China is moving toward a cashless society. Fewer people are carrying cash in their wallets and increasingly rely on digital payments. According to a study by Ipsos Research, 40 percent of Chinese consumers normally carry less than 100 RMB in cash, and this is particularly true of younger people.[4] About half of Chinese people use cash for 20 percent or less of their monthly consumption. Digital payment options are used more widely in the more developed regions of China, namely, in eastern and northern China. The mobile payment penetration rate was 77 percent in China in 2016, compared with only 48 percent in the United States. Figure 2.1 shows the rapid growth of mobile payment utilization in China.[5]

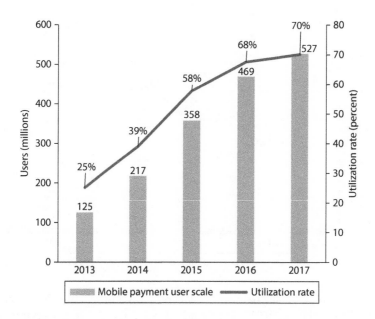

Figure 2.1 User scale and usage rate of mobile online payment apps (user size/ million people internet users usage rate). *Source*: China Internet Information Center, China.org.cn.

Mobile payments are widely accepted at dining institutions, particularly at fast food restaurants. Digital payments are commonly used at movie theaters as well. Use of digital payments is easier than traditional electronic payments requiring a POS terminal. Although a POS terminal can be used for Alipay and WeChat Pay, usually at larger retailers, it is not necessary.[6]

Figures 2.2 and 2.3 show China's online payment transaction size statistics between 2011 and 2017, and the comparison of online to offline payments in 2017. According to figure 2.2, the total volume of online payments reached 2,085 trillion RMB in 2016 and 2,075 trillion RMB in 2017.[7] Figure 2.3 reveals that about 85 percent of payments were made online in 2017.[8]

Digital payments continue to expand in public transportation. For example, the national subway and public transportation systems now accept digital payments. WeChat Pay can be used through the Tencent Bus Code applet. This service is available in nearly fifty cities. The offline penetration rate in sectors such as entertainment, hospitality, and medical services is relatively low, however, in which digital payments lag bank card use.

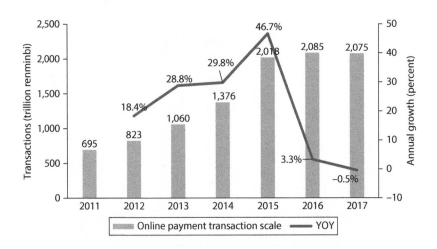

Figure 2.2 China's online payment transaction size statistics, 2011–2017. *Source*: Ai Media Consulting, "2017–2018 China Third Party Mobile Payment Market Research Report" (in Chinese), Ai Media Report, April 23, 2018, http://www .iimedia.cn/61209.html.

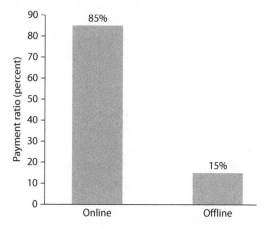

Figure 2.3 Comparison of online and offline scale and payment penetration ratio, 2017. *Source*: National Bureau of Statistics of China, Annual Data, 2017, http://www.stats.gov.cn/english/Statisticaldata/AnnualData/.

In some locations, it is harder to pay with cash than to pay using a payment app. This may leave out some individuals who have trouble using mobile payments, including the elderly, illiterate, and disabled. For these social groups, cash continues to be an important means of payment, which is essential to remember as mobile payments revolutionize commerce. This reality, however, underscores the idea that increasingly, particularly in young, urban areas, cash usage is becoming the exception rather than the rule.

Risks and Rewards in the Digital Payments Sector

The digital payments industry has risks as well as rewards. One of the major risks in this sector is payment security. Maintaining customer security is paramount to a successful online payments company. For example, the U.S. firm PayPal announced a security vulnerability and potential breach in its newly acquired TIO Networks in November 2017 that might have affected 1.6 million users.[9] A full security review of the TIO network was required to determine how extensive the security violation was. This type of security breach lays bare the need to safeguard customer data and prevent the risk of having databases hacked and consumer financial data stolen.

Indeed, Gu and Yang identify mobile payment platform risks as the great risks in the digital payments sector.[10] Mobile payment platform risks are like traditional network security risks of online finance, including website tampering, phishing, and backdoor intrusion. The security issue is great because there is an interaction between mobile terminals and open networks. During the payment process, an intelligent terminal collects transaction information using user identity authentication. The transaction data are transmitted in real time using a mobile network operator. Data must be protected during this procedure, as failing to do so can be costly. Research has shown that in 2016, the per capita network security loss of Chinese consumers reached 9,471 RMB per individual. The total amount involved was as high as 43.35 million RMB.

Even if the mobile payment platform is secure, users can be scammed and must be educated. One story published in the Chinese media illustrates this issue:

> Mr. Zhang attempted to purchase mobile phone software from the internet. The seller told him that in order to make the payment, he could not use WeChat Pay directly but would have to provide the seller with his WeChat wallet barcode. Mr. Zhang reported the barcode to the seller, who took 2,800 RMB from his digital wallet. The seller later sent him a WeChat voice message stating that he had to return the funds and needed to be paid again. Mr. Zhang told the seller the 18-digit barcode once again and was then defrauded of 2,700 RMB. When he realized that this was a scam, Mr. Zhang tried to ask the seller to refund the money but found that he had been blocked by the seller.[11]

This story shows that digital payments users need to be informed about possible scams and prevented from misusing the payment application. In China, fintech users often lack an understanding of how the technology and business work together, so they are vulnerable to fraud. Measures to educate and protect consumers are essential to reduce the risk of user deception.

Despite these risks, the rewards are sufficient to maintain the industry's attraction. Digital payments firms have enjoyed steady fee income flows. This means that the industry enjoys strong liquidity as long as firms choose to take advantage of charging fees for their services. Fee income sources include merchant charges, in which merchants pay a fee to payment institutions. The industry standard rate is 0.6 percent, but it is lower for merchants with many transactions. As the number of merchants using digital payments spreads, the amount of income from this fee source rises. Digital payments companies also can charge customers a cash withdrawal fee. Alipay and WeChat both charge for withdrawals above a certain quota.[12]

Digital payment companies generate rewards through advertising. With many user groups and high daily traffic, large third-party payment platforms tend to have a higher advertising value. Therefore, for the industry, the profitability of the advertising business is considerable. With high commercial value, large third-party payment platforms often use multiple effective channels to conduct advertising business. Alipay, for example, has a large advertising company that uses exclusive subchannels to conduct advertising business. In each administrative region, Alipay cooperates with many small and midsize advertising companies, using multiple firms. The level of agency is engaged in related advertising business. The advertising revenue from this multichannel advertising business has generated significant revenue for third-party payment platforms.

Competition in the Digital Payments Sector

Digital payments are payments made electronically. Generally, these payments are made their online. Internet payments are those made online through a PC from a user to a merchant. Mobile payments also can be used to make payments using mobile communication networks. Payments may be made through a digital television—users can connect their bank cards using the television remote control.

In contrast, the previous generation of digital payments could be used without access to the internet. Fixed-line payments allowed regular telephones to be used as sales terminals if the user had a smart terminal phone combined with a POS terminal device. Digital payments could be made through prepaid cards, with a value specified by the card issuer. Bank card payments made use of bank credit cards through POS and self-service terminals.[13] Some overlap exists between previous-generation payment technologies and present-day payment technologies. Online payments, for example, can be made using prepaid cards.

Ant Financial's Alipay and Tencent's WeChat Pay dominate the digital payments sector. Woetzel et al. refer to the two apps as "super apps."[14] Large third-party payment platforms, such as Alipay and Tenpay, have a transaction volume of more than 10 billion yuan a year, and the resulting income amounts to tens of millions of yuan. In addition, WeChat's app had forty functions, whereas Alipay's app had ninety functions as of 2017. This number of functions is expanding, and customer uptake is rapid. Notably, WeChat Pay was launched ten years later than Alipay and is catching up rapidly in terms of functionality.

Alipay has attempted to compete better with WeChat Pay by offering a chat application. That app, called Laiwang, allows users to chat with up to five hundred people. The program, however, does not allow users to send money within it, as does WeChat. Alipay recently rolled out a service called Quanzi, or Circle, which helps to build online communities. Users can receive updates on topics in which they are interested and can connect with others who share similar

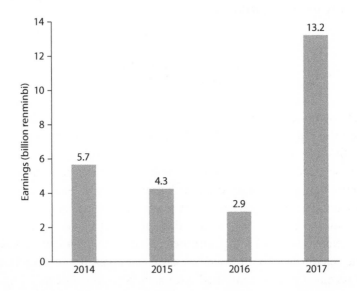

Figure 2.4 Ant Financial earnings before tax. *Source*: "Ant Financial Development Report" (in Chinese), *Beijing Time*, 2018, https://item.btime.com/40kea81aac r9d1bsrm0hnscgpfe?page=1.

interests. Despite Alipay's efforts, it has been a challenge to attract users at the same level as WeChat, which was an early entrant into the social media industry.

Alipay and WeChat Pay are competing to determine which company can gain a greater market share (figure 2.5). In the area of taxi payments, for example, each company is striving to break ground at a faster pace than the other. Both companies rolled out payment services in Hong Kong taxis in November 2017. One month later, two thousand five hundred of the forty thousand taxis had signed up for the service, which included incentives such as no administrative fees.[15] Both Alipay and WeChat Pay expanded usage of their general services in Hong Kong in 2016.

WeChat Pay and Alipay are also expanding to other countries. WeChat Pay and Alipay are available in forty countries and regions around the world.[16] Alibaba and Tencent also have invested in payment apps in other countries. Tencent has invested in PayU, a payment application that is viewed as the PayPal of the developing world. Alibaba has invested in overseas wallets, including PayTM in India, Ascend Group in Thailand, Kakao Pay in South Korea, Mynt in the Philippines, Hellopay in Singapore, and Emtek in Indonesia.

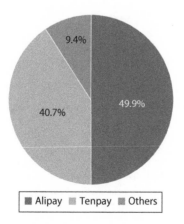

Figure 2.5 Market share of China's third-party mobile payment transaction size, first quarter 2018. *Source*: Ai Media Consulting, "2017–2018 China Third Party Mobile Payment Market Research Report (in Chinese)," Ai Media Report, April 23, 2018, http://www.iimedia.cn/61209.html.

WeChat Pay provides city service to 362 cities with 310 million users.[17] WeChat Pay can be used for several services, including education, transport, and social security. The aim is to improve customer service and access to city services. Alipay also has close association with some cities; for example, the company rolled out a government-certified identity card in three cities in China: Zhangzhou, Hangzhou, and Fuzhou. The identity card can be used for certain administrative services, such as hotel check-ins and ticket purchases.

The payments firms have replaced some traditional practices with financial technology. For example, WeChat's Hong Bao, or *red envelopes*, combined the digital payment system with local culture, allowing users to send red envelopes as digital money gifts during Chinese New Year (figure 2.6). Red envelopes are traditionally given during Chinese New Year as a money gift. WeChat's adaptation of the tradition to digital technology has been wildly successful, resulting in 14.2 billion Hong Bao sent on New Year's Eve in 2017.[18] Some view this innovation in 2014 as a turning point in the popularity of WeChat Pay because of its powerful interaction with important social relationships. After this period, WeChat Pay boomed in online to offline transactions, including with some important firms like Didi Chuxing, a ride-sharing service in which Tencent is an investor.

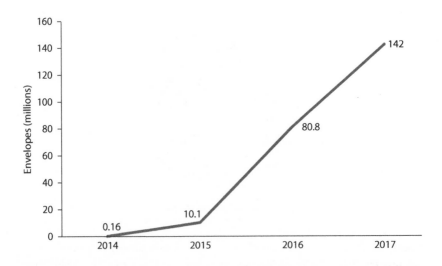

Figure 2.6 Number of WeChat red envelopes issued on New Year's Eve (one hundred million). *Source*: Guojin Securities Research Institute.

Other digital payment companies have created some domestic competition. UnionPay Quickpass is another digital payments application that allows customers to open debit and credit accounts, make QR payments, manage bank cards, shop online, pay bills, and conduct business overseas. The card implements discounts from users' banks. Banks can partner with the company to better compete with Alipay and WeChat Pay. Many online and offline shops now offer the ability to pay with UnionPay Quickpass. China UnionPay has advantages over its competitors in allowing customers to use more than one card easily under the same application.

In the short term, the intensive competition, especially between Alipay and WeChat Pay, may benefit merchants and consumers to a certain extent, but this also has pushed down the profit margin in the industry.[19] Third-party payment platforms are facing competitive pressures from traditional banks, which have attempted to expand their business into this new field. Although third-party payment platforms have many links with traditional banks, such as through pure gateway interfaces that payment institutions use to connect to banks during the payment settlement process, it may be beneficial for banks to launch their own payments business. Some time ago, traditional banks, such as China Merchants Bank, Guangfa Bank, and Industrial and Commercial Bank of China, made large-scale investments in online payment services, focusing in particular on the business-to-consumer field. The central bank has approved more than ten foreign banks to conduct online banking through the internet. Banks may have an advantage compared with third-party payment platforms, because traditional banks have great financial strength and a more mature management model. Therefore, if traditional banks join the online electronic payment industry on a large scale, it could be devastating for third-party payment platforms, especially small and midsize payment institutions.

Intense price wars and operational homogenization have intensified vicious competition within the industry. This heavy competition has spurred the rapid development of the entire industry. In the long run, it is possible that one payment platform will occupy the monopoly position of the industry, at the expense of the consumer. Therefore, each third-party payment platform needs to be innovative and carry out diversified investment, thereby improving the development level of the entire industry. Specifically, payment institutions can take the following diversification measures. First, third-party payment platforms can broaden the scope of business operations and extend the original business scope to administrative agencies and public sectors. For the administrative agency, basic work such as tax collection and payment can be completed through a third-party payment platform; in the public sector, payment institutions can establish a one-stop service platform with a bank, allowing the user to use a mobile terminal. The platform can be used to pay for utility, natural gas, and property fees. Second, the third-party payment platform can cooperate with high-tech companies to introduce new internet financial products using high-tech electronic technology to meet the specific needs of different consumers in other service departments to form a unique competitive advantage.

Adding to this competitive atmosphere, the Chinese government stated in March 2018 that it would open its digital payments sector to foreign competition. This would be carried out in 2020. PayPal already has ties to China through Venmo as well as through Baidu and Alibaba. The UK payment company WorldFirst has applied to enter the Chinese market through its subsidiary, Yuefan Business Information Consulting Shanghai. Apple Pay is already in use in several locations in China on public transit, although its use has trailed that of WeChat Pay and Alipay. Apple Pay has invested a great deal in hardware throughout China as well as in its relationship with Union Pay, but as a latecomer, it is at a serious disadvantage.

Regulation

Since 2005, China has successively introduced laws and regulations related to payments. One of the first regulations was Electronic Payment Guidelines (No. 1), which defined electronic payments and stated how banks and customers should conduct the electronic payment business.

The Administrative Measures for Payment Services of Non-financial Institutions Order, People's Bank of China Bank (PBOC 2010) No. 2, defined payment services provided by nonfinancial institutions and stated that such firms needed a payment business permit from the central bank, which supervises the industry. The Implementation Rules for the Management of Payment Services for Non-Financial Institutions, PBOC Announcement (2010) No. 17, provided rules for managers and investors in payment businesses.

The Provisions on the Administration of Testing and Certification of the Payment Service Business System of Non-financial Institutions [Effective], PBOC Announcement (2011) No. 14, was established to guard against technical risks and ensure compliance with technical standards. The Payment Agency Customer Deposit Payment Procedures, PBOC Notice (2013) No. 6, sought to regulate customer deposit payments, requiring that such deposits be paid into a reserve fund. The policy also described the requirements for the reserve fund bank.

The central bank laid out the Administrative Rules for Network Payment of Nonbank Payment Institutions in December 2015. These rules created tiers of payment accounts provided by nonbank digital payment companies. The rules required that low-transaction-volume customers be identified by a legal external database, that medium-transaction-volume customers be identified in person or by three external databases, and that high-transaction-volume customers be identified in person or by five external databases. These rules revealed the position of the PBOC, the Ministry of Commerce, and other institutions.

The Guiding Opinions on Promoting the Healthy Development of Internet Finance of 2015 clarified the role of regulators in creating guidelines and encouraging innovation for internet finance.

In 2017, China intensively introduced laws and regulations on the regulation of third-party payment, aggregation payment, and other institutions. These included the Notice on Conducting the Cleanup and Remediation of "Aggregated Payments" Services, the Notice on Further Strengthening the Remediation of Unlicensed Payment Services, Notice of the People's Bank of China on Regulating Payment Innovation Business, and Bar Code Payment Service Specification (Trial).[20]

These new rules stated that aggregate payments should not be disguised to settle special merchant funds; should not collect sensitive information; should obtain a network payment service license if using a bar code; should adjust bank cards and transaction limits to be accepted according to the risk of small merchants; should not allow the payment amount of all small microbusinesses to exceed 1,000 yuan; and should not take part in securities, insurance, credit, financing, wealth management, guarantee, trust, currency exchange, or cash access based on barcode technology.

In August 2017, the PBOC required payment firms to submit all digital payments to the central bank clearing platform Wanglian.

Starting in 2018, the clearing platform was intended to track capital outflows and illegal transactions.

QR code generation, payment transmission, and security present several potential risks. To combat these risks, China's central bank laid out regulations in December 2017 that require QR encryption, transaction verification, and information protection. Online payment service providers also need a permit to operate. Additional regulations implemented in December 2017 state that digital payment firms must change their reserve funds ratio from 20 percent to 50 percent. In addition, foreign third-party electronic payment firms must store client data in China as of March 2018.

Overseas Digital Payment Transactions

Overseas digital payment transactions follow a slightly different business procedure than do domestic digital payments transactions. Cross-border third-party payment involves a domestic third-party payment institution that obtains a nonfinancial institution's payment service license issued by the central bank to provide cross-country or regional internet payment services to facilitate trade or service transactions between domestic and foreign payers.[21] The business model has two channels. First, domestic consumers purchase overseas goods, and funds are remitted abroad, paid in renminbi, and settled in foreign currency. Second, overseas consumers purchase domestic goods, funds are remitted into the country, and payment is settled in renminbi. With the rise of the global payment status of the renminbi, the recognition of the renminbi abroad is also increasing. The Chinese currency now plays an important role in promoting the increased use of cross-border renminbi payment business of third-party payment institutions.

Overseas digital payments began in 1998, when China launched e-commerce. China Merchants Bank first introduced its online banking services, which was a landmark event, triggering the development of e-commerce payment services. With the expansion of third-party payment services, the business scope of payment institutions has shifted gradually from domestic to cross-border payments. In August 2007, Alipay launched its overseas acquiring business to provide Alipay customers with the purchase of foreign exchange and payment services for cross-border shopping, realizing the exchange of renminbi into foreign currency and payment to overseas sellers in real time. Alipay's cross-border payment business has expanded to hundreds of overseas merchants, and the settlement currency is carried out in more than ten currencies, including U.S. dollars, British pounds, and Swiss francs. Demand for such services has increased in recent years.

Third-party payment institutions that carry out cross-border payment services require a payment service license issued by the PBOC. In 2010, the PBOC promulgated the Measures for the Administration of Payment Services for Non-Financial Institutions. In recent years, the scale of transactions in China's cross-border e-commerce market has increased steadily, but the growth rate has slowed down. In 2016, China's cross-border e-commerce transactions reached 6.3 trillion yuan, a growth rate of 23.5 percent. In 2017, cross-border e-commerce transactions reached 7.6 trillion yuan, a growth rate of 19.0 percent.[22]

Ant Financial Profile

Background

Ant Financial, which traced its root to Alipay, was founded in October 2014. Alipay is an online payment service launched in 2004 to facilitate e-commerce transactions on Alibaba's Taobao shopping platform. Ant Financial's business goal is to build an open and shared credit system and financial service platform through technological innovation capabilities to provide safe and convenient inclusive financial services to individual consumers and small and micro-enterprises worldwide. Currently, the business units operated by Ant Financial include Alipay, Ant Fortune, Ant Financial Cloud (upgraded to Ant Financial Technology since 2018), Zhima Credit, and MYbank.

Ant Financial's Alipay began the Chinese third-party payment industry and has been sharing the industry's leading role along with Tencent's WeChat Pay. Since its inception in 2004, Alipay has partnered with more than two hundred financial institutions to provide payment services to more than ten million small and microbusinesses. Alipay has extended its payment services to the businesses offline, using QR codes to ease the process of payments with a quick scan using a mobile phone. Alipay has invented creative ways to make payments. For example, Ant Financial's Smile to Pay system captures customer's biometrics to make a payment. The system was debuted at KFC's KPro restaurant in Hangzhou.

As a pioneer in the online payment space, Alipay created an infrastructure that is scalable and expandable to other financial service offerings. Alipay has amassed a vast quantity of customer transaction data. Since the first year it offered payment services in 2004 through Singles Day (or Double Eleven Day, a major online shopping day) in 2018, Ant Financial has accumulated risk management and customer behavior experience through a massive number of financial transactions. On Double Eleven Day in 2017, the total number of Alipay transactions reached a high of 170 million. In addition, Alipay has more than one billion active users worldwide. It has developed into an open platform that integrates multiple services and industries, including payment, living services, government services, wealth management, insurance, and public welfare.

In terms of payments, the cost to Alipay merchants is considerably low. Merchants pay an annual fee between 0.4 percent and 0.6 percent. These fees are lower than those charged by PayPal, MasterCard, and Visa, and vary with the value of the transaction. Alipay holds a large amount of funds on deposit to the PBOC (China's central bank), and, as a result, it is no longer viewed as a major competitor to banks. Payment deposit funds were estimated to have reached 400 billion RMB in 2018. Ant Financial derives its revenue from three areas: income from payment services, income from technical consulting fees to partners such as financial institutions, and income from financial services. With the transformation of Ant Financial from an integrated financial service platform to an open technical service platform model, the proportion of revenues from payment and direct financial services is expected to decrease, and the proportion of technical service revenue is expected to increase.

Ant Fortune is the mobile wealth management platform of Ant Financial. Users can log into the Ant Fortune app or the "Ant Wealth" section in the Alipay app to invest in wealth management products, such as Yu'ebao; regular wealth management offerings, such as Cunjinbao; and mutual funds. At the same time, users can access financial information, market conditions, community view exchanges, and other services. With the more diversified and higher-yielding investment expectations from users, Ant Fortune gradually has developed from a platform marketing only Yu'ebao into a full wealth management platform covering product categories, such as bond funds, index funds, equity funds, and gold exchange-traded funds. To date, the platform has more than one hundred fund companies and more than three thousand fund products. Ant Fortune uses artificial intelligence (AI) to make personalized recommendations for customers, and in 2019, Ant Future started to offer advanced robo-advisory services.

Ant Financial also creates insurance products through advanced technology and massive data to address customer insurance needs. For example, the first commercial application in the field of auto claim adjustment that is combined with AI and computer vision, Dingsunbao, can automatically analyze traffic accident pictures for car damage and submit accurate claim evaluation results in just a few seconds.

Ant Financial is involved in public welfare insurance as well. In January 2018, Ant Financial and Trust Mutual Life officially launched the public welfare platform Xianghubao. Xianghubao members share the claim costs using the following formula:

$$\text{Claim cost contribution amount} = (\text{guarantee} + \text{management fee}) / \text{number of participating members}$$

The management fee is 10 percent of the completed claim costs in each period. This public mutual assistance product provided basic major illness coverage and a valuable inclusive insurance offering to customers.

Business Strategy

To achieve its mission, Ant Financial has employed three major strategies to compete in a fiercely competitive global arena: globalization, service to small and micro-enterprises, and improvement of the credit system.[23] As early as August 2007, Alipay expanded beyond mainland China into Hong Kong. Later, Ant Financial invested in several overseas payment services, located mainly in South and Southeast Asia. Expansion into these regions has huge potential, as the current supply of finance services is inadequate to meet growing demands. Ant Financial invested in and transferred technical know-how to PayTM in India in 2015. As a result, the number of users in India rose from less than thirty million in 2015 to more than three hundred million in 2018. Since 2015, Ant Financial has launched a series of overseas local e-wallets through strategic investments. In three years, it has entered nine countries and regions including India, Thailand, South Korea, Philippines, Indonesia, Hong Kong, Malaysia, Pakistan, and Bangladesh, which created what became known as the "1 + 9 payment network" (i.e., Alipay China plus nine local digital wallets), serving more than one billion people worldwide.

In June 2018, the company announced the world's first cross-border remittance network based on blockchain through a partnership between AlipayHK and GCash, the leading digital wallet in the Philippines. Traditionally, sending money home for Filipinos working in Hong Kong involved a long process of physically going to a remittance booth, queuing in line for hours, and filling out forms. With blockchain-powered remittance service, it now can be done securely on mobile phones in a few seconds.

Ant Financial has provided loans to millions of small and micro-enterprises, lending to more than sixteen million small firms in 2018. This business is part of Ant Financial's online merchant banking activity, with credit decisions being based on sales data collected from e-commerce platforms operated by Alibaba Group. These loans are small and generally unsecured. This platform can process a loan application in three minutes using AI and big data analytics. Ant Financial services small firms through MYbank, one of the first batch of privately owned banks licensed in China. MYbank is a privately owned commercial bank approved by the China Banking Regulatory Commission. This internet bank officially opened for business on June 25, 2015. With the mission of serving small and micro-enterprises, supporting the real economy, and practicing inclusive finance, MYbank practices inclusive finance and provides finance for small and micro-enterprises as well as for individual entrepreneurs. Therefore, Ant Financial is playing an important role in increasing lending to these small and micro-enterprises, which aligns with government policy goals.

Finally, Ant Financial's credit rating system, Zhima Credit (also called Sesame Credit), uses big data analytics. Cloud computing is used to process vast amounts of data. Sesame Credit holds both personal and corporate credit licenses. Zhima (Sesame) Credit is an independent third-party credit institution and an important part of the Ant Financial ecosystem. Zhima Credit quantifies the credit worthiness of individuals and companies using technologies such as cloud computing and machine learning. The company uses big data from more than three hundred million registered users. With permission from users, data are collected from Alibaba Group's various services, combined with information from social media, transactions on Alibaba platforms, and usage of Alipay, to feed into analytics. Merchants can access Sesame Credit for a small fee to better understand customer credit risks.

The company has operated on several factors that have been proven to be essential to online financial service success according to David (Kuo Chuen) Lee, director and practice professor of quantitative finance at Singapore Management University.[24] Known as LASIC, these principles include low profit margin, asset light, scalability, innovative, and ease of compliance. Low profit margin refers to the idea that fintech services must achieve a critical mass of customers using high network effects and low profit margins, as customers use online information to find the lowest costs. This approach suggests that the secret to turning a profit is to have high volumes of transactions and a critical mass of users. Asset light means that fintech businesses must have low fixed costs so that they can easily adapt to new situations. The principle of scalability states that fintech businesses that start small must be able to grow while maintaining efficiency and keeping the costs down. Innovative fintech firms must continue to change and adapt to new circumstances. A benign compliance environment allows fintech firms to grow and change without the high costs of a tight regulatory environment.

Ant Financial meets all these standards.[25] The firm charges low fees to merchants for payment receipts and provides low fees for high-quality wealth management products. Therefore, the firm has provided more benefits to its customers without a high margin. Ant Financial is also asset light in most business lines, with few costs stemming from building the technological infrastructure. Alipay's architecture has scaled up from serving one hundred million users in 2005 to one billion worldwide in 2019. The company constantly searches for better ways to process payments both online and offline while allowing customers to make payments with ease. Alipay performed well in a tolerant yet prudential regulatory environment imposed by the Chinese government until more recently. The company obtained the first Third Party Payment license issued by PBOC in a market it helped to create.

Technologies

As a technology company, Ant Financial is strategically focused on the core technology capabilities of BASIC—that is, blockchain, AI, Security, Internet of Things (IoT), and computing. On the basis of these five areas, three major capabilities are extended: credit, risk management, and professional connections. Ant Financial also cooperates in six dimensions: financial intelligence, mobile development, blockchain, financial security, financial distributed architecture, and financial distributed database. The cooperation mechanism helps participants in the ecosystem to improve customer retention and promote resource sharing (such as big data analytics, customers' direction), while in turn helping Ant Financial to strengthen its position. Ant Financial is developing additional cooperation mechanisms under the Alipay Applets Ecological Development Plan and the Ant Blockchain Partner Program.

Recently, Ant Financial announced the opening of a financial cloud, biometrics, blockchain, and other capabilities to partners such as financial institutions. Capacity enablement is becoming a long-term driving force for the company's future growth. The use cases of blockchain applications include charity traceability, product traceability, urban services, cross-border payments, judicial confirmation, and rights protection. At the same time, the Ant blockchain partner program was launched to enable small and medium-size entrepreneurs to directly develop and apply various scenarios on the underlying blockchain technology.

Ant Financial has been using blockchain technology to tackle real-world problems by making financial services and commerce more efficient. It has developed 831 projects on this platform, which has raised more than $187 million from two hundred million donors since 2008. For example, Ant Financial has applied blockchain technology in its Ant Love charity platform to make it more transparent. The lack of trust in the charitable sector in China has been an issue in the past. Blockchain helps to build this trust. Ant Financial applies blockchain technology to the Ant Love charity platform as a "transparency ledger," on which donations can be tracked in real time.

Blockchain has been applied to Ant Financial's food supply chain tracking as well. On September 30, 2017, Alipay launched a program jointly with Cainiao Logistics and Tmall to allow customers who purchased certain imported products from Australia to scan the QR code on the product and access information about the producer, the quality inspector, and the delivery status. All relevant parties participate in a blockchain-enabled platform, ensuring the reliability of the information and food safety.

Ant Financial has made three technological advances in the field of financial security. These include (1) ZOLOZ, (2) IFAA, and

(3) AlphaRisk. The ZOLOZ biometric face recognition system has reached 99.99 percent accuracy. The IFAA local biometric certification framework covers 1.2 billion terminal devices and supports 380 types of Android phones with high security at the trusted execution environment level. The AlphaRisk intelligent risk control engine has been upgraded to the fifth generation, and its accuracy and computing performance have improved significantly. Alipay's payment fraud loss rate is less than five-tenths of a million, far below the two-thousandths risk level of leading international payment agencies.

Ant Financial Cloud is a platform that provides financial institutions with cloud computing services based on online financial technologies amassed over the years. Since its release in September 2015, it has opened its technical capabilities to provide basic financial technical services to its ecosystem partners. As of 2018, the Ant Financial cloud was fully upgraded to Ant Financial Technology, and its more than eighty products included financial intelligence, financial security, financial distributed architecture, mobile development, blockchain, and financial distributed database. Ant Financial has served more than two hundred partners, including more than one hundred banks, sixty insurance institutions, and forty mutual funds and securities firms.

Financial intelligence is another focus, and the number of use cases is gradually increasing. The financial institutions that Ant Financial empowered with financial intelligence include Harvest Fund, Zhonghe Rural Credit, and Guiyang Bank.

Risk Control

Ant Financial has complied with changes in regulation and aims to stay at the forefront of risk control methods. Regulatory policies aim to keep industry development on track and control risks. Ant Financial abides by business ethics, relevant laws and regulations, regulatory requirements, and best business practices. The company pays much attention to risk prevention and control and actively participates in establishing new industry standards and international standards to reduce potential regulatory uncertainties. Adhering to the idea of compliance operation, Ant Financial has established a smooth communication channel and a sound supervision mechanism to promote fair competition, protect intellectual property rights, safeguard human rights, oppose discrimination, and eliminate any form of corruption and commercial bribery.

Through biometrics, machine learning, and other cutting-edge technologies and an industry-leading professional risk control team, Ant Financial proactively carries out safety checks for users. Ant Financial has passed a variety of domestic and international safety testing standards. Ant Financial also has set up an emergency response team and established a clear contingency process to ensure that in the event of major information safety incidents, it can respond in a timely manner and report to relevant regulatory authorities.

Ant Financial not only reinforces its own risk control system but also cooperates with the industry's leading enterprises to improve the risk control system of the fintech ecosystem. Ant Financial actively communicates with regulatory agencies, such as People's Bank of China, China Banking and Insurance Regulatory Commission, China Securities Regulatory Commission, and Ministry of Industry and Information Technology; participates in setting industry standards; and adjusts safety and compliance strategies to proactively control related compliance risks. With the rapid growth of its overseas business, Ant Financial has helped international regulators conduct related research before the revision of international standards.

Innovation

Ant Financial continues to innovate. The Alipay applet is a new open model of Ant Financial. It runs on the Alipay client and can be easily accessed and distributed without downloading. As one of the largest apps in the mobile internet ecosystem, Alipay's small programs allow more external developers and merchants to reach hundreds of millions of customers through Alipay, further allowing the platform to expand its service capabilities to meet the diverse needs of users and providing a better user experience. On September 20, 2018, Alipay released the Cloud Security Token Service program, which is to invest 1 billion RMB over three years to promote the development of Alipay applets.

Some emerging challenges demand innovative solutions, including the following: (1) providing real-time secure computing of IoT massive data, (2) providing machine intelligence with financial capabilities, (3) ensuring that services never go down, (4) making the digital world safe and trustworthy, and (5) providing everyone with a digital identity.

China's Place in Global Digital Payments Development

China's place in global digital payments development is rising rapidly. China is expected to overtake the United States in the digital payments sector by 2020. Global noncash transactions are expected to grow at the fastest rate in emerging Asia, led by China and India, at 30.9 percent.[26] Ant Financial and Tencent are top payment firms in China and are attempting to expand globally. Ant Financial is considered to be the largest fintech company in the world, and it is continuing to expand overseas to increase its market share in the industry. In June 2018, Ant raised $14 billion to expand globally. Ant Financial holds stakes, for example, in bKash, a fund transfer service in Bangladesh, and Telenor Microfinance Bank of Pakistan, as well as helloPay Group in Singapore and EyeVerify in the United States. In January 2018, Ant Financial was blocked from acquiring MoneyGram by the U.S. government, which failed to approve the deal. Alipay is already present in the United States, however, having entered the market in 2016. In 2018, Ant Financial made an agreement with First Data to allow more than four million U.S. merchants to accept Alipay.

Tencent has had a smaller presence overseas, as it has attempted to target mainly Chinese users overseas rather than to expand to foreign customers. WeChat Pay executives have stated that developing local wallets for overseas users is difficult.[27] Currently, WeChat Pay provides digital wallets for local users in Hong Kong and Malaysia. WeChat Pay has eight hundred million users that have set up the service, linking it to their bank accounts or credit cards.

Digital payments go hand in hand with an expanding e-commerce industry. China accounts for 40 percent of global e-commerce transactions. Users move between digital payments, social media, and e-commerce apps on their mobile phones. E-commerce includes an increasing number of cross-border transactions, as online sales and purchases become increasingly global.

CHAPTER THREE

Peer-to-Peer Lending and Crowdfunding

PEER-TO-PEER (P2P) lending provides a platform on which borrowers and lenders can meet. P2P platforms allow small businesses and individuals to obtain loans in an environment in which they often are unable to secure loans from banks. In China, the P2P sector was popular at its inception, but it later experienced ongoing issues with fraud and poor management. Regulatory action shook up the industry in 2018, and at the time of this writing in 2019, the future of the industry was unclear.

Crowdfunding platforms have provided another means of raising funds and have become an important method of borrowing in China. Chinese investors are interested in obtaining returns that they cannot receive from bank deposits, so providing funds through crowdfunding platforms is an attractive investment alternative. Borrowing through a crowdfunding platform allows smaller firms and individuals to obtain funds potentially more easily and quickly than through the formal banking system.

In this chapter, we explore the development of China's P2P lending industry and the subsequent emergence of the crowdfunding industry.

Background

Globally, the first P2P lending company began in London in 2005 with the advent of Zopa. China's P2P lending sector began in 2006 with the establishment of CreditEase in Beijing, and it grew more rapidly starting in 2011, with the initiation of PPdai. This was followed by the emergence of the P2P firms Hongling Capital, Renrendai, and Lufax. Over time, the industry has become more concentrated, with larger firms taking on a greater market share. In July 2018, the P2P industry had a total of 1,662 normal operating platforms. China's online lending volume went from $3.3 billion U.S. dollars in 2012 to $41.1 billion in 2014, more than the United States ($10.4 billion) and the United Kingdom ($2.4 billion) to $420 billion (2,804.8 billion RMB) in 2017. Total investors and borrowers in 2013 were numbered at four hundred thousand, exploding to forty million by 2017.[1] More than 80 percent of borrowers are between the ages of twenty and forty, with a monthly income of 4,000 RMB ($600).

The number of P2P lending platforms increased greatly in 2015 and remained relatively high through 2017. Figure 3.1 illustrates this

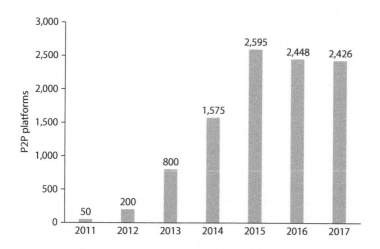

Figure 3.1 Number of national P2P lending platforms. *Source*: Prospective Industry Research Institute, "2016 P2P Online Loan Market Volume and Platform Statistics" (in Chinese), Qianzhan, 2018, https://bg.qianzhan.com/report/detail/459/170116-76b6eb15.html.

fact, showing that the number of P2P platforms in existence surged over 300 percent between 2013 and 2015.[2]

Indeed, both borrowers and lenders have found the P2P lending model appealing. Borrowers are attracted to these platforms' cost-effective pricing, flexible repayment channels, and financing discounts, whereas lenders and investors are attracted to the associated registration rewards, cash back for credit-based purchases, and competitive returns.[3] According to a 2015 survey of 935 borrowers and lenders on the P2P lending platform Paipaidai, 87 percent of users were attracted to the easy application process and low borrowing threshold, and more than half stated that they were borrowing to build up a credit history because they did not have one.[4] In July 2018, the number of active investors and borrowers in the P2P industry totaled 3.34 million and 3.75 million, respectively.

Loans could be priced either based on credit risk or based on the lowest bidder in an auction. In July 2018, the comprehensive rate of return for the P2P industry was 9.76 percent, and the average borrowing period for the P2P industry was 12.99 months. Figure 3.2

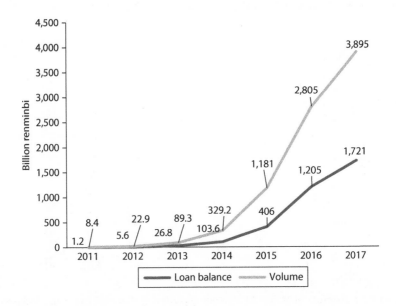

Figure 3.2 National P2P loan balance and turnover (billion renminbi). *Source*: Report Hall, First Online Loan, "P2P Online Loan Industry Status and 2017 Development Trend Analysis: The Number of Platforms Shrinks" (in Chinese), Chinabgao, July 31, 2018, http://www.chinabgao.com/freereport/76214.html.

shows the loan balance and turnover volume in the industry between 2011 and 2017.[5]

During the period of heavy development in China, several P2P lending business models arose. These models included the direct model, the automatic bidding model, the self-guarantee model, and the risk diversification model.

Under the direct model, the platform acted as an intermediary by providing information and rating borrowers based on their creditworthiness. The platform was required to review the borrower's qualifications and eliminate unqualified borrowers, displaying the information about the good borrowers to match investors and borrowers. If the borrower defaulted, the platform helped the investor follow-up with the borrower. One or more lenders could finance a loan. Most loans tended to be of relatively short duration, around ten months.[6]

Using technology, some P2P platforms also adopted a model in which there was automatic bidding on loans and a transfer of claims to investors. This allowed platforms to reduce the waiting period between the request for funds and funding. This reduced the amount of idle funds. This model could meet challenges, however, if the number of investors was insufficient.

Other business models included the guarantee model, the risk diversification model, and the agency model. Under the guarantee model, the platform guaranteed the payment to investors. This model was common in the early years of P2P lending but has since been banned because of excessive risks. The practice of using third-party credit guarantee companies to guarantee the funds also has dissipated, as the credit guarantee industry faced mounting risks when multiple P2P loans defaulted. Currently, however, it is increasingly common to use insurance to guarantee the funds.

Under the risk diversification model, the platform did not provide guarantees, but rather distributed revenues and risks among investors. This model used risk pricing methods to cover potential losses stemming from defaults. In the agency model, firms sold the credit assets of financial institutions to investors on the platform. Examples of these types of firms include lu.com and yooli.com.

China's P2P lending industry faced serious challenges in 2018, as more stringent regulations were put into place to control risks. Protests against failing P2P lenders rocked the country. The situation was so threatening that China's bad banks, its four largest asset management companies, were ordered to intervene in the sector to bail out failing P2P lending companies. These asset management companies—Huarong, Cinda, Great Wall, and Orient Asset Management—were asked by the China Banking and Insurance Regulatory Commission to purchase nonperforming loans of firms in this sector to stem social unrest.[7] Figure 3.3 shows that the number of active investors and borrowers declined in 2018 because of enforcement of regulations.[8]

China's largest P2P companies control for risk in a number of different ways. For example, Hexindai controls risk by analyzing big data. The company reviews borrowers' credit history with the banking system, which all banks hold. GBG software is used to reduce the risk of fraud.[9] The firm uses the FICO decision-making engine and credit scoring to determine how risky customers are. Yirendai uses its own risk management system, which is similar to a FICO score, and has five levels of pricing. Both Hexindai and Yirendai also use credit insurance.

Renrendai follows a similar model, using its own credit rating system that incorporates borrower information. Renrendai assigns a

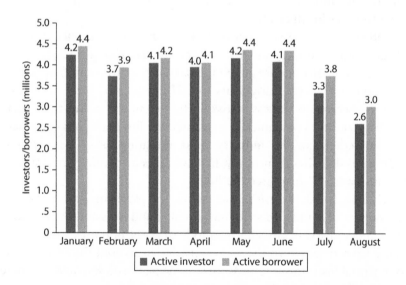

Figure 3.3 P2P active investment and borrowings in 2018 (January through August). *Source*: Online Loan Home, "P2P Active Investment and Borrowings" (in Chinese), Online Loan Home, 2018, https://www.wdzj.com/wdzj/front/search/index?type=12&referer=//www.wdzj.com/front/search/index&key=%25E6%25 9C%2588%25E6%258A%25A5.

credit score to each borrower and classifies every loan application into one of seven risk grades starting with the safe Grade AA, followed by Grades A through E, and finally HR (high risk). Renrendai also offers an offline credit-checking process through its sister company, Ucredit. In 2015, 89 percent of loans sourced were authenticated offline. Many borrowers also were backed by approved credit guarantee companies. Renrendai loans do not use collateral and have a fixed interest rate.[10] The company has a risk reserve fund to cover delinquent payments. Payments overdue for two months or longer are transferred to a collections agency.

Weidai is the largest P2P auto loan platform in China, maintaining strong risk management procedures using big data. Weidai conducts risk analysis by capturing authorized user information, such as credit information, social welfare, and consumption data. The company then standardizes the data to compare online and offline data, providing applicants with an automated message after the loan is given. Offline enforcement and feedback supplement online risk analysis.

Paipaidai has its own credit rating system called the Magic-Mirror System. This system analyzes big data, covering more than two thousand borrower characteristics to evaluate their credit score and risk of default. Borrower information includes personal information, third-party data, repayment history, personal debt, and credit history. Borrowers are assigned credit ratings ranging from AAA to F.[11]

Figures 3.4–3.7 show the net income for Paipaidai, Yirendai, China Rapid Finance, and Lexin, respectively.[12] China Rapid Finance is in the least attractive position financially, with negative net income year after year. China Rapid Finance has struggled to keep up with regulations and to make its business model more profitable. The other firms appear to be relatively healthier.

The P2P firms that have remained in the industry despite the regulatory crackdowns have developed better credit rating systems than in years past. At the beginning of the development of the P2P industry, credit rating required a lot of staff power and often fell short because of the lack of information. This was particularly difficult for the P2P industry, which, rather than servicing regional or local borrowers, had to investigate the credit background of borrowers nationwide. Due diligence often was overlooked because of the high costs of examining customers for credit risk. Over time, automated risk modeling based

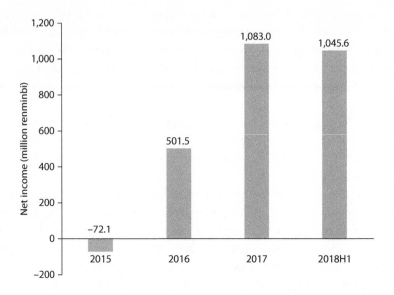

Figure 3.4 Paipaidai's net income (2018 data for first 6 months). *Source*: WIND, Wind Data, 2018, www.wind.com.cn.

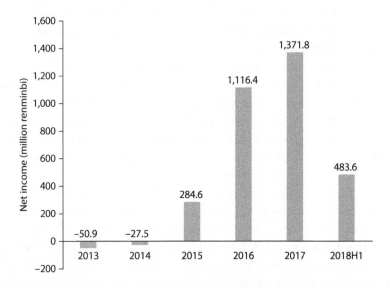

Figure 3.5 Yirendai's net income (net profit/million yuan; 2018 data for first 6 months). *Source*: WIND, Wind Data, 2018 www.wind.com.cn.

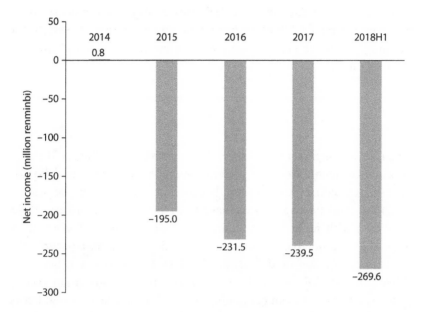

Figure 3.6 China rapid finance's net income (2018 data for first 6 months). *Source*: WIND, Wind Data, 2018, www.wind.com.cn.

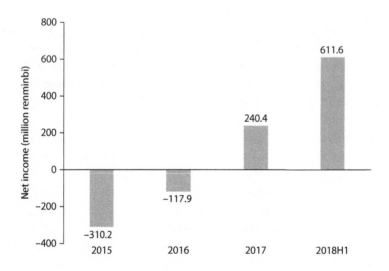

Figure 3.7 Lexin's net income (2018 data for first 6 months). *Source*: WIND, Wind Data, 2018, www.wind.com.cn.

on the use of big data allowed P2P companies to better assess credit risk. The largest P2P lending firms tend to have a distinct system for assessing customer credit scores and determining which clients are most creditworthy.

Riskiness in the P2P Lending Sector

The P2P lending sector has several major risks, including credit risk, information technology risk, operational risk, legal risk, and liquidity risk.[13] Credit risk is present because the credit appraisal system is lacking, and borrowers may have poor or no credit history. Risks associated with information technology make online P2P companies particularly vulnerable to hacking. Operational risk may occur from managerial mistakes or downright fraud by employees or other individuals, and P2P firms require internal controls and governance controls to prevent this from happening. Legal risks may arise as regulators impose additional regulations over time and firms may be required to meet new standards. Finally, liquidity risks may come about as P2Ps experience increasing fund requirements resulting from a run on the company or maturity mismatches. Such events can leave P2Ps without enough money to pay obligations.

Controlling for credit risks was a major challenge at the outset of the industry because of the lack of borrowing information for many individuals and firms. The movement of lenders from offline to online made understanding credit risks an even more challenging task for creditors. To properly assess customer creditworthiness, these creditors often still had to follow up with customers offline. In many cases, platforms lacked the expertise to appropriately assess credit risks even when information was available, although some firms were savvy enough to outsource credit risk analysis to expert firms. In addition, on some platforms, lenders were able to obtain loans themselves using their creditors' rights as a security. This led to increased leveraging by many platform lenders, which then faced the risk of potential default.

Furthermore, according to one study, investors spend only twenty to thirty seconds evaluating the viability of a P2P loan entry. Because the amount of borrowing is relatively small, and the analysis process is too complicated for individual investors, investors intentionally ignore details when making decisions. This also has occurred when loans have been guaranteed, as investors know that they will be repaid even if the credit risk is high.[14] When complete information is lacking, lenders tend to look at and mimic the behavior of other investors, creating a herd mentality in which multiple investors are vying for similar loans. All of these actions have a disastrous impact on proper credit risk assessment.

Credit risks can be amplified when borrowers lack experience with properly using credit. This risk can be exemplified using an anecdote first printed in the *Securities Times* that represents a typical online borrower.[15] According to the story, a woman called Wang Sufen (not her real name) borrowed 140,000 RMB from a P2P lending company to open a clothing store. She quickly lost all of the capital. Each month, Wang Sufen received text, phone, and WeChat reminders to repay the loan, but as she had no income, she was forced to borrow money to pay off the loan. Four years later, the 580,000 RMB she had borrowed to pay off the initial loan had itself not yet been paid off.

Wang Sufen had borrowed funds from several places, including small loan companies, P2P lending companies, microfinance companies, and banks. As she had little experience with loans, Wang Sufen at first didn't see the harm in obtaining them, as all she had to pay was a monthly installment of a few hundred RMB. However, as she got deeper and deeper into debt, she realized that she had a problem. According to her contract, Ms. Wang's calculated annualized interest was between 7.56 percent and 23.64 percent, which is considered to be a normal private loan interest rate. What Wang Sufen had not realized before obtaining the first loan is that she had to pay a monthly fee of over 2,000 RMB for a platform service fee and repayment liability insurance. This increased her debt significantly. These small firms also continued to charge interest based on the entire principal, rather than the principal that remained. As a result, the interest payments were also quite high, increasing the actual interest rate by many times.

According to the central bank's credit records, Wang Sufen was delinquent on 20 loans, but this did not affect her ability to continue to obtain loans. Some small loan company employees even helped Wang Sufen borrow money on other platforms for a fee. The December 2017 "Notice on Regulating and Regulating the 'Cash Loan' Business" (No. 141) attempted to prevent financial companies from getting borrowers overindebted, but the practice is taking time to implement. Also, in December 2017, the "Notice on Printing and Distributing the Implementation Plan for the Special Remediation of the Microfinance Business Risk of Small Loan Companies" stated that the real interest rate must include all borrowing costs such as interest, expenses and insurance premiums. The current crackdown on the P2P lending industry seeks to force P2P lending companies to properly implement these measures.[16]

Another major issue stemmed from the use of credit guarantees. If borrowers defaulted on loans, P2P lending platforms often compensated the lenders for their lost funds. Before regulations were put in place to stop the use of guaranteeing loans, this was the mainstream practice. A study by Yin found that 78 percent of the top-one hundred platforms by outstanding loan amount used loan guarantees.[17] Many of the P2P lending firms guaranteed the loans or used credit guarantee companies. Credit guarantee companies were exposed to a string of loan failures. Many of them shut down when their capital was depleted because of the lack of repayment. Chains of credit guarantees among nonfinancial firms led to a major contagion in some areas. The top credit guarantee companies in 2017 were Zhonghe Guarantee, China Bond Development, China Investment Insurance, Chongqing Three Gorges Guarantee Group, and China Securities Development. The *Regulations on the Supervision and Administration of Financing Guarantee Companies* laid out by the State Council in August 2017, however, stated that the government wanted to guide guarantee companies back into the traditional loan business.

China clearly defined the minimum registered capital, establishment procedures, business scope, and restrictions of the financing guarantee company in *the Interim Measures for the Administration of Financing Guarantee Companies.* P2P companies must be approved for establishment and are not allowed to engage in deposits and loans. The balance of P2P lending platforms' guarantee liability is limited to 10 percent of the net assets. Affected by these factors, to attract funds, some online lending platforms have established a system of self-guarantee or use of platform capital reserves to provide protection for investors' principal and interest income. Under the national policy of de-guarantee, this behavior of the P2P online lending platform likely constitutes a violation of regulations.

Because of the failure of some credit guarantee firms and new regulations, insurers stepped in to provide a stronger type of guarantee to guard against risk. Insurance companies provide risk protection for P2P lending companies.[18] The insurance company and the P2P platform separately agree on a counter-guarantee clause. If a borrower fails to repay the loan according to the contract, the P2P platform provides the counter-guarantee through the insurance premium paid by the insurance company. In the P2P platform counter-guarantee model, the borrower's overdue repayment responsibility ultimately is covered by the P2P platform through insurance premiums. Therefore, the guarantee insurance contract is aimed at reducing the risk of default and diversifying risks.

Some experts have viewed this type of insurance as both insurance business as well as credit guarantee business. This classification matters during the litigation process. The judicial practice community, however, is divided on this issue. For instance, the Supreme People's Court stated in a reply to the Hunan Provincial Higher People's Court that although this is a kind of insurance for the insurer, its essence is of a credit guarantee transaction. This means that, even if the enterprise goes bankrupt or fails, the bank can claim rights to the insurance company, and thus it should deal with the loan guarantee contract dispute and apply the relevant guarantee law.

We next turn to a discussion of operation and liquidity risk. Operation risk arose before P2P lending platforms were required to hold funds in escrow accounts. P2P lending companies were holding investor funds in their private accounts. The danger was that funds could be abused and used for self-financing. Capital pooling often was carried out to increase liquidity by matching yields with loan maturities. Liquidity risk was a major issue because of the presence of maturity mismatches between lender and borrower accounts. Lenders expected to see returns in a short period of time, whereas borrowers needed the money for a longer period of time. Borrowed funds generally were repaid in installments, increasing the possibility for maturity mismatches to arise.

Some P2P lending platforms found a solution to this mismatch. Investors with a short time horizon could transfer creditors' rights through the platform, if necessary. For example, if investors signed a three-year contract with a borrower but wanted to exit after six months, they could transfer the contract to another investor, if the platform allowed.[19] This process smoothed operations and reduced the conflict of maturity mismatches, in which investors wanted to lend short and borrowers wanted to borrow long.

Despite marginal improvements along the way, P2P lending fell into disrepute as platforms failed to control for risk or used their own funds to lend to borrowers. P2P firms lent to riskier sectors, including the real estate and mining industries. Platforms also collected cash from investors, who sought large profits. A model that was later banned under regulations implemented in August 2016 allowed P2P platforms to bundle loans to sell to investors under an "originate to distribute" model.[20] This approach aimed to increase platform liquidity, but at the same time, it greatly compounded risks, because risks of the underlying loans were passed on to a larger group of investors.

Another issue was that lenders could register on several P2P lending websites and borrow on multiple platforms, sometimes borrowing more than they could afford. When the lender defaulted on their borrowed loans, this could lead to defaults on several P2P lending platforms.

Fraud also became a problem, as some platforms used money for their own purposes and set up Ponzi-like business models. For example, Ezubao launched a Ponzi scheme that collected 59.8 billion yuan ($9.14 billion) from more than nine hundred thousand investors.[21] Ding Ning, chair of Anhui Yucheng Holdings Group, which launched Ezubao in 2014, received life in prison and was fined 100 million yuan ($15.29 million).

Ezubao, or Jin Yirong Beijing Network Technology Co., started in 2014, was a wholly owned subsidiary of Anhui Yucheng Group, and had a registered capital of 100 million RMB. The expected annualized rate of return ranged from 9.0 percent to 14.2 percent, with maturities of three, six, and twelve months. The platform would sign an agreement with another company through an equipment leasing firm and issue financing in the form of creditors' rights, which transferred on the Ezubao platform. After funds were received, leases were made, and when the company paid rent, the leasing company paid the investor income and principal. Ezubao became quite popular, running advertisements on television channels and sponsoring variety shows.

Ezubao seemed to be in compliance with risk maintenance, signing a contract with the People's Insurance Company of China to insure transactions. As of August 2015, the total turnover had reached

74.568 billion RMB. Most of the information on the financing leases, however, turned out to be false. Only one of the more than two hundred leased companies had a real business relationship with the lessor. In December 2015, Ezubao was placed under investigation. In January 2016, the police announced that the company had illegally raised more than 50 billion RMB.[22] The P2P lending industry overall struggled with fraud:

> Underlying many of these issues was an overall absence of transparency. Information disclosure was lacking, as was capital movement through the action of creating cash pools from investors. Sources of loan repayment were unspecified, making it difficult for investors to understand how reliable the loan repayments were received. In addition, risks have arisen in the P2P lending sector due to low barriers to entry. The lack of a standardized credit reporting system and poor platform management also contribute to rising risks.[23]

Risks resulting from fraud are exemplified in the following story:

> Mr. Shao, a citizen of Kunshan, Jiangsu Province, discovered an online investment scheme that not only doubled its investment. After investing more than 70,000 yuan, he learned that the a self-proclaimed "investment company" did not possess the qualification to operate an online banking business.
> Mr. Shao first invested more than 10,000 yuan. On the morning of the 3rd, Mr. Shao recharged 20,000 yuan for investing in a mobile phone. However, when Mr. Shao asked the company when they would send a mobile phone, the customer service staff stated that to obtain a mobile phone, the customer must be VIP, and that members need to recharge more than 30,000 yuan at a time. At noon on June 4, Mr. Shao recharged nearly 40,000 RMB to the platform. At this time, the customer service staff said that after the event is over, Mr. Shao sent his mobile phone and asked for his delivery address and bank card identity information. On June 5, Mr. Shao found that his account showed a sum of more than 4,000 yuan for "Project repayment," and that there was also a "return of principal" of 20,000 yuan. Mr. Shao felt that the investment in this platform was reliable. However, when he went to obtain his money, a platform staff member said that Mr. Shao's withdrawal channel was

frozen and needed to be activated. In order to activate the account, Mr. Shao would have to invest a total of 80,000 yuan. Mr. Shao calculated that he only had to invest a few thousand dollars to reach 80,000 yuan, so he would recharge 8,000 yuan.

After Mr. Shao saw that there were a few more rebates on his account, but that he was still unable to withdraw his funds, he contacted the customer service staff again, the another party said that he needed to immediately deposit 80,000 yuan to withdraw cash. At this time, Mr. Shao began to doubt himself. After some investigation, Mr. Shao found that the company did not have an online financial platform.[24]

At present, many investors and people already have experienced the same experience as Mr. Shao. To end these fraudulent practices, the government cracked down on the industry in several rounds, detailed in the next section "Regulations."

Regulations

The P2P industry has gone through several regulatory crackdowns that have winnowed the number of viable firms. In August 2011, the China Banking Regulatory Commission (CBRC) issued the Circular on Risks Associated with Peer-to-Peer Lending to identify risks, including money laundering and fraud.

In July 2014, the State Council released the Guiding Opinions on Advancing the Healthy Development of Internet Finance. This required P2P platforms to hold customer accounts at custodian banks and to refrain from guaranteeing returns by covering losses themselves. In July 2015, the Guidelines for Healthy Development of Internet Finance, which moved past the opinion stage, were promulgated, and in August, the Supreme Law clarified the red line of 24 percent for interest rates, with an absolute ceiling of 36 percent for private lending, including for P2P lending companies. Additional rules were set out in December 2015.

An internet finance "rectification campaign" was launched in April 2016 and the CBRC imposed rules on the P2P sector in August 2016.[25] The August 2016 rules launched an institutional framework for the online lending industry that would be elaborated upon through 2017.

New requirements forced P2P firms to set lending and borrowing caps on individual accounts and to hire a custodian bank to hold investors' funds. Regulations also restricted P2P platforms to matching lenders and borrowers and not to acting as a financial intermediary.

The National Internet Finance Association of China (NIFAC) implemented two rules on information disclosure in October 2016, the Standard on Internet Finance Information Disclosure and the NIFAC Rule on Self-Regulation of Information Disclosure, requiring online lenders to provide information on their platforms, including basic information, statistics, and information about projects seeking funds.[26] In October 2016, the Guidelines for the Registration and Licensing of Internet Lending Information Intermediaries were issued. These measures aimed to provide guidelines for registration of online lending information for intermediary institutions and P2P lending companies.

Additional regulations introduced in February 2017 outlined rules for custodian business, stating that only commercial banks can provide custodial services for online lending.[27] Regulations established in April 2017 limited annual interest rates and fees to a total of 36 percent. In June, the government issued the Notice on Further Improving the Cleanup and Rectification of Internet Financial Risks. This notice required provincial groups to submit summary reports at the end of each month. These reports needed to contain classification of internet financial activities according to rectification requirements. On August 25, 2017, the CBRC China Banking Regulatory Commission stated that online lenders must disclose particular information, including deposit and filing information. Disclosure frequency and recipients also were stipulated.

The Circular on Regulating "Cash Loans" Business laid out in November 2017 stated that interest rates should align with the borrowing interest rate required by Supreme People's Court and prohibited illegal fundraising. Loans were barred from being used for the purpose of student loans, investment speculation, or property down payments. The regulation also stated that lending businesses could not deduct the interest, handling fee, management fee, or security deposit from the stated costs. In December, regulators required local governments to improve the P2P industry in their areas, registering major online lending platforms, under the Notice on Doing a Good Job in P2P Network Lending Risk Special Rectification and Reconstruction and Acceptance.

As a result of the regulations, many P2P companies went out of business as they found themselves unable to comply with the new rules. In 2015, the number of P2P platforms reached five thousand, but declined to less than two thousand by 2017.[28] Many P2P firms have failed to remain in business, and the sector continues to consolidate as platforms attempt to control credit risk and improve efficiency.

Some of the worst P2P risks have been related to criminal activity, which is barred by the Criminal Law of China. Article 192 of the Criminal Law prevents fundraising fraud. Article 225 of the law sets out against illegal business operations. Money laundering is banned by Article 191. The crime of selling and illegally providing citizen information is stated in Article 253 of the Criminal Law.[29] Article 176 of the law prevents illegal deposit taking.

Firms that have stayed afloat have been some of the first to comply with new regulations, even though the new standards have not always assured them of greater profits. For example, Yirendai and Hexindai are two P2P firms that have stayed in business in large part by anticipating future regulations. These firms consult with regulators to recommend new regulations and are part of the Beijing Internet Finance Association, an industry self-regulating body that works closely with the government. Managing risks has been a key component of self-regulation for firms that have survived the regulatory process.

P2P firms have used guarantee insurance to manage risks, but this area also has its own regulation and interpretation. The Supreme People's Court defined the nature of guarantee insurance in the Interpretation of Several Issues Concerning the Application of Laws in the Trial of Insurance Dispute Cases (Draft for Comment), which was established in December 2003. This interpretation stated that the guarantee insurance contract was established to guarantee the performance of contractual debts. The China Insurance Regulatory Commission indicated in the Reply on the Case of Guaranteeing Insurance Contract Dispute (the Insurance Supervision Law [1999] No. 16) that guarantee insurance is a kind of property insurance, a form of insurance in which a person provides a guarantee to a right holder. If the rights holder suffers economic loss because of a failure to perform the contractual obligation resulting from an act or omission of the insured, the insurer is liable to the insured or the beneficiary.

In general, authorities have taken a cautious approach to insurance protection of transactions. The government laid out the Interim Measures for the Supervision of Credit Guarantee Insurance Business,

Acting on the Insurance Company's Service Network Lending Industry to issue a warning about the use of insurance of P2P lending platforms. These measures constrain the insurance liability in terms of the amount and activities insured. Certain activities, such as asset-based securities operations and creditors' rights transfers, may not be insured.

Empirical Studies

Many empirical studies have been published in Chinese-language scholarly literature on Chinese P2P lending platforms. These studies have examined different aspects of this sector, including credit risk, efficiency, discrimination, rationality, and regulation. The scholarly literature seeks to analyze data and provide solutions to a particular set of problems.

Credit Risk

To better understand credit risk, several scholars have studied Paipaidai. Zhang et al. examine Paipaidai data to understand the factors that determine the likelihood of obtaining a loan through P2P lending.[30] Using a binary logistic regression, the authors find that such factors as gender, annual interest rate, credit grade, repayment period, description, failed loan number, borrowed credit score, and successful loan number determine whether an individual is successful in receiving a loan.

Feng, Fan, and Yoon also examine Paipaidai data to measure the popularity of loans in terms of borrower strategy.[31] Borrowers are categorized into three types: novice borrowers, pure borrowers, and mixed borrowers (as both borrower and lender). The authors show that applying for larger loans can increase the probability of receiving the loan. Credit-related information is a big determinant in whether borrowers will obtain a loan across all three types. More experienced borrowers propose loans at lower interest rates, whereas mixed borrowers tend to emphasize the loan period.

Chen, Lai, and Lin use Paipaidai data to understand the role of trust in the lending and borrowing decisions.[32] The authors find that trust is important, particularly trust in borrowers. Borrowers must overcome this issue by providing high-quality information, and intermediaries must provide high-quality services as security protection.

The initial system of credit risk assessment requires on-site visits or credit guarantees. Tao, Dong, and Lin examine Renrendai data to understand how the offline credit risk assessment affects whether bor-rowers can obtain loans.[33] The authors find that those who own cars or earn higher incomes are more likely to obtain a loan and pay lower interest rates. Some lenders do not trust the credit rating assigned to the borrower by the P2P platform, but third-party screening offline can mitigate this distrust and improve borrowers' access to credit.

Peng and Xu use binary logistic regression analysis on Renrendai data to analyze the efficiency of the platform's interest rates.[34] The authors find that only the 12.18 percent interest rate is accurate, that the interest rates of high-credit loans are overestimated, and that the interest rates of low-credit loans are mostly underestimated. This underestimation results from the limited fluctuation in the interest rate. Those with underestimated interest rates belong to low-value-added service industries, and those with overestimated loans belong to labor-intensive industries like agriculture and manufacturing.

Li, Li, and Wang use Renrendai data to show that the non-fully market-based interest rate does reflect the borrower's default risk, but that a fairly high percentage of default risk still is not reflected in interest rates.[35] This inconsistency reveals the difference between the real interest rate of the loan project and the ideal interest rate, which should fully reflect the default risk premium of the loan project.

Sun and Fan examine the loan data published by Renrendai.[36] This paper empirically studies the value of borrowing quota and financial heterogeneity in the personal lending market through empirical analy-sis. The authors analyze the relationship between the amount of bor-rowers' borrowings and their success rate and examine the role of borrowing in the personal small-credit market. The empirical results show that, as the amount of borrowing increases, the success rate of borrowing increases first and then decreases. This paper finds that bet-ter experience and high education can reduce the amount the loan decreases by to a certain extent.

Song Weishi analyzes the risk preference of investor groups in P2P lending patterns based on the actual transaction data of P2P lenders.[37] The empirical results show that P2P investors are risk averse. When the interest rate is more than 11 percent, the risk-aversion characteristics of the investor group rise. Risk-averse investors show that the increase in interest rates results in investors making greater effort to select the quality subject matter, so that the potential default risks of borrowers do not increase along with the rise in the borrowing rate. Because the real default rate does not show a positive correlation with the interest rate, the borrowing rate cannot reflect the default rate effectively, thus resulting in an imbalance between the profits and risks of products.

Jiang, Wang, and Ding show that the integration of valuable soft information into the default prediction model of a P2P platform can significantly improve the prediction accuracy.[38] P2P users upload or generate a lot of nonstandard and personalized data, such as basic demographic information and loan descriptions (soft data), when making a loan application and repayment. Rich soft information provides more value factors for default prediction, which can alleviate the impact of insufficient hard information on default prediction. Existing research has found that in the absence of hard information, the impact of soft information on the behavior of lending users is more pronounced.

Hu and Zhang examine the data of 845 P2P platforms to determine the influencing factors of platform default risk and operational risk from a shareholder's perspective.[39] The research finds that the default risk and operational risk of P2P lending platforms with public state-owned assets are lower than that of private platforms, because of differences in reputation and managerial backgrounds.

Efficiency

Gao, Yu, and Shiue examine efficiency in the Chinese P2P lending industry, finding that some companies perform better than others.[40] Those with higher levels of performance (including listed firms), those with venture capital investment, and those funded by state-owned capital exhibit higher growth efficiency. Firms with diversified ownership and financial group involvement show increased operating efficiency. Factors that do not improve efficiency include management incentives and the economic level of the platform location.

Discrimination

Chen, Li, and Lai analyze data collected from ppdai.com to determine whether a gender bias exists in lending on the large lending platform.[41] The authors find that, although females are more likely to obtain funding, they do so at a higher interest rate than males, even though their default rate is lower. The authors suggest that the reasons for discrimination vary.

Dou, Meng, and Zhou look at gender discrimination in Chinese internet borrowing using data from Renrendai platform from 2011 to 2015.[42]

The empirical results show that female borrowers' loan default rate is lower than that of male borrowers. The female borrowers, however, find loans to be less available and suffer from irrational discrimination.

Rationality

Zhang finds that investors in P2P online lending platforms in China are not rational.[43] This is clear because P2P investors do not maximize their expected return, which is affected by both systematic risk and idiosyncratic risk. By contrast, Hu and Song show that Renrendai investors are rational, efficiently matching the supply and demand for loans.[44] Investors shy away from risks associated with lower levels of income and education levels, as default risks are higher for these borrowers.

Regulation

Lei writes about the regulation of China's P2P lending system, noting that multiple regulatory bodies can oversee the industry as long as functional regulatory theory is applied to ensure that similar financial services receive the same regulation.[45] Lei notes that the P2P lending industry offers the same traditional services as the financial industry and therefore should accept the same regulations. The author's view is that financial innovation brought about by the industry is generally positive because it can bring additional efficiency to the financial system.

College Students

About one in four college students cannot repay loans. These students often lack financial knowledge and may overestimate their ability to repay the loan. Those who do repay the loans earn funds through part-time work, receive funds from their parents, or borrow from friends and classmates. In general, research shows that college students with a better credit record or access to external support have a stronger repayment ability.

Wang Xudong examines college students' online lending habits.[46] In 2015, the Renmin University of China Credit Management Research Center surveyed nearly fifty thousand college students from 252 colleges and universities nationwide and published the "National University Student Credit Cognitive Research Report." According to the survey,

8.77 percent of university students use loans to make up for a shortage of funds, of which online loans account for nearly half. One reason for this is that the process of online student lending is convenient.

Currently, college students obtain loans from three types of online lending platforms. The first is a staged shopping platform specifically targeting college students, offering a lower amount of cash withdrawals. Generally, such platforms will mark the price and interest of various stages. Users can enjoy the loan service by purchasing goods from the platform. In this model, interest rates tend to be higher. Many traditional offline lending companies or entrepreneurs with e-commerce experience adopt this model. The second type of platform targeting college students is the credit service provided by the traditional large e-commerce platform. For example, Alibaba's Ant Financial Service and Jingdong's White Bar, based on the existing e-commerce platform, provide one-month interest-free lending or installment services. At the same time, the platform can provide a lower amount of cash withdrawals. Such platforms have a more favorable interest rate. The third type of platform targeting college students is the P2P lending platform, which is used to help students start businesses. This category should not be used for consumption, and loan approval time can be rapid.

Li Wei analyzes the results of an online survey conducted in August 2017 on 404 undergraduate students in Jiangsu Province.[47] The author finds that the consumption pattern of college students determines whether they obtain internet financial loans. College students who have a negative attitude toward early consumption usually do not obtain loans and are less prone to premature consumption. People who think that online loans can solve some urgent needs usually obtain short-term loans to improve their purchasing power. Campus online loans are easier to obtain than other loan methods, so students are more likely to prefer online loans. College students who aim to start a business, however, usually do not obtain campus online loans. In general, college students' entrepreneurship will be supported to some extent by relevant institutions such as schools. Therefore, when entrepreneurs encounter financial difficulties, they often use some relatively formal loan channels, such as from schools, banks, or family support.

Ping and Sun write that college students may suffer from threats to their personal or financial safety after providing much personal information online for a loan application.[48] Undergraduate students in particular may lack an understanding of finance but want to try new things. They may see the benefits of financial products without understanding the consequences of using them. It can be appealing to use loans to purchase goods for a better life without understanding the associated security risks and the potential for being defrauded.

Crowdfunding

The crowdfunding model works well for high-tech or small and micro-enterprises producing goods and services. It is mainly composed of the platform, investors, and fundraisers. Crowdfunding fundraisers list projects on the platform, and the platform is responsible for promoting these projects to investors. This process can be challenging, as the personal reputation of the fundraising company and the ability of the project implementer are essential to attracting investment. The biggest shortcoming for the crowdfunding model is that the financing process may result in insufficient financing, which could result in the inability to carry out the project. Crowdfunding credit for small firms, however, can be more efficient than credit extended by traditional banks. This is because, as Zhang and Xu show, traditional financial institutions implement credit rationing for small and micro-enterprises to reduce costs.[49] The crowdfunding platform is connected with the small amount of funds of individual investors, and once the platform is built, the cost of platform operation and management required is converted into fixed costs. These platforms can expand and achieve economies of scale.

The crowdfunding business model has four modes of funding: service return crowdfunding, equity crowdfunding, bond crowdfunding, and donation or public welfare crowdfunding.[50] In product or service crowdfunding, investors raise funds for a product or service. Product or service crowdfunding may face issues when goods differ from investors' expectations, which can lead to investor complaints about false advertising and lead to legal proceedings. Investors may lose confidence in the platform and refrain from financing companies on the platform in the future. In equity financing, the fundraiser raises money in exchange for investor ownership in the company. This mode is relatively rare because it can bring about a loss of firms' management rights in the future.

In the case of bond crowdfunding, product financing is issued in the form of debt, and the fundraiser must repay the principal and interest after the expiration date. Under this model, the interest cost of repayment is much higher than that of equity crowdfunding or product or service crowdfunding, which can lead small and midsize companies to invest less in research and development (R&D) and production in the future to repay their loans. Donation crowdfunding is used for public welfare projects, and investments are not returned to the investors. In this model, a WeChat friends circle may be used, but the fund use is not monitored.

Public welfare crowdfunding can broaden the development of financial affairs and public welfare.[51] This has become a hot term in the field of internet finance. The advantages of public welfare crowdfunding include existence of a variety of projects, wide coverage, high efficiency, low cost, and high transparency.

Public welfare crowdfunding can harness a large amount of idle funds and create social value. It has a low public participation threshold and represents bottom-up social welfare. Social media can enhance the spread of public welfare crowdfunding and increase interaction between individuals. Risks are associated with this type of finance, however, including potentially poor fund management, lack of legislation, weak supervision, and information asymmetry. The potential also exists for criminal legal risks to arise, leading to fundraising fraud. Even when fraud is not present, the possibility exists that moral hazard can arise through mismanagement of funds and lack of transparency.

Internet equity-based crowdfunding allows individuals to invest in small businesses through online platforms. Small businesses can describe business characteristics online, including their business type and model, financial information, and fund target, to reach potential investors. According to the statistics of the Zero2IPO Research Center, as of the end of 2015, there were 141 Chinese equity crowdfunding platforms, which had raised nearly 10 billion yuan to promote mass entrepreneurship, innovation, and development. Because of the current imperfect internet financial investment environment and unsound regulation, equity crowdfunding faces some risks.

Although the legitimacy of equity crowdfunding has been recognized in the national policy, it has not cleared legislative obstacles and may be suspected of illegal fundraising and unauthorized issuance of shares. For example, Xiamen Credit Platform always claimed to be an equity crowdfunding platform, but it did not follow the corresponding legal operating rules. As a result, it encountered trouble when two hundred people were suspected of illegally issuing stocks.

Equity crowdfunding platforms pose other potential risks.[52] The user information and financing information that may affect the rights and interests of investors in the equity crowdfunding platform may be concealed or false project information may be released. Individuals may disappear after the investment, or misappropriate funds, to the detriment of investor interests. Insufficient privacy protection of investors can result in the acquisition of personal information by third parties, such as hackers, for abnormal use. At the same time, in light of the current asymmetric information of equity crowdfunding, the relevant regulatory legislation lags, rendering the operation of equity crowdfunding unstandardized. Thus, it is easy to enable some bad financiers to obtain investors' investments using false information.

Equity crowdfunding regulations were issued in July 2011, and China's first crowdfunding website platform was officially launched that year.[53] A few equity crowdfunding platforms followed. In September 2011, Dreamcatcher was launched in Shanghai; in March 2012, Taomeng began operation; in December 2013, the Taobao crowdfunding platform was established; in July 2014, Jingdong crowdfunding was launched; and in 2015, Suning crowdfunding was launched.

In terms of regulation, the Administrative Rules on Private Equity-Based Crowd-Funding Financing was issued by the Securities Association of China (SAC) at the end of 2014. A number of regulations followed thereafter, including the Guiding Opinions on Promoting the Healthy Development of Internet Finance of July 2015, which proposed a series of measures to support the development of internet finance, including equity crowdfunding; the Circular on Conducting Special Supervision on Institutions Engaging in Equity Financing via Internet of August 2015, which required that all internet equity-based crowdfunding platforms in China be open only to qualified investors; the Guiding Opinions on Accelerating the Construction of Volkswagen Entrepreneurship and Innovation Support Platform of September 2015, which called for promoting equity crowdfunding; the Implementation of Optimizing the Financial Structure to Further Increase the Ratio of Direct Financing of December 2015; the Notice on Printing and Promoting the Inclusive Financial Development Plan (2016–2020) of January 2016, which proposed to promote the revision of the Securities Law and to strengthen the legal basis for equity crowdfunding; and the Outline of the Thirteenth Five-Year Plan for National Economic and Social Development of March 2016, which proposed to improve the supervision of various types of crowdfunding. Despite all of this regulation, China still lacks the conditions for the real growth of equity crowdfunding because of its younger stock market, lack of compliant institutional investors, and insufficient legal environment for equity crowdfunding. Equity crowdfunding has not been approved by the Securities and Futures Commission.

Zhu and Zhou explore the ability of blockchain to improve equity crowdfunding for startups in China.[54] Even though SAC issued the Measures for Private Equity Crowdfunding in 2014, equity crowdfunding still lacks protection for the rights of investors. Blockchain can resolve this issue. The authors find that the technology can offer a low-cost solution for registration of equity shares in crowdfunding, simplify equity crowdfunding transactions, and improve regulatory compliance.

Figure 3.8 shows the number of internet crowdfunding platforms between April 2017 and March 2018.[55] The overall number declined over this period as regulation increased.

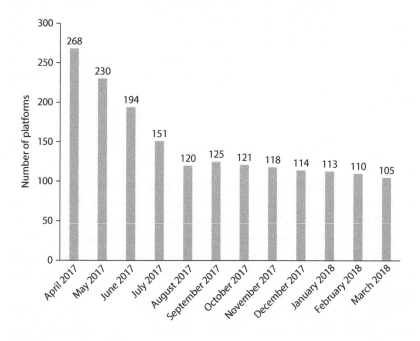

Figure 3.8 Number of Internet crowdfunding operations platforms. *Source*: *Beijing Times*.

China's Place in Global P2P Lending Development

China's P2P lending market boomed much more rapidly than that in any other country, but after regulation, it also faced hundreds of failures. As a result, the sector has been much more volatile than in other countries because of the emergence of risks and fraud in the industry. Compared with the U.S. P2P lending industry, which has boasted successful companies such as Lending Club and Prosper, China's P2P industry was far more chaotic and undisciplined. Investors in Lending Club and Prosper have enjoyed returns of between 5 percent and 9 percent since 2009, whereas returns on investment in China faced volatility and inconsistency in many companies.

A major reason for this volatility is that P2P lending companies in the United States generally have acted only as strict information intermediaries rather than as lenders or asset managers, whereas in China, some P2P companies participated in the lending process or used Ponzi-like financing structures to fund loans. The Chinese P2P lending industry was riddled with insufficient credit risk assessment, resulting in higher rates of loan failure. At present, China's place in the global P2P lending market has significantly diminished. Although some major P2P lending companies remain active, the industry continues to be rationalized, and as of June 2019, more firms were likely to fail.

Yiren Digital Profile

On July 10, 2019, Tang Ning, founder and CEO of CreditEase, announced that Yirendai Digital (a P2P platform) and CreditEase would be merged and that he would assume the role of both businesses. The aim was reportedly to create a digital wealth management solution for affluent investors through Yiren Wealth Management and to provide consumer credit services, with online and offline lending products and services through Yiren Credit.

Tang founded CreditEase in 2006, as China's first marketplace lending company. The company was set up to cater to micro-enterprises and other individuals whose financial needs were not covered by traditional financial institutions. Over the past decade, CreditEase developed into one of China's leading fintech companies, specializing in small business and consumer lending, as well as wealth management for China's rapidly growing mass affluent and high-net-worth investors. Use of technology was essential in working with customers who lacked credit histories.

Tang began his career in finance as an investment banker with Donaldson, Lufkin & Jenrette in New York, where he participated in initial public offerings (IPOs) and bond issuances as well as advised on merger and acquisition transactions in the areas of financial services, telecommunications, media, and technology. Upon returning to China in 2000, he joined U.S.-listed Chinese technology company, AsiaInfo, as the director of strategic investments focusing on opportunities in emerging technology ventures. After his tenure at AsiaInfo, he became one of China's early angel investors and made a series of successful angel investments that later grew into major technology companies such as Tarena International (NASDAQ: TEDU) and Emay Softcom (Shenzhen Stock Exchange: 300085). He also established China Growth Capital, a venture capital firm investing in early-stage consumer and enterprise technology startups.

Under Tang's leadership, CreditEase expanded its nationwide network to include more than 280 cities and rural areas in twenty provinces across China, as well as abroad, in Hong Kong, Singapore, Israel, Europe, and North America. In December 2015, CreditEase successfully listed its online consumer finance and wealth management subsidiary, Yiren Digital, on the New York Stock Exchange (NYSE: YRD), becoming China's first publicly listed fintech company in the global market.

Tang has stated that he believes the success of Yiren Digital is predicated on its tight risk control, operational capabilities, and very large market potential in China. The IPO, in turn, has induced Yiren Digital to become more transparent and to conform with strict financial supervision.

Background

Yiren Digital specializes in marketplace lending serving underserved prime borrowers, online wealth management for the mass affluent population, and a fintech platform servicing other financial services providers.

China has become the largest market in fintech and the undisputed center of global fintech innovation. China's financial services industry has shown a state of imbalance between supply and demand for a long time and a large population remains unserved. The fintech industry has served the financial demands of groups that previously were underserved by traditional banking. Yiren Digital captures this market opportunity to achieve long-term development. The firm is fundamentally a technology-driven company and continues to invest heavily in data science and artificial intelligence, both of which have been providing tremendous efficiency gains and have been driving forward all aspects of business, including customer acquisition, customer services, risk management, and antifraud.

Globalization capabilities, investing capabilities, technology capabilities, and general service capabilities are Yiren Digital's core competencies. In 2014, Yirendai used proprietary risk analysis tools, combined with the data accumulated by CreditEase, to launch the world's first mobile borrowing app. The app has a rapid credit evaluation speed, using mobile phones to allow users to obtain the borrowing amount within one minute, credit approval in ten minutes, and loan receipt within hours.

In June 2015, Yirendai worked with China Guangfa Bank to create an innovative model for fund custody. The model created by Yirendai and Guangfa Bank differs from the industrial standard models. It maintains P2P fund custody and monitors the transaction process between the borrower and lender, completely separating the platform's funds and P2P transaction funds. Yirendai and Guangfa Bank's custody standards have been used widely as references for setting standards in the industry. The innovative model has decreased the risk for "runaway money," allowing the platform's operation information to be more transparent and traceable. Since then, increasing platforms have begun to refer to the Yirendai model, built on the new fund custody model with traditional banks to enhance the platform's security capabilities.

This has become particularly important when the Chinese online lending industry experienced some major setbacks. The Chinese government initiated regulations on P2P lending after high-profile instances of fraud, particularly in the case of Ezubao, which in late 2015 robbed some nine hundred thousand investors of 50 billion RMB. Compared with the U.S. consumer lending sector in which only 10 percent of the potential losses come from fraud, in China, the fraud loss could be as high as 70 to 80 percent. Some dishonest borrowers registered and borrowed money from many P2P companies. An underground industry arose just for this purpose, with many professional fraud companies producing fake data in batches.

Managing risk therefore has been a major focus. To reduce credit risk, Yirendai launched a credit-scoring system, the Yiren Score, in 2017, to deliver a more precise and accurate characterization to enhance its risk management capability. Like the FICO score in the United States, the new system has a score range that corresponds to the credit quality of a borrower. This proprietary risk management system enables the company to effectively assess the creditworthiness of borrowers, appropriately price the risks associated with borrowers, and offer relevant loan investment opportunities to investors.

Yirendai has explored the use of alternative data for underwriting. For example, the company has used underwriting data based on a consumer's housing allowance. The housing allowance data of Chinese citizens is not centralized but rather is maintained by each different city. Adding more data points to the underwriting process has allowed Yirendai to gain better insight into a customer's risk profile.

Meanwhile, Yirendai has become one of the first fifteen lending companies to connect to China's first unified credit reporting platform, Baihang Credit. Yirendai has been reporting data to the National Internet Finance Registration and Disclosure Services Platform, and it shares data with other platforms in the association. The platform has built a long-term mechanism combining positive incentives and public supervision over information disclosure.

In addition to Yiren Credit, Yiren Wealth aims to fill the gap in China's financial sector. CreditEase Wealth Management previously targeted high-net-worth individuals and ultra-high-net-worth individuals and is now focused on the mass affluent market. Currently, Yiren Wealth's target clients include the thirty million mass affluent people with 1 million to 10 million RMB investable assets. Most of them are thirty to fifty-five years old with a college degree. An ideal asset allocation portfolio should be well diversified by investing on different regions and countries as well as across different asset classes through an automatic investment plan and fund portfolios with a long-term focus. To enhance the standard of living and achieve various life goals, such as retirement, education, and succession planning of the mass affluent investors, the asset allocation plan should include cash and short-term fixed income and similar products, medium- to long-term fund portfolios, and insurance protection and estate planning.

Hexindai Profile

Background

Hexindai is an online consumer lending marketplace based in Beijing. It facilitates loans to meet the increasing consumption demand of the emerging middle class in China. The company offers borrowers a variety of products based on customer segmentation data and tailors those products to meet the specific needs of this emerging middle class. Hexindai matches borrowers with investors seeking various types of investment products with appropriate risk levels and risk-adjusted returns. The company is funded entirely by individual investors, providing loans that mainly are used for "consumption upgrades."

Hexindai's online and offline user-acquisition capabilities combined with an online platform with extensive offline networks, an advanced risk management system, and strategic cooperative relationships with a custodian bank and an insurance company allow the company to realize faster growth in China. The company facilitates primarily midsize loans to borrowers on the online marketplace. Loan products can be generally categorized as credit loans. These credit loans are offered in amounts ranging from 20,000 RMB ($3,188) to 200,000 RMB ($31,885) with terms of typically twelve to thirty-six months. Hexindai offers five main types of tailored credit loan products: (1) provident fund loans, (2) property-owner loans, (3) car-owner loans, (4) insurance-holder loans, and (5) premier customer loans.

Hexindai also offers investors investment services and products, including portfolio investments and individual investments. The company has two types of portfolio investment products: (1) Freedom Wallets and (2) Stable Wallets. These wallets cater to different needs of investors and offer a variety of risk-based returns. Hexindai also allows investors to make loan transfers on the marketplace so that they can flexibly transfer their creditors, rights associated with specific loan products to other willing investors and therefore exit their investments, if desired.

Notably, Hexindai is a pure information and service platform that matches investors with individual borrowers. Loans are not held on balance sheets and the company bears no default risk. The company provides a secure portal for both borrowers and investors to access an independent online banking platform for the payment, settlement, and clearing of loan proceeds. Jiangxi Bank, a national commercial bank in China, is the company's custodian bank for fund management, payment, settlement, and clearing services. All funds from borrowers and investors are managed by Jiangxi Bank to ensure security and compliance with the relevant laws of the People's Republic of China and its regulations. Jiangxi Bank administers payments among borrowers, investors, and the company and performs the related clearing and fund settlement actions associated with these payments.

Hexindai has entered into an insurance agreement with Changan Insurance, a third-party insurance provider to provide insurance coverage to investors. In practice, if the borrower fails to repay the investor, Changan Insurance compensates the investor for the principal investment amount and accrued interest. Hexindai is responsible for assisting Changan Insurance's collection of late payments, making a phone call and sending a text message to the defaulting borrower to request repayment. Changan Insurance may take legal action, if required, to collect on outstanding larger, long-term loan obligations.

Hexindai is compliant with online lending industry guidelines. In particular, it is compliant with the August 2016 measures. Hexindai recently fulfilled the submission of the P2P Compliance Self-Inspection Report to the Beijing Municipal Bureau of Financial Work, marking the completion of one of three key steps for compliance with industry reforms from the National P2P Rectification Office.

Hexindai has begun focus on the next two steps in the process, including an inspection conducted by the Beijing Internet Finance Industry Association. This inspection will be followed by verification of inspection by the Beijing Municipal Bureau of Financial Work, along with a field inspection, and a possible final check by higher level government organizations.

The strengthened regulation will raise the barriers to entry, which Hexindai believes will benefit compliant platforms. Only compliant platforms can survive going forward. During this process, top P2P platforms will have significant opportunities for growth.

The P2P industry has experienced a significant growth period and is under the supervision of the China Banking and Insurance Regulatory Commission (CBIRC). Currently, the P2P section has about 10 million active investors and about 130 million A-share accounts. Given the overall lack of investment channels for domestic individuals, P2P platforms can be a useful channel for their investments. In addition, with the completion of filing and registration and given the fierce competition, investors likely will be more inclined to invest only in the top P2P platforms.

During the P2P regulatory crackdown, many lenders became overly cautious, leading to liquidity issues. P2P companies focusing on small and midsize enterprises have suffered because of deleveraging. This became an industry-wide problem, even in the face of strong demand from borrowers. As a result, investors switched to lending to those who could suffer liquidity risk, albeit with a lower expected rate of return. Hexindai has, through the regulatory turmoil, continued to focus on the midsize consumer loan market. Customers must have a stable job with a stable monthly income and a strong credit record. Customers must also have a plan for the next three years of their lives.

Compared with other P2P platforms, Hexindai claims to offer the following competitive advantages:

1. On the asset side, over the past four years, the company has built multiple online and offline borrower acquisition channels that span the entire nation. Its online borrower acquisition channels cover Android and IOS apps, search engines, and vertical websites focusing on consumer loans. As of August 29, 2018, Hexindai's offline cooperation partners had a total of 253 branches in 130 cities.
2. The company has a sound risk control system that incorporates the following:
   a. Credit review: Hexindai cross-checks the information provided by the borrower, the credit information authorized by the borrower, and the credit information provided by third party credit partners.
   b. Antifraud system: The company uses "Instinct Application Fraud Detection Solution," a powerful antifraud solution provided by GBG DecTech, a reputable Australian antifraud, anti-money-laundering, and decision management services

provider. In addition, Hexindai has a dedicated antifraud call center team.

   c. FICO Decision Engine: Hexindai has incorporated a FICO Decision Engine into its current systems.

   d. Credit rating system: Hexindai has built a credit rating system based on its founding team's more than ten years of experience in consumer banking and microfinance. The company's risk control system is well regarded by Changan Insurance, which provides default insurance on both existing and new loans on the platform.

3. On the funding side, Hexindai has a wide and stable lender base. As of June 30, 2018, the company has provided services to 236,000 lenders since the inception of the company. For the first quarter of fiscal year 2019, Hexindai served about sixty-eight thousand lenders. More than 82 percent of its customers are repeat lenders.

In August 2018, the company acquired an equity stake in the Indonesian P2P firm Musketeer, marking its first cross-border investment as part of its going out strategy. Hexindai took a 20 percent stake in the firm, which offers consumer installment loans. Indonesia is viewed as a market with strong potential because of its youth and level of economic growth. Many of Indonesia's consumers are underserved by traditional banks. At the same time, Indonesia has a solid internet infrastructure and expanding mobile penetration rate that allows potential clients to access online financial services.

Yilongdai Profile

Background

Beijing Tongcheng Yilong Network Technology Co., Ltd., was established in 2005 with a registered capital of 100 million RMB, and its website was launched in 2007. The company currently has 710 employees.

   Yilongdai is an internet financial platform focusing on the three areas of agriculture, rural areas, and farmers. The company aims to provide fast and timely financial information matching services for urban lenders and rural borrowers.

There are four products for lenders: Yinong Plan, Sesame Blossom, Private Customization, and Novice Exclusive. The core product, Yinong Plan, offers thirty-day, ninety-day, and other loan terms from which lenders can choose. In September 2018, for example, the loan amount of this product accounted for 87 percent of all products. The Sesame Blossom product packages and releases claims with the same borrowing period. These product terms are thirty days, sixty days, ninety days, and other loan terms. After the closing period, the lender can transfer credits. The Private Customization product is a personalized asset allocation tool that helps lenders lock in the scope of returns, personal preferences, and spread risk. Novice Exclusive is a short-term product designed to allow lenders to quickly experience the entire lending process of Yilongdai.

The company's income is generated by two parts: one is the transaction fee and the withdrawal fee charged to the borrower; and the second includes the transfer fee, withdrawal fee, and management service fee charged to the lender.

As of late September 2018, the business of Yilongdai covered more than one thousand districts and counties and tens of thousands of villages and towns across the country, helping 710,000 rural families, individual industrial and commercial households, and small and micro-enterprises to obtain effective financial support. As of the end of June 2018, Yilongdai had provided more than 46 billion RMB in matching funds to the rural sector. About 9.34 billion RMB of funds flowed to 212 poverty-stricken counties, accounting for 35.8 percent of China's 592 poverty-stricken counties.

In terms of performance, the company achieved a net profit of 4.96 million RMB in 2017 and a net profit of 3.72 million RMB in 2016.

Compared with the average borrower, the major problem for agricultural, rural, and farmer groups is a lack of collateral. In addition, credit records are scarce, and it is difficult to manage risks according to traditional bank lending methods. After a long period of visits, investigation, and research, Yilong Loan pioneered the online and offline (O2O) lending model in the country, combining online information matching with offline risk prevention and control.

To attract more lenders to agriculture, rural areas, and farmers, Yilong Loan launched the Mid-Autumn Carnival· Celebrate Harvest Festival from September 18 to 27 on the occasion of the first Chinese Farmers' Harvest Festival. This recent innovation attracted a large number of urban surplus funds to the countryside.

In the process of borrower selection in poor areas, Yilong Loan has needed to pay more attention to projects' extended impact. Rural projects should obtain industrial returns based on land advantages, as well as potentially improve the rural environment, which in turn can attract people to return to the countryside to participate in the rural industrial activities, or to otherwise resolve rural problems, such as those of left-behind children, poor education, and insufficient medical infrastructure.

Funding

Sicong Wang is the founder of Yilong.com and one of the founders of the Internet Finance Society. Like the development of internet technology, Wang's road to entrepreneurship has not been smooth.

Established in Beijing in 2007, Yilongdai Network was the earliest internet lending platform in China. It was the first high-tech enterprise in China to promote P2P, P2C, and B2C internet e-lending transactions. It is invested in by Beijing Tongcheng Yilong Network Technology Co., Ltd. In 2009, Wang transformed his lending website into a P2P network lending model and officially changed its name to Yilongdai. In the first few years of P2P online lending, he stopped the original practice of private lending offline business, focusing instead on internet finance. As the company was new and faced unclear market prospects, Yilongdai first earned very little income and was not profitable.

Part of the problem was the result of Wang's philosophy: rather than making money in the first five years, a company should focus on building the platform technology foundation. Years later, Yilongdai is now at the forefront of its peers in platform construction. Through cooperation with the Ministry of Public Security, major banks, and third-party payment companies, the company has established smooth information inquiry, fund transfer, and fund supervision mechanisms.

Wang Sicong proposed the concept of local lending early on, which meant that borrowers could apply for loans only on the local Yilongdai platform and could not apply across regions. This improved due diligence. The franchisees in different places can obtain the right to use the Yilongdai network platform, conduct regular business management online, conduct due diligence offline, and gradually form an online and offline (O2O) operation mode.

The business of Yilongdai is essentially a networked and informationized business of private lending. If the private lending is poorly managed, it may be viewed as being involved in "illegal fund-raising" and "illegally absorbing public deposits." In the past, private lending companies did not have financial licenses, and most of them registered their businesses in the name of investment consulting companies. Wang Sicong understands that private lending must be formalized and operated in a positive manner, and it must be recognized by the government. On September 1, 2011, Wang came to the Central University of Finance and Economics to communicate with Professor Li Jianjun, deputy dean of the School of Finance, and Dean Li Wei, dean of the training college, to speak about the prospects of the online lending platform. He was quite upset and felt that his company's prospects were uncertain. Li Jianjun suggested that he should seize the favorable opportunity of the country's financial reform and innovation and make the network lending bigger and stronger, so that the company could be recognized by the financial regulatory authorities. Wang liked this idea.

In 2011, Yilongdai became a pilot enterprise under the Wenzhou Golden Reform program, and in 2012, it entered the Wenzhou Financial Comprehensive Reform Experimental Zone. After entering Wenzhou, Wang's business performance improved significantly. In 2012, the State Council approved Wenzhou's comprehensive financial reform plan, and Yilongdai was given an opportunity to transform. At the beginning of March of that year, Wang went to Wenzhou to investigate and negotiate with the local government financial authorities. Finally, the Wenzhou Municipal People's Government determined that Yilongdai would be the first internet finance enterprise to enter the financial comprehensive reform pilot zone and the only company that could carry out P2P matching services. Entering the Wenzhou Financial Comprehensive Reform Experimental Zone has become a key point in the transformation and upgrading of Yilongdai, and its business scale has achieved rapid growth.

In the rapid development of internet finance in 2013, Yilongdai became one of the leaders in the P2P online lending industry. Wang accepted an exclusive interview with CCTV and introduced the same local city O2O model of Yilongdai network, which attracted a great deal of attention. In 2014, the number of franchisees of Yilongdai network exceeded five hundred, and the scale of business greatly increased. As of October 2014, more than 150 online lending platforms had experienced risk events. These risks stemmed from moral hazard and fraud based on the lack of a sufficient funding pool, false projects, and poor integration. Therefore, improving the governance structure and strengthening regulation became urgent problems for the P2P industry.

By 2013, many P2P companies were able to obtain an A round of financing, and some had entered the B round of financing. As one of the leading companies in the industry, Yilongdai attracted the attention of private equity and venture capital. Wang also contacted a number of investment institutions to discuss capital cooperation matters. Among these institutions, Wang negotiated with Lenovo Holdings, and on November 3, 2014, Legend Holdings officially invested in Yilongdai.

After Lenovo's investment in the company, the governance structure of Yilongdai underwent major changes. Legend Holdings sent an executive to serve as the president, injecting the management experience of a state-owned enterprise into the originally private online loan platform. At the same time, according to the agreement of both parties, the founder and team of Yilongdai network retained most of the decision-making power, relying on its original industry experience to manage the daily operation of the platform. This combination model was similar to the governance structure of Alibaba after it was listed in the United States. The managerial layer and the original shareholders of Yilongdai maintained control over the company's operations and used modern governance structures, such as shareholders' meetings.

After Lenovo's investment, the business and assets of Yilongdai were to be operated as the core asset business of Legend Holdings. The new Yilongdai network reduced the bottleneck of the original geographic layout. Using Lenovo's business networks, Yilongdai services were deployed in first-tier cities, such as Shanghai, Shenzhen, and Guangzhou, to expand the financial services access of urban communities and promote inclusive financial services. After the strategic cooperation was established between Yilongdai and Legend Holdings, the first city to receive services was Shanghai, China's largest financial center. The Yilongdai network in Shanghai offered many offline community wealth experience stores, which were deployed to serve the surrounding residents, helping individuals who have the willingness to increase their wealth but lack information and channels to do so. In addition, Yilongdai designed credit products that were suitable for large cities and expanded new customer bases for supplementary products, such as "three rural" credit loans and small and micro-enterprise loans. The layout of the Fortune Experience Store allowed customers to explore new modes of urban community banks.

After Legend Holdings invested in Yilongdai, its valuation surged from several billion renminbi before the negotiations between the two sides to more than 5 billion RMB. Lenovo Holdings invested less than 500 million yuan in cash (additional funds later invested) for less than half a year, with high returns. The original shareholders of Yilongdai also received substantial returns as a result of the integration of the characteristics of the Yilongdai model and Lenovo's reputation.

Previous venture capitalists were not optimistic about the Yilong-dai model, and some private equity fund managers viewed Yilongdai as being used for online loans to the agricultural sector, with high risks, small loans amounts, and limited profitability. Some investment fund managers believed that the Yilongdai's O2O model had higher labor costs and was not sustainable. Wang stuck to his original business model, however.

The Yilongdai network platform provides basic services for franchisees everywhere, and franchisees are responsible for P2P online loan operations in their respective regions. The franchisee system has gradually improved risk control in practice. For example, in addition to the franchise fee, a certain amount of risk reserves needs to be paid, the franchisee's interests are linked to risk management and control responsibilities, and the cooperation of all parties is responsible for the matching of rights.

After seven years of operation, Yilongdai's franchise program had formed a three-level management system. The company had set up operation centers in twenty provinces across the country, covering more than 120 first, second, and third tier cities across the country, with more than five hundred franchisees. To enhance corporate value and social credibility, Yilongdai planned to open lending and wealth management businesses in towns and villages, close to the most basic economic units such as small and micro-enterprises, farmers, individual industrial, and commercial households.

An important feature of Yilongdai has been its insistence on providing funds for microfinance. Wang Sicong believes that financial risks should be mitigated to reduce impact, especially in rural finance. Microfinance is the most economical option to solve farmers' cash turnover problems. Therefore, over the years, every single loan has been limited to a maximum of 60,000 RMB. The benefits of setting this limit are to spread the risk and broaden the service distribution, benefiting a large number of rural people. Wang said that in 2012, Yilongdai network transactions amounted to tens of millions of renminbi. In 2013, it exceeded 300 million RMB. In 2014, it reached 2.3 billion RMB. In 2015, the target was 30 billion RMB. In 2014, the Yilongdai service served more than three hundred million people in rural areas. It has had a positive effect on solving the three rural issues through inclusive finance.

CHAPTER FOUR

Online Consumer Credit, Online Supply Chain Finance, and Internet Banks

IN THIS CHAPTER, we examine online consumer credit coming from commercial banks, internet finance giants, licensed consumer finance companies, and innovative companies. We then turn to a discussion of online supply chain finance, and finally, we look at internet banks.

As China moves toward a consumption-based economy, consumer credit is becoming increasingly important. Obtaining such credit online makes it much easier for consumers to access loans and to obtain a faster loan decision.

Supply chain finance allows firms to access a variety of funding, including accounts receivable financing, warehouse financing, and general financing. Providers of the financing may include banks, firms, supply chain companies, and business-to-business (B2B) platforms. For firms that are part of a supply chain, this can be a key source of funding, as relationships in the supply chain reinforce the lender–borrower ties.

Finally, we discuss the role of internet banks in China's fintech sector. Internet banks are characterized by the absence of physical outlets and their use of data, resources, and technologies to provide a series of internet-based financial services.

Online Consumer Finance

Online consumer finance refers to the consumer finance business that uses the internet for online application, review, lending, and repayment. Broadly speaking, internet consumer finance includes the internetization of traditional consumer finance. The narrow sense of internet consumer finance refers only to the consumer finance platform established by internet companies.

The consumer finance business can be divided into consumer loans and cash loans. Types of consumer loans depend on various life scenarios—for example, Ant Check Later relies on the shopping scenario of the Taobao website. Cash loans issue funds directly to users. Most consumer financial institutions provide both consumer and cash loans.

Background

Relative to other countries, China's consumer finance started late; in 2007, China began to pilot consumer finance in Guangdong. In 2009, the China Banking Regulatory Commission issued the Measures for Pilot Management of Consumer Finance Companies, which allowed for the establishment of a consumer finance company in four cities—specifically, Beijing, Shanghai, Tianjin, and Chengdu—officially marking the concept of consumer finance companies' growth in China. The business operations of the first four consumer finance companies was rapidly expanding in the short term, but most of the consumer finance business in the early stage of development continued the traditional commercial bank credit card business and did not cover marginal groups that cannot apply for credit cards even though they have consumer credit needs.

Since 2013, the China Banking Regulatory Commission has revised the Measures for the Pilot Management of Consumer Finance Companies, lowering the entry threshold for consumer finance companies and expanding the number of pilot cities to sixteen. A series of industrial consumer finance companies was approved by the China Banking Regulatory Commission. In 2014, with the rise of internet finance, Jingdong and Tmall, large-scale e-commerce platforms, officially entered the consumer finance market with their consumer financial products JDbaitiao and Tmall Staging. Many other internet financial platforms also have begun to enter the consumer financial market.

In June 2015, the State Council decided to encourage qualified private capital, domestic and foreign banking institutions, as well as internet companies to initiate the establishment of consumer finance companies. In March 2016, the People's Bank of China and the China Banking Regulatory Commission proposed to speed up innovation in the consumer credit sphere. Driven by policy encouragement and industry innovation, consumer finance has ushered in rapid growth; however, at the same time, problems have emerged, such as excessive credit and insufficient protection of personal information. In 2017 and 2018, various qualifications and business supervision policies were introduced, and the industry entered a period of rectification. By 2018, domestic licensed consumer finance companies rapidly increased to twenty-six companies.

Currently, consumer finance players are broadly divided into four categories, including commercial banks, internet finance giants, licensed consumer finance companies, and innovative companies.

Commercial banks are involved primarily in the transformation of traditional credit, focusing on product innovation and extension. Commercial banks' consumer financial products include credit cards, auto loans, and consumer loans. Banks issue loans to customers based on their application materials.

Internet finance giants have strong customer bases and rich data accumulation. Relying on rich consumption scenarios and multidimensional credit information, internet firms allow customers to conveniently apply for consumer loans. At the same time, online shopping and social behavior on the customer platform make credit evaluation more accurate. Typical examples of these internet firms include JDbaitiao and Ant Check Later, which are supported by the consumption environment of the e-commerce platform.

Licensed consumer finance companies rely on license advantages. As of late December 2018, twenty-three licensed companies had officially opened. The China Banking and Insurance Regulatory Commission defines the model of the internet consumer finance company as expressly existing not to accept public deposits, but to provide consumer loans to residents on an individual basis.

Innovative companies provide a variety of fintech services, such as microfinance companies, financial leasing companies, financing guarantee companies, pawn companies, and nonlicensed companies. Examples of some of the many innovative companies include Weixin Jinke (the Viscon Jinke Group) and 51credit.com.

The following discussions highlight several consumer finance platforms founded by internet companies.

Ant Check Later

Ant Financial Services Group owns Ant Check Later, which provides consumer loans for customers to purchase goods from Alibaba Group Holding Limited's Taobao and Tmall websites without paying immediately. Ant Check Later brings great convenience to the users, while also promoting Taobao and Tmall products. Ant Financial makes use of customer credit history and payment records to assess customer creditworthiness.

Ali Small Loan (Xiaowei), which specializes in microfinance, was set up in 2010. Ali Small Loan has four aspects to its business process: loan application, loan review, loan issuance, and loan recovery and management. The company uses information from e-commerce platforms and merchants on the platform. Merchant information is collected, integrated, and processed to create a risk profile. Risk pricing takes the risk profile into account when laying out the amount of loans, the period of use, and the interest rate of loans. Ali's credit risk reflects the borrower's potential default risk, solvency risk based on past repayment information, credit rating, and presence of any breach of a previous loan contract.[1]

JD Baitiao

JD Baitiao was launched in Jingdong Mall in 2014 to allow users to consume first and pay later under a 30-day interest-free installment loan service. This service allows customers to purchase goods immediately and make their payment later. JD Baitiao first relied on the shopping platform at the Jingdong Mall and later expanded to cover rental, tourism, decoration, education, and wedding industries as well as other consumption scenarios. The business became popular with customers, particularly on Singles Day.

Aiyoumi

Aicai Group owns Aiyoumi, an online consumer loan company launched in 2014 that provides consumers with multiple scenario consumer financial services, such as installment shopping, education and training, and mobile phone rental. Customers can paste the link to a product they wish to purchase into their loan application and can choose the repayment period.

Risks and Rewards

China's internet consumer finance industry has passed its initial stage and gradually has entered a period of rapid development. Various business models are maturing slowly. Improving the risk control mechanism is essential for the development of consumer finance. The potential of consumer finance business is huge; at the same time, however, China's consumer finance services are still maturing and more uncertainties and difficulties in risk control remain. On one hand, the current consumer finance business is expanding too fast for subprime consumers, resulting in a rising rate of nonperforming assets. On the other, this continuous innovation of consumer financial products is introducing more unsecured products. The large-scale, high-risk consumer finance business is quite dependent on the automatic approval mechanism and is prone to collective default.

A strong personal credit system is the basis for the effective control of credit risk by consumer financial institutions. Compared with the developed credit system in Europe and the United States, China's credit reporting system has many shortcomings. The traditional credit coverage is insufficient and lacks dynamic adjustment. The development time of internet credit reporting is short, and problems, such as the lack of unified evaluation standards and nonsharing of credit data, persist.

The United States and the European Union have introduced a series of laws to address consumer finance development and now have a comprehensive set of laws and regulations to regulate consumer credit. China's consumer finance remains in its infancy, and relevant laws are imperfect. In addition, China's personal credit legal system is insufficient, which has created obstacles for the development of consumer finance.

Regulation

From 2015 to 2017, consumer finance policies at the national level were introduced to encourage industry development and innovation in technology and business models. In the second half of 2017, the supervision became stricter, which led to a negative impact of innovative institutions on products and business models. Generally speaking, however, guidelines helped to standardize the online lending industry and to improve information disclosure. These have helped to reduce risks and improve the sophistication of the industry.

On February 23, 2017, the China Banking Regulatory Commission officially issued the Guidelines for the Deposit and Management of Online Lending Funds, which required funds to be deposited in a third-party financial institution with a clear principal and depositor. In May 2017, the Ministry of Education, the China Banking Regulatory Commission, the Ministry of Human Resources, and Social Security jointly stated that no online lending firm could grant loans to college students.

In July 2017, the China Banking Regulatory Commission and other departments issued Interim Measures for the Management of Business Activities of Internet Lending Information Intermediaries, which required the strengthening of online lending information intermediary management, proposed a filing system, and standardized information disclosure and supervision.

In November 2017, the Office of the Leading Group for the Special Remediation of Internet Financial Risks issued the Notice on Immediate Suspension of the Establishment of Network Microfinance Companies to suspend the issuance of online small loan licenses. Just one month later, the Office issued the Notice on Standardizing the Reorganization of the "Cash Loan" Business (No. 141), which banned particular cash loans, clarified the 36 percent annual interest rate limit, and restricted the form of finance loan cooperation to banking financial institutions.

In August 2018, the Banking Insurance Supervision Committee issued the Notice on Further Improving Credit Work to Improve the Quality and Efficiency of Service Entity Economy, which encouraged the development of consumer finance and enhanced the role of consumption in driving the economy.

In early January 2019, the Office of the Leading Group for the Special Remediation of Internet Financial Risks and the Office of the P2P Network Loan Risk Special Rehabilitation Leading Group jointly issued the Notice on Further Implementing P2P Network Loan Compliance Check and Follow-up Work (No. 1). The core requirements of this notice include launching real-time data access work for the national peer-to-peer (P2P) platform, realizing full and real-time access to transaction data of various online lending institutions, and emphasizing information disclosure.

Internetization of Traditional Consumer Finance

Most Chinese consumers have a debit card, as the first debit card was issued in China in 1985 by Bank of China. The Jinka Gongcheng program was used to make electronic payments using these debit cards.[2] The number of debit cards rose from 2.6 billion in 2011 to 6.9 billion in 2018 (see figure 4.1).

China has had a low credit card penetration rate despite its high debit card penetration rate. This rate is changing, however, as fintech evolves. Credit card use is on the rise, moving from five million in 2002 to three hundred million in 2017. First, virtual credit cards allow consumers to purchase goods using credit instead of cash. Second, new fintech companies are being established to improve credit card risk management.

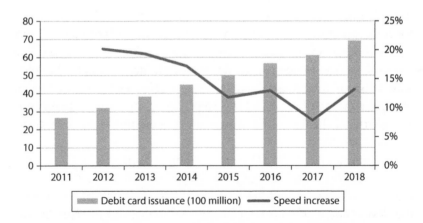

Figure 4.1 Number of debit cards used in China. *Source*: International Bank for Reconstruction and Development, World Bank, and People's Bank of China, *Toward Universal Financial Inclusion in China: Models, Challenges, and Global Lessons* (Washington, DC: World Bank Group, February 2018), https://open knowledge.worldbank.org/bitstream/handle/10986/29336/FinancialInclusion ChinaP158554.pdf?sequence=9.

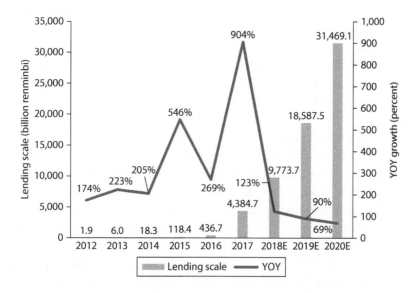

Figure 4.2 Internet consumer finance lending scale and growth rate. *Source*: Prospective Industry Research Institute, "2018 China's Internet Consumer Finance Development Status and Market Trends Analysis of the Explosive Growth of Lending Scale" (in Chinese), Qianzhan, February 8, 2019, https://www.qianzhan.com/analyst/detail/220/190201-20f83e47.html.

As data becomes richer, financial firms can use credit modeling programs to assess customer creditworthiness without establishing an extensive credit history with each person individually (see figure 4.2).[3]

Online Credit Firms

Many online credit firms have arisen since 2011. Fintech companies like Samoyed Financial Service have been able to carry out credit scoring online, which has vastly reduced costs for banks in credit card issuance.[4] Such companies make use of available data, such as phone payment information, to analyze consumer credit risk. For its part, Samoyed Financial, founded by Jianming Lin, has targeted prime consumers to reduce risks and maintain low prices. The firm does not require consumers to meet with bankers in person and, as a result, can reduce transaction costs. Samoyed Financial's risk control process is extensive, as bankers check for differences between online and offline information and using artificial intelligence (AI) to review for potentially fraudulent applications.

Mintech, founded by Mickey Li in 2015, is an online credit card company that uses consumer data to analyze credit risks. The firm analyzes the credit risk of potential bank borrowers and underwrites the loans, allowing banks to fund the loans. Using an interface with multiple capabilities, including balance transfers and provident fund inquiries, Mintech targets consumers aimed at both online and offline consumption. Mintech categorizes its functions into four cloud-based services: the marketing cloud, which uses big data to reveal customer needs; the capital cloud, which matches borrowers and lenders at an appropriate price; the underwriting cloud, which maintains risk assessment based on proprietary algorithms; and the collection cloud, which assesses consumer behavior to forecast collections. Mintech also uses the blockchain to record credits, which are exchangeable. Shareholders include venture capital firms Redpoint Ventures, Angel Plus, and Amap, an Alibaba subsidiary.

51credit.com is another online credit card firm that helps banks address the high costs of risk management in the need to expand online inclusive finance. As a Hong Kong–listed company, it is one of the largest online credit card platforms, with 110 million active users of credit cards. 51credit aims to have three types of relationships with banks: joint development of products to improve access to mature products; joint risk control; and joint modeling, including strategy and antifraud modeling. The company aims to obtain high-quality customer users. 51credit can provide standardized procedures and platforms, provide individual credit reports, supply voice recognition and account monitoring, and integrate its risk control system with banks to prevent fraud. The service allows models and data to be seamlessly integrated with banks.

Risk control is an essential component of online lending. HC Financial Service Group is an online lending and investment company focusing on small loans, which was established in 2011. Founder and CEO Qin Hongtao noted at the Lendit Fintech conference in September 2018 in Shanghai, China, that institutions should hire accountants to carry out auditing to ensure that firms are in full compliance with the law. HC Financial Service Group was audited in 2016 and 2017 and has continued to remain in business. The firm has a good flow of cash and capital as well as authentic creditors' rights. For the company, risk control plays a central role in its business model.

Samoyed Financial Profile: An Interview
with Chair Jianming Lin

Samoyed Holding Limited (Samoyed) is a financial technology service company in China that was founded in 2015 by experienced executives in China's consumer finance industry. Samoyed partners with financial institutions to provide loan facilitation to credit-proven millennials, who have established a credit history with prime credit quality. Samoyed offers more affordable financing alternatives for its customers and provides financial institutions with access to high-quality consumer finance assets with low-risk profiles. Its registered users reached seventeen million by the end of 2017 and further increased to more than twenty-four million as of June 30, 2018. Its net operating revenue increased 353.5 percent to reach 240.4 million RMB ($36.3 million) in 2017, from 53.0 million RMB in 2016.

Samoyed is the only loan facilitator in China focused on facilitating credit card balance transfer products with a weighted average annual percentage rate (APR) lower than 18.25 percent, the annual interest rate cap for credit cards set by the People's Republic of China regulators. Samoyed believes that competitive pricing is the key to its success.

Samoyed's business model is an independent third-party platform, matching broader customers and financial institution partners. On this platform, financial institution partners directly lend money to and collect money from the customers. Samoyed charges a service fee to its financial institution partners in return for this facilitation service.

Not all the customers registered on the platform, however, have passed the risk assessment procedures. Those who failed the procedures are recommended to other credit platforms, such as, VCREDIT, X Financial, or Finvolution Group (formerly PPDai). Samoyed also recommends registered users to some non-credit-related platforms, providing them with insurance products, wealth management products, and online bank account services. The company charges these third-party service providers a recommendation service fee, which can offset the customer acquisition cost. For those customers who pass the risk assessment procedure, Samoyed offers a loan facilitation service.

The company is guided by managers who allow customers to strategically establish a virtuous cycle, by offering low-APR products that attract prime customers, which in turn provide high-quality assets to financial institution partners, in turn reducing their risk. With this lower risk, Samoyed's financial institution partners can continue providing low-cost funding, which further allows the company to continue facilitating products with a low APR.

To remain competitive, Samoyed has established a full matrix of proprietary technology systems, called the "Seven Swords," which are applied across its entire business process, covering customer acquisition, fraud detection, credit assessment, postfacilitation management, cooperation with financial institutions, and customer servicing. Leveraging its AI capabilities, Samoyed has distilled more than 2,600 features from customer data and has developed a comprehensive set of proprietary models, including the Orion antifraud model, the DNA credit-scoring model, the location-based service recommendation model, and the Alpha S credit decision bot, all of which buttress its ability to offer enhanced risk management solutions to its financial institution partners.

Samoyed widely applies AI-driven systems, accurately predicts delinquency, and adjusts customer credit approval strategies in a timely manner. As of December 31, 2017, and June 30, 2018, the 90-day delinquency rate by credit card balance transfer and cash advance facilitated by the company was 0.82 percent and 1.66 percent, respectively. As of June 30, 2018, the historical 90-day delinquency rate for credit card balance transfer and cash advance facilitated through the platform was below 1.5 percent.

The biggest challenge Samoyed has faced is maintaining profitability in the face of a low pricing strategy. Because of its comparatively low profit margin, a loss period was unavoidable in the first two years. Customer acquisition costs were not low, and the company did not profit from every borrower's first loans, although subsequent loans were expected to be more profitable because of the credit life cycle.

In the short run, however, most of the company's competitors were following the reverse strategy, providing high-APR products to subprime users, although their default rate was very high. Because the high pricing could cover their delinquency losses, they still could make a profit from the start. This brought severe pressure to Samoyed's low pricing strategy. Some of the company's colleagues doubted its business model, which posed a significant challenge to management.

Samoyed's core founding team chose to continue with the low pricing strategy, believing in their vision and potential for greater success.

To make the strategy viable, the management team paid attention to both the revenue side and cost side, attempting to innovate new products for their users. The company launched its cash advance and credit loan businesses in 2016 and 2017, and these margins were comparatively higher than the credit card balance transfer business and better served customers' tailormade financial needs.

The firm also launched several new products for revenue growth, including online credit card applications, online insurance recommendations, wealth management products, and online bank account initiation. These new businesses increased the stability and robustness of its business model, which gave the company room to prove the viability of its low pricing strategy.

China's Place in Global Credit Card Issuance Development

In 2018, China's per capita credit card ownership was only 0.47, whereas the United States and Japan each had 2 and 2.5 credit cards in use per capita (see figure 4.3).[5]

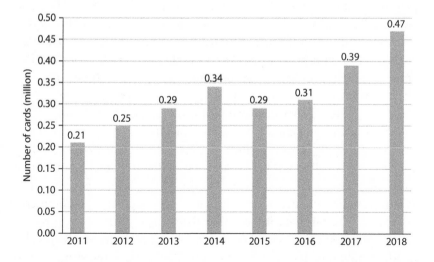

Figure 4.3 Credit cards per capita (one hundred million). *Source*: People's Bank of China, 2018, www.pbc.gov.cn.

Compared with other countries, China's credit card penetration rate still has room for improvement. According to Oliver Wyman's data, in 2017, 66 percent of adults (fifteen years and older) in the United States hold credit cards, compared with only 21 percent in China. As of 2018, the number of credit cards issued by the Chinese banking industry had reached 686 million, an increase of 16.7 percent compared with 2017.

China's UnionPay, however, is considered to be the world's largest card issuer and is expanding into other countries. The company recently made a deal with Tribe Payments in the United Kingdom to expand in the country and mainland Europe.

Online Supply Chain Finance

Supply chain finance allows banks to connect firms to access a variety of financial services, such as accounts receivable financing, warehouse financing, and general financing. Providers of the financing may include banks, firms, supply chain companies, and B2B platforms. According to data from the Prospective Industry Research Institute, China's supply chain financial market reached 13 trillion RMB in 2017.[6]

Traditional supply chain finance faces some difficulties, especially in providing funds for small and medium-size enterprises (SMEs) that lack credit data and that may be secondary suppliers. Many SMEs are used in the manufacturing industry as part of a supply chain that reduces core enterprise costs. The flexibility required, including discounts, longer purchase deadlines, and shorter lead times, places a huge burden on manufacturing SMEs. The traditional supply chain finance also faces issues in sharing information and even fraud.

Online loan companies have faced difficulties in meeting the needs of SMEs' supply chain finance because they have fewer funding sources and smaller funds. Banks have a disadvantage in obtaining large amounts of credit information for SMEs, which is costly. The solution is for online lenders and banks to cooperate.[7] E-commerce companies use big data information from their platforms to provide credit enhancement services to those who demand finance. Banks also conduct offline review and grant credit. Banks pay interest income to the e-commerce enterprise in a specific proportion. In this cooperation strategy, banks and e-commerce companies conduct online and offline multidimensional credit review, which optimizes bank loan quality, improves loan recovery rate, and increases revenue.

Digital supply chain finance can reduce risks by controlling advance payments, inventory, and receivables. Compared with traditional bank financing channels, digital supply chain finance has improved the financing problems of SMEs in the manufacturing industry from the following aspects: first, the bank's real estate guarantee pledge is transferred to accounts receivable during the transaction process. The transaction may include movable property mortgages, such as inventory, future cargo rights, and trade relationship certificates. Second, trade information is used to complement the lack of information on manufacturing SMEs, and trade information replaces individual credit information. Third, trade conditions are verified, cargo rights are controlled, the credit endorsement of core enterprises, and the third-party logistics supervision are used to carry out perfect risk management and control. Fourth, group purchase sales are adopted for core enterprises and industrial supply chain clusters to reduce the overall operating cost of the supply chain.

Core enterprises use their own information on the core goods or services in the supply chain, supply and marketing channels, and transaction history, providing a package of financial services for upstream and downstream SMEs and end users. By controlling the trading of goods, trading prices, trading frequency, and trading changes in the market, the trading market, e-commerce platform, and logistics centers provide financial services to market participants, consumers, and others.[8]

Financial Institutions Involved

In the past ten years, the competition faced by the banking industry for supply chain finance has become increasingly fierce.[9] Through supply chain finance, banks can ensure that credit funds are effectively injected into the relatively weak upstream and downstream small and micro-enterprises in the industrial chain, while also preventing funds from going to speculative purposes. Several banks have been involved in the online supply chain finance sector. For example, China Merchants Bank has launched an online supply chain financial solution for e-commerce and logistics industries. Shanghai Pudong Development Bank and China Mobile launched an online supply chain financing platform. Some city commercial banks also have begun to actively develop supply chain finance. To some extent, small and midsize city banks that have geographical and human advantages, particularly the microcredit franchise, benefit from advantages in online supply chain finance that are not inferior to large and medium-sized banks.

Consider an example of a liquor transaction. A commercial bank provides a liquor producer with guarantees under online prepayment financing for downstream distributors. The liquor manufacturer and the dealers sign an electronic contract online to ensure the real trade deal; then, the bank signs a tripartite cooperation agreement with the liquor manufacturer and distributor, and the dealer makes the first deposit according to regulations. Next, the bank will pay the remaining amount of the contract (or the ticket delivery) to the liquor manufacturer. Finally, the liquor factory owner issues some goods to the dealer. The dealer needs to repay or add a deposit when applying to the bank for redelivery. The bank tells the liquor manufacturer to reissue the goods. In addition, fifteen days before the credit expiration, if the customer fails to repay the goods in time, the bank will issue a refund payment notice to the liquor producer to make up for the corresponding amount of the undelivered part of the payment.

Then, the liquor manufacturer produces according to the amount of the dealer's separate delivery, which avoids the overstocking cost of the liquor manufacturer's inventory. Commercial banks have injected crucial funds into the supply chain and thus have effectively controlled for risk based on the credit of liquor manufacturers. This approach has earned them more business and entrepreneurial innovation opportunities for their downstream distributors.

A number of financial institutions have risen to meet the demands of online supply chain finance. In 2005, Shenzhen Development Bank (now Ping An Bank) introduced its "1+N" supply chain financial product to the market and signed agreements with China Ocean Shipping Company, China National Materials Storage and Transportation Group, and China National Foreign Trade Transportation Corporation. The bank created a credit line of 250 billion RMB, contributing 25 percent of business profits to the product, while maintaining a nonperforming loan ratio of only 0.57 percent. Hundreds of companies received financing services from this strategic cooperation.

In 2007, China Construction Bank and Alibaba jointly launched supply chain financial products, including network provider financing and network joint insurance loans. To obtain financing services for online merchants on the e-commerce platform, Alibaba and the banks each set up a "risk pool" of 20 million RMB to implement a risk- and revenue-sharing cooperation model.

In 2012, Jingdong (JD.com) began to engage in supply chain financial services, developing the Jingbaobei and Jingxiao Loan products. Jingdong is both an e-commerce platform and a provider of supply chain financial funds in the business ecosystem. Suppliers rely on the Jingdong platform to receive capital financing as well as to provide financing services. The two sides create value through interaction.

Jingbaobei allows a supplier to apply for financing online according to its needs; Jingdong's highly integrated and automated information system accepts applications online and approves them within three minutes. To assist these processes, Jingdong Data Platform has accumulated a large amount of customer information so it can respond quickly and provide efficient financing services. Supply chain finance not only increases the speed at which suppliers receive financial support but also increases the capacity of suppliers, thereby increasing the efficiency of the entire Jingdong supply chain ecosystem and achieving value creation.

The Jingxiao Loan model provides a full range of financial services to help suppliers improve capital turnover, ensure smooth supply channels for Jingdong, and increase the retention of Jingdong customers. Jingxiao Loan can provide financial services, such as order loans, early receipts, and credit loans. Order loans allow the supplier to release the amount of the in-transit order, speed up the withdrawal of funds, and increase sales turnover. The early payment service helps merchants recover in-transit funds if the seller has shipped goods but the buyer has not confirmed receipt.

In 2016, the Agricultural Bank of China officially launched the Bee Cloud Internet Financial Supply Chain Financing Platform.[10] Bee Cloud can make loans to SMEs upstream and downstream of the supply chain to address their financing problems. Bee Cloud was established in February 2014 with a registered capital of 5 million yuan and a paid-up capital of 3 million yuan. The company was jointly funded by Jiangsu Huabo Industry Group and its subsidiary Beestar Telecom, of which Huabo Group invested 4.5 million yuan. Equity accounted for 90 percent of this investment, and Beestar Telecom invested the remaining 10 percent (500,000 yuan). As of 2017, Bee Cloud's total assets reached 21.2 million yuan, including current assets of 18.25 million yuan, long-term investment of 2.55 million yuan, and fixed assets of 400,000 yuan. The company's total liabilities totaled 22.4 million yuan. From February to September 2017, the company's operating income was 9.69 million yuan.

The platform's supply chain financing model combines credit products and sales products for its downstream dealers by connecting the Agricultural Bank of China's e-commerce platform to the Bee Cloud's B2B sales platform. The Agricultural Bank conducts a credit system review of the customer list submitted by Bee Cloud and returns an assessment of the credit status of the customer.

The borrower must (1) open an account in the Agricultural Bank and open the online banking function; (2) fill in the relevant information on Bee Cloud's B2B platform and apply for credit on the Agricultural Bank e-commerce platform; and (3) select the contract on the Agricultural Bank e-commerce platform, designate a repayment of interest and interest account, and sign the agreement. The Agricultural Bank handles the credit inquiry and issues a notice of the person's credit information to Bee Cloud. Bee Cloud's B2B platform receives data, approves the credit line, and informs the Agricultural Bank, which notifies the customer.

Bee Cloud can monitor the entire process of financing and repayment of collaborative enterprises on the platform. Except for the collaborative enterprises that need to open settlement accounts and online banking services at the Agricultural Bank counter, all other processes are online. On the completion of the operation, from the application for financing to the final loan, the collaborative enterprise does not need to provide any paper materials, and the consumer can complete the financing without leaving the house. The entire process requires only one to two working days. Because the loan is issued to the downstream dealers in the supply chain, a close cooperation relationship with the company is formed, thus omitting the need for the cooperative enterprises to provide collateral.

Blockchain and Supply Chain

Blockchain can reduce some of the challenges faced during the supply chain financing process by enhancing trust among the parties. Blockchain can verify and confirm the bill and validate the credit certificate, allowing secondary suppliers to obtain credit. Smart contracts can be provided and stored on the blockchain.[11]

Tencent Holding Limited's Blockchain and Supply Chain Financial Solutions has been used by supply chains to connect core enterprise accounts receivable with financial institution funds. Accounts receivable are used as underlying assets and receive creditor's rights certificates through Tencent's blockchain technology. When the original assets are registered, the supplier's accounts receivable are audited and confirmed to ensure the authenticity of the listed assets. The creditor's certificate can be transferred as needed within the supply chain. Original assets of the registered chain can be traced to allow credit to flow between the core enterprise and multilevel suppliers. Financial institutions can help provide funds and support small and micro-enterprises within the supply chain.

In April 2017, Yijian and IBM China Research Institute jointly released Easy Block, a blockchain supply chain financial service system, focusing on the pharmaceutical industry. The system is integrated with supply chain management and commercial factoring. Through blockchain technology, the company's collection period can be shortened from a typical 180 days to just a few days.

In June 2017, China Zheshang Bank launched its Receivables Chain Platform using the underlying blockchain platform Hyperchain. The platform was established to solve the problem of enterprise accounts receivable. The platform uses blockchain technology to transform corporate accounts receivable into online payment and financing tools to reduce company costs. The technology is used for the issuance, acceptance, confirmation, payment, transfer, pledge, and redemption of corporate accounts receivable. More than six hundred companies were using the platform as of May 2018. The system offers several benefits:

- decentralization realizes the unique signature of the enterprise, and the key cannot be changed once it is generated on the blockchain;
- distributed ledger technology records receivables information, technically eliminating various possibilities for data being tampered with and forged; and
- smart contract technology ensures that all types of transactions of receivables are automatically and unconditionally fulfilled according to the rules of smart contracts.

China Minsheng Bank launched a blockchain-based domestic letter of credit information transmission system in July 2017 to link the opening, notification, delivery, acceptance, and payment of the letter of credit. This has reduced the transmission time for the letter of credit and supporting documents. The system also takes advantage of the tamperproof features of the blockchain, improving the security of the letter of credit business.

Suning Financial Services assisted its subsidiary, Suning Bank, to launch the blockchain domestic letter of credit information transmission system in September 2017. The system uses Hyperledger Fabric blockchain technology to ensure strict online compliance, with full encryption and domestic credit card online issuance, notification, and delivery.

This area has not gone unnoticed by the government. The Guiding Opinions on Actively Promoting Supply Chain Innovation and Application laid out in October 2017 stated that the use of emerging technologies such as blockchain and AI should be studied to connect the supply chain with the internet.

In the 2018 semiannual report of the financial industry in the Shanghai and Shenzhen stock markets, at least ten financial institutions discussed supply chain finance in the application of blockchain technology, including the Industrial and Commercial Bank of China (ICBC), Ping An Bank, Bank of Communications, Nanjing Bank, and Guiyang Bank. Examples of this technology include ICBC's ICBC e-xin and Ping An Bank's Supply Chain Receivables Service Platform.

At present, China's supply chain finance is still in its infancy. The many pain points include information islands, distrust of core enterprises' ability to be transmitted effectively, lack of credible trade scenarios, and financing difficulties. Because the blockchain is tamper resistant and transparent, it has the potential to make breakthroughs in financing convenience and reducing financing costs.

Internet Banks

The Definition of Internet Banks

China has not officially defined internet banks. Internet banks are a type of private bank approved by the China Banking Regulatory

Commission since 2014. Such banks are characterized by the absence of physical outlets. Internet banks rely on powerful networks, data, resources, and technologies to provide a series of integrated internet-based financial services. Internet banks' deposits, loans, and settlements are all based on the network. They focus on using big data, the internet, AI, and other high-tech means to complete acquisition and lending processes. Internet banks are relatively dependent on data and scenarios.

The three internet-only banks in China are WeBank, MYBank, and XW Bank. These online banks cater to individuals and SMEs and offer the same advantages as licensed banks. WeBank also can obtain business from smaller banks in credit card and consumer finance transactions.

The Business Model and Development Status of Internet Banks

WeBank Profile

WeBank was the first internet bank in China. WeBank was established by several well-known enterprises, including Tencent, Shenzhen Baiyeyuan Investment Co., and Shenzhen Liye Group. In December 2014, the company obtained a financial license issued by the Shenzhen Banking Regulatory Bureau and was formally established. WeBank relies on WeChat Pay to focus on serving consumers and providing personal loan business.

The mission of WeBank is to serve the underserved. The business strives to be affordable, appropriate, and accessible. Costs are kept low using AI, cloud computing, and blockchain technologies. Artificial intelligence does the repetitive review work that people otherwise would have to do, and customer service requirements are fulfilled using robots. Artificial intelligence helps to identify abnormal transactions. WeBank uses the blockchain ecosystem, Financial Blockchain Shenzhen Consortium, which is a national open-source blockchain. Cloud computing and the cloud architecture are central to the company, creating an agile bank without significantly increasing marginal costs.

WeBank achieved an operating income of 226 million yuan in 2015, 2.449 billion yuan in 2016, and 6.748 billion yuan in 2017. After a

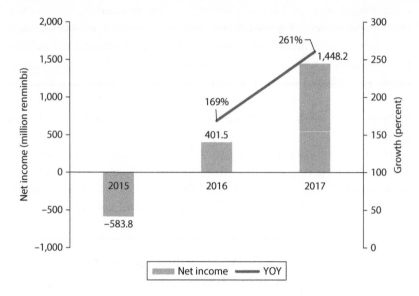

Figure 4.4 WeBank's net income. *Source*: WeBank, *Annual Report of WeBank 2017* (WeBank, 2018), https://www.webankcdn.net/s/hjupload/app/pdf/annual _report_2017.pdf.

net loss of 584 million yuan in 2015, it achieved a net profit of 402 million yuan in 2016 and 1.448 billion yuan in 2017 (figure 4.4).[12]

The core product of WeBank is the Weili Loan. The Weili Loan is a purely online small consumer loan product launched by WeBank for WeChat Pay users and mobile QQ (instant messaging) users. The service was launched on mobile QQ in May 2015 and on WeChat in September 2015. Weili Loan adopts a system in which users are invited into the Weili Loan entrance through the QQ wallet of mobile QQ and through the WeChat wallet of WeChat Pay. Consumers can apply for a loan amount of up to 300,000 RMB. Users must be in good standing at WeBank to be invited as a borrower.

As of the end of 2017, WeBank had more than sixty million registered users, in 567 cities, and more than thirty-four million credit customers. WeBank has distributed a total of 870 billion yuan in loans to twelve million people online, meeting the needs of customers for consumption, operation, car purchases, and emergencies. According to WeBank's annual report, 78 percent of the bank's major loan customers are junior college graduates or younger, 76 percent are non-white-collar workers, and 92 percent of the loan balances are less than 50,000 yuan. This reflects the concept of inclusive finance, targeting low- and middle-income individuals.

In terms of the core net interest margin indicator of commercial banks, the net interest margin of WeBank in 2017 reached 7.02 percent, which is much higher than the average level of 2 percent for ordinary commercial banks. Hence, despite catering to less wealthy customers, WeBank has performed exceptionally well. In addition, in 2015–2017, the provision coverage ratio of WeBank was 2,376.61 percent, 934.11 percent, and 912.74 percent, which was significantly higher than the average of 200 percent in the banking industry.

In addition to being much more profitable than ordinary commercial banks, WeBank has better risk control capabilities. As of the end of 2017, WeBank's nonperforming loan ratio was 0.64 percent, which was much lower than the average of 1.74 percent of ordinary commercial banks. This was possible because WeBank can gather and analyze data from Tencent's more than one billion QQ and WeChat users.

Since its inception, WeBank has positioned itself as a "connector"— connecting individual consumers, small and micro-enterprises, and financial institutions. The joint loan created by the micro-loan is the embodiment of this concept. As of the end of 2017, WeBank's core product Weili Loan had established a joint loan business relationship with fifty financial institutions that share the associated benefits and risks.

Through its Joint Loan Platform, about 20 percent of the loan funds are issued by WeBank, and 80 percent of the loan funds are issued by the cooperative banks. WeBank provides customer screening and risk control services for partner institutions and maintains an interbank joint loan clearing platform based on blockchain technology to provide back-office support for clearing and reconciliation.

As of the end of 2017, WeBank's customer deposits totaled approximately 5.3 billion yuan, accounting for only 7.3 percent of total liabilities. At the end of 2017, interbank liabilities amounted to 46.7 billion yuan, accounting for 64 percent of total liabilities. These amounts show that the funds are derived mainly from other banks. As a result, WeBank has stimulated a large-scale loan business with limited capital. From this point of view, the success of WeBank is based on the usage of Tencent's data ecosystem.

MYBank Profile

MYbank is a competitor of WeBank that opened on June 25, 2015. It is one of the first five private banks piloted in China and the first bank in China to have a core system embedded in the financial cloud. As such, it can take advantage of the internet and big data to provide financial services to more small and micro-enterprises.

The largest shareholder of MYBank is Ant Financial, accounting for 30 percent of share ownership. MYbank is positioned as the preferred financial service provider for internet merchants, an innovator of internet banking, and a practitioner of inclusive finance, providing services for small and micro-enterprises, mass consumers, rural operators and farmers, and small and midsize financial institutions.

The current development strategy of the network merchant bank includes the strategy of serving small and micro-customers as well as the rural market. Using the advantages of Alibaba's database, Ant Financial's rich online e-commerce platform and Ant Financial's offline payment transaction scenarios, MYBank has issued small and short-term loans to small and micro-customers who usually cannot obtain loans through traditional financial channels.

Since its start in 2018, MYBank has provided unsecured, nonguaranteed pure credit loans to farmers to support the production and operation of farmers, based on an original data-based supply chain model, combined with data generated by the government in the administrative and public service processes.

From 2015 to 2018, MYBank realized operating income of 2.529 billion yuan, 2.637 billion yuan, 4.276 billion yuan, and 6.284 billion yuan per year, respectively. After a net loss of 609 million yuan in 2015, the bank achieved a net profit of 316 million yuan in 2016, 404 million yuan in 2017, and 671 million yuan in 2018, respectively (figure 4.5).

By late 2018, MYBank had served 12.27 million small and micro-enterprises and individuals with an average loan balance of 26,000 yuan.

As of late 2018, the total assets of MYBank were 95.9 billion yuan, the total liabilities were 90.5 billion yuan, the capital adequacy ratio was 12.1 percent, and the nonperforming loan ratio was 1.3 percent. As a bank catering to small and micro-enterprises, individual operators, and rural customers, the nonperforming rate was at a very good low level.

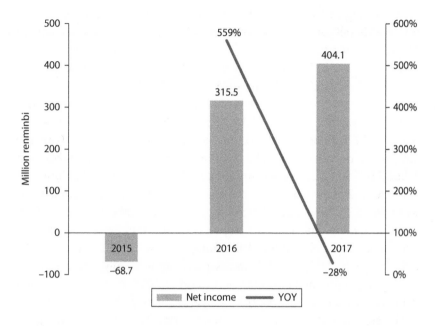

Figure 4.5 MYBank's net income. *Source: Annual Report of MYBank.*

According to data disclosed by the central bank, as of March 2018, the average nonperforming loan rate of small and micro-enterprises in China was 2.75 percent.

XW Bank Profile

XW Bank officially opened on December 28, 2016. The registered capital of XW Bank is 3 billion RMB. This internet-only bank was initiated by shareholders including the New Hope Group, Xiaomi Corporation, and Chengdu Hongqi Chain Company. It is the seventh private bank approved by the China Banking Regulatory Commission and the first private bank in Sichuan Province.

XW Bank positions itself as a "mobile internet and inclusive" bank that strives to use digital technology. The bank relies on leading financial technology capabilities, including robust big data risk control and efficient internet open-platform operation. The bank serves small and micro groups, supporting the real economy and practicing inclusive finance.

According to XW Bank's 2018 financial report, its operating income was 1.335 billion yuan and the net profit was 368 million yuan. In 2017, the operating income was 359 million yuan and the net loss was 169 million yuan. The new network bank's operating income in 2018 increased by 271.9 percent compared with 2017.

In 2018, the new network bank's business and scale of operations developed rapidly. By late 2018, the total liabilities of XW Bank had reached 32.986 billion RMB, an increase of 144 percent from the end of the previous year. The total amount of deposits absorbed was 13.638 billion yuan, accounting for 41.34 percent of total liabilities, an increase of 291 percent from the end of the previous year; total assets were 36.157 billion yuan. Year-end growth amounted to 122 percent.

Relying on its internally developed antifraud system, credit risk decision-making model, and big data-mining system, XW Bank realized the effective control of risks while its asset scale grew rapidly, and the bank's asset quality remained good. As of the end of 2018, the nonperforming loan ratio of XW Bank was 0.39 percent, the loan provision rate was 2.71 percent, and the provision coverage ratio was 693.03 percent.

As of October 30, 2018, XW Bank had more than eighteen million users, with a total loan amount of more than 130 billion yuan, a total of nearly fifty million loans, and assets under management of more than 46 billion yuan.

Among its loans, the per capita loan amount of its product called "Good People Loan" is 3,300 yuan, and the average loan period is seventy-five days. Some 99.6 percent of online loan applications of XW Bank are automated and batch-approved by machines. Only 0.4 percent of large-value loans and suspicious transactions require manual intervention. At present, the fastest credit approval time of the new network bank is seven seconds, with an average of only forty seconds. The amount of loans approved daily exceeds 330,000 at its peak.

The current business highlight of XW Bank is P2P deposit funds. At the beginning of the bank's establishment, it used P2P fund deposits as its strategy. Its participation in the custody business was quite deep, and it was also well known in the P2P industry.

The fund depository business is only part of a new cooperative network of XW Bank. It obtained connections with many internet financial platforms through fund depository business. This is why XW Bank can distribute a total of 100 billion yuan of loans in two years without relying on traffic driven from WeChat and Alibaba.

Challenges Facing Internet Banks

On December 25, 2015, the People's Bank of China issued the Notice on Improving Personal Bank Account Services to Strengthen Account Management, and classified bank accounts into Class I, II, and III accounts. The biggest difference between Class II accounts and Class I accounts is that Class II accounts cannot access cash and cannot transfer funds to unbound accounts. Class III accounts can handle only small purchases and payments.

As pure internet banks, WeBank, MYBank, and XW Bank have no physical outlets and cannot meet the conditions for opening Class I accounts. Therefore, their deposit accounts are all Class II accounts. The limited function of the Class II account has led to the weaker ability of internet banks to absorb deposits, and as a result, interbank liabilities have become the main source of funding for internet banks.

The regulatory authorities stipulate that interbank liabilities should not exceed one-third of total bank liabilities. These liabilities, however, are the primary means of bank asset expansion, and the limitation of debt through interbank liabilities limits the expansion of internet banking assets.

At the customer level, leading internet-only banks currently rely on shareholder advantage to obtain massive customer resources. For example, WeBank and MYBank have relied on WeChat Pay and Alipay to obtain low-cost customers. Other banks, however, that do not rely on strong shareholder resources will have to learn how to diversify and improve their ability to acquire customers.

CHAPTER FIVE

Online Investment
and Insurance

CHINA'S FINTECH sector is well established in the area of digital payments, and the sector increasingly has regulated and legitimized its online lending practices. It lags, however, in online investment and wealthtech as well as insurance and insuretech. These areas fall behind the traditional offline investment and insurance industries, which are moving forward but remain underdeveloped.

Few of China's financial investment outlets provide substantial returns for investors. Its stock and bond markets are underdeveloped and subject to government intervention. As a result, many people invest in real estate, but this type of real investment requires a large amount of capital and is frequently a target of regulatory restrictions.

This doesn't mean that Chinese investors are uninterested in these areas—in fact, demand is great. For this reason, in recent years, new types of investment vehicles, including wealth management products, have become popular as a means to obtain higher returns, even though Chinese regulators have cracked down on risky behavior in this sector, reducing potential gains. Online investment in wealth management products and other types of products also has become an attractive option for investors who want to see substantial gains without having to possess high levels of capital. New online investors are often not high-net-worth individuals (HNWIs) but rather are middle-class investors looking for a place to hold their savings.

As in other areas of fintech, online investment helps to improve efficiency and attract additional users through the convenience of managing wealth online. Big data are mined to reduce credit risk and prevent fraud, whereas artificial intelligence can be applied to improve customer service. The traditional know your customer (KYC) process is used in online investment, as it is in online lending, to create a better customer profile. These technological applications can make up for the lack of know-how among some financial firms in understanding and marketing to customer needs.

In addition, online investment can be more cost effective for individuals who do not possess high levels of wealth, providing much needed information. Traditional wealth management has required HNWIs to hire knowledgeable investment experts, but less wealthy clients now can use robo-advisors to understand where to place and grow their savings. Robo-advisors may assist customers by asking questions about investment objectives, investment time horizon, and risk tolerance to guide them toward the correct investment decision. Research reinforces the idea that customers have found robo-advisors to be a satisfactory and less costly form of investment advice; BCG Research conducted a survey of 3,200 individuals and found that middle-class customers accounted for the largest client segment of internet wealth management.[1] Investors who use robo-advisors feel comfortable with technology and often desire a simple investment solution.

In addition, the BCG survey found that most clients of online investment are investing their wages and salaries rather than existing wealth or inheritance. These customers demand investment information or advice. Such clients also demand relatively high levels of liquidity to shift funds around.

Assets in online products account for about 35 percent of China's investment market. Banks make most of these sales, along with some independent online firms, with sales by Alibaba Group Holding Limited's Ant Financial.

Background

China's online investment industry is growing because of the limited good options available overall for investments. Demand is pent up in the investment industry. Increasingly, online investment products and wealthtech companies have expanded to meet this demand, although products and firm channels have much room to expand.

Underdeveloped Investment Industry

China's investment industry is underdeveloped. Even though China was able to leapfrog the use of credit cards in the payment and credit industry, the country may not be able to do so in the investment industry. To some extent, the online investment industry is helping to develop certain aspects of the investment landscape. Investment in money market funds, for example, has become popularized by Alipay's wealth management offering.

Chinese investors have insufficient access to profitable assets. This group of middle-class investors is interested primarily in placing their funds in fixed income products, such as money market funds and bank wealth management products. Despite this apparent penchant for fixed income products, traditionally viewed as less risky, online investors have a slightly higher tolerance for risk than offline investors—with almost half aiming for moderate risk and steady growth. The problem with this tolerance is that some of these clients are less risk averse because they believe that their investments will be guaranteed by the financial institution. A typical client is looking for a liquid investment and professional advice.

Investors remain unsophisticated and lacking in sufficient investor education. Investors have been trained to believe that large financial institutions provide implicit guarantees for their assets because the government has rarely allowed investors to suffer large losses. This means that investors lack a sufficient understanding of risk. They often look only at the returns and evaluate risk based on potential profits. For online investment firms, technology will have to fill this gap by understanding clients' needs and providing investors with enough information with which to make decisions. This will require greater transparency among investment firms.

Online Investment Products

Despite investors' lack of sophistication, they can invest online in stocks and bonds. Government bonds can be purchased online through several traditional banks, including Bank of China, Industrial and Commercial Bank of China (ICBC), Agricultural Bank of China, China Construction Bank, China Merchants Bank, Bank of Communications, and Guangfa. Users can open a national debt account and purchase three- or five-year bonds. Stocks also can be purchased over the internet after opening an account online or offline with a securities company and downloading trading software. Customers can trade during the four trading hours per day.

Stocks and bonds do not offer strong returns, however, and stocks may embody excessive risk in a stock market upswing and corresponding downturn, as was demonstrated during the stock market crash of 2015–2016. China's reliance on direct financing through the stock and bond markets is quite low compared with Western countries. Hence, this area has room for improvement before it becomes a prime area of focus for online investors.

One class of investment products has striven to provide a diversity of offerings to customers to meet different demands. These wealth management products, although recently more strictly regulated, have shown high levels of innovation. Innovations in wealth management products arise from term innovation and structural innovation. Term innovation refers to providing customers with different products of different terms. Structural innovation is associated with profit, and products can be structured according to risk level, bringing high profits to some customers. These products became popular for several years with the rise of shadow banking but have since been more strictly controlled. Despite that control, they do provide an example of how to create innovative products.

Wealthtech Companies

Many traditional securities firms are lacking in digital technology, and much of the industry is focused on brokerage functions. The focus is on improving technological innovation in the area of wealth management, and smart investment is becoming increasingly popular.

One reason for the popularity among investors of smart investment firms is the much lower commission rate paid to brokers, which makes it cheaper for the middle class to invest.

Two companies that are participating in smart investment are GF Securities and Huatai Securities. In June 2016, GF Securities launched a robot investment service in the securities industry. According to the company, as of February 2017, the service had three hundred thousand active users. Even though the company boasts the largest team of wealth management advisors in China, robot investment services have improved the ability of the firm to cater to its clients.

Huatai Securities acquired a 100 percent equity stake in AssetMark Investment Services, an American fintech firm that provides digital asset management services to investment managers, investors, and brokers. AssetMark assists online customers with simple questions and fee sensitivity. Both of these companies have found that robot advisors are more accessible to online users and are far less expensive than human investment advisors.

Automated Investment

Automated investment processes have gone even further into developing China's wealthtech industry. Digital asset securitization is a current trend. In this process, blockchain technology has been used to connect assets on the blockchain. For example, the Jianyuan Car Loan Asset Securitization Project, under the Jianyuan Capital Car Purchase Mortgage Loan Project, uses an incremental lending model. After the original equity owner and the investor sign the contract, the investor transfers his or her special account to the plan supervision account through the trust account.

Next, after the borrower submits the loan application to the original equity owner, the original equity owner submits the loan data to the investor, and the investor screens for risk. Once the loan is confirmed, it is linked in the blockchain. Then, after the original equity party provides instructions to a third party, the loan is paid into the reserve fund account by the third party and is transferred from the reserve fund account to each borrower's account. When the borrower repays the loan, they submit the repayment to the third-party payment account and notify the equity owner. The third party will make the repayment one day later.

Information then is sent to the original rights holder, who sends the information to the investor for verification. Finally, the supervising bank will transfer the funds to a trust account after receiving the payment, and the payment information and repayment funds will be linked.[2] Although this may seem complex, digitization of this process has improved the ease of securitization and has allowed more sophisticated financial processes to operate through financial technology.

Risks and Rewards

Because China's investment landscape is underdeveloped, it has suffered from high levels of risks resulting from investor perceptions of government guarantees, insufficient investor education, herd behavior, and lack of transparency. Some of these issues have carried over to the online environment as well.

Academic research has shown that investor education is positively correlated to effective financial decision-making.[3] Chinese investors need to understand some basic information about investment risk, asset allocation, and fees.

Unfortunately, China's internet environment is rife with illegal investment recommendations. Investors were warned last year by the China Securities Regulatory Commission (CSRC) to avoid false stock recommendations on WeChat, Weibo, Webcast, Forum, Shares, and QQ. Fake stock advice firms may seek a fee or funds from customers. Social networks have been advised to prevent such false advertisements.

Fraud is a major issue in China, especially with the rise of online lending and investing. Some fintech firms that appeared to be legitimate defrauded customers of their savings. Authorities have been challenged with the task of cracking down on these firms.

In several cases, white-collar criminals have engaged in such practices. The case of Xiamen Express Currency Exchange's fraudulent Electronic Reservation Platform illustrates this phenomenon.[4] In this case, the founder, Chen Lijian, acquired Xiamen Expressway Business Services Co. in 2013, with the following result:

> Chen Lijian hired Wang Di and others to work in the company. In July of the same year, Chen Lijian called Wang Di and others to agree to build an online foreign exchange trading platform for

foreign exchange margin trading. In August 2013, according to Chen Lijian's arrangement, Wang Di and Shanghai Aolin Software Technology Co., Ltd., purchased some trading software in order to accomplish this and signed a transaction agreement with the Industrial Bank to establish a virtual foreign exchange. Chen Lijian and Wang Di and others concealed the qualifications of their personal currency exchange franchise business. To deceive customers, the team also designed a simulation platform. Because the simulation platform provides a spread, the customer feels that the platform allows them to make money, but when the customer invests in the foreign exchange trading platform, they must pay a deposit of 8,000 RMB when they purchase 100,000 currency units.

From September 2013 to August 2015, the number of customers signed by the Shuihui platform reached 11,277, and the number of trading customers was 5,905. The deposits amounted to 8.7519 billion RMB, and the total balance of customer accounts reached 32.79 million RMB. The fraudsters were soon found out, however. The Xiamen Municipal Branch of the State Administration of Foreign Exchange sent a letter to the Quick Cash Corporation indicating that it had set up a branch outside Xiamen without approval. In March, the Xiamen Branch held a meeting attended by Chen Lijian and others, and announced the suspension of the franchise business qualification of the Expressway Currency Company, requiring it to stop the online exchange business of currency exchange, and prohibiting the operation of the foreign exchange trading platform in this name.

However, despite the request of SAFE to cease the operation of the express foreign exchange platform, Chen Lijian, Wang Di, and others did not end their participation in the operation but continued to recruit agents to attract customers to enter the platform and carry out transactions. On August 14, 2015, Wang Di was arrested. After the case was prosecuted by the Fifth Branch of the Chongqing Municipal People's Procuratorate, the Fifth Intermediate People's Court of Chongqing Municipality heard on July 31, 2017, that the defendant Wang Di and others had defrauded the clients' funds in a total amount of RMB 346.7 million. Wang Di was sentenced to 15 years in prison for fraud, deprived of political rights for 2 years, and fined 1 million yuan.

After the verdict was pronounced, Wang Di refused to accept the appeal. The Higher People's Court of Chongqing Municipality held a public hearing on the case on November 15, 2017. The court found that agents and platform customer groups seriously opposed the express foreign exchange platform and its member units. Wang Di and others used their personal foreign currency exchange franchise business license, cash transactions, renminbi settlement, and third-party deposit of funds for false propaganda. The court found that concealing the platform was like gambling and insider trading, as the firm founders enticed ordinary investors to enter the platform for foreign exchange margin trading.[5]

There are other stories like this. For example, Qianbao, or Qbao.com, promised up to 80 percent returns. The founder of the site, Zhang Xiaolei, was taken into custody by the police after being accused of illegally raising 70 billion yuan ($11 billion).[6]

Despite the risk of fraud, there are also rewards for investing online. Investors have been educated about and accustomed to investing in products through online sales. The first wave of online investments was accomplished through safe money market funds like Yu'ebao, and the next wave contained somewhat riskier investments such as equity and bond funds. In this way, investors have gained a better understanding of how to invest. Users are becoming accustomed to interacting with robo-advisors and increasingly trust the online investment process.

Investing online has opened the investment process to millions of new individuals, as investment websites are much easier to access than traditional methods. This has made it much easier for China's growing middle class to find suitable assets with solid returns. As long as risks can be controlled, online investment makes sense for China's mobile-friendly population.

Independent Investment Firms

China's *baobao* (wealth management) products assist customers with cash management. Ant Financial's Yu'ebao has been extremely successful in attracting investment, becoming the world's largest money market fund. The fund began as a way for customers to invest money left over from online shopping. Yu'ebao places funds in bank deposits, short-term investments, policy bank bonds, company bonds, and interbank deposits. Much of the funds are invested on the interbank market.

Yu'ebao has grown rapidly since many customers use Alipay to pay for transactions on the Taobao and Tmall marketplaces as well as to pay for offline transactions. Yu'ebao offers a low investment threshold of 1 RMB, an almost nonexistent minimum for investment. Before the advent of Yu'ebao in 2013, most wealth management products required a minimum investment amount of 50,000 RMB.[7] To encourage the use of Yu'ebao, Alipay charges customers to transfer funds from Alipay into their bank accounts.

Figure 5.1 shows that Yu'ebao's quarterly cumulative income has remained strong since its inception in 2013.[8]

Figure 5.2 illustrates the fact that Yu'ebao's user scale is rapidly growing, almost doubling between 2017 and 2018.[9]

Yu'ebao therefore has been successful in earning income and attracting investors. Other online firms like CreditEase offer a variety of fintech services, including wealth management. Yirendai, a subsidiary of CreditEase, offers wealth management services to the mass affluent with investable assets ranging from 600,000 RMB ($92,840) to

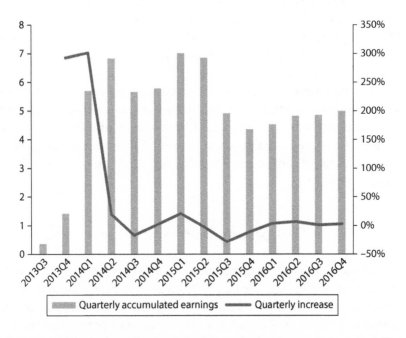

Figure 5.1 Yu'ebao's quarterly cumulative income (quarterly cumulative gain/billion quarterly gains). *Source: Beijing Time.*

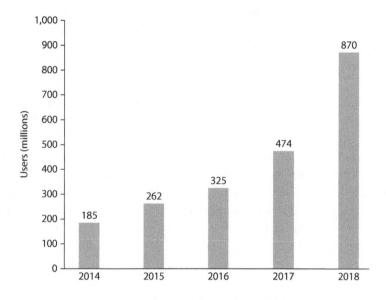

Figure 5.2 Yu'ebao user scale (per million people). *Source: Beijing Time.*

6 million RMB.[10] The company uses robo-advisors to assist customers, although the biggest challenge to increasing the use of wealth management services is overcoming costs resulting from high trading fees and increasing the number of exchange traded funds available.

Robo-advisors are increasingly capable of handling customer requests. Currently, they can carry out performance reviews, provide account status alerts, assess risk tolerance, gather client information, open client accounts, and develop a financial plan, although they fall short in other areas, particularly in explaining complex topics and persuading customers to take action.[11]

Guotai Junan Securities aims to create a one-stop financial service platform to provide investors with investment advisors, financial information, and audio and video support through the Junhong app. Video broadcasts streamed through the app provide easy-to-understand investor education that has been well regarded. Investor usage also allows Guotai Junan to analyze customer data and preferences. The more investors use the app, the richer the accumulated data, and the more accurate the push, thus forming a virtuous circle. According to reports, Guotai Junan Net Gold previously proposed that the app should attempt to reach thirty million users by the end of 2018. By the end of 2017, this number already had reached twenty-three million.

Similarly, Zhongtai Securities Network Finance said that its focus in 2018 was to continue to promote the combination of online and offline business models. Zhongtai Securities proposed a process-oriented centralized operation plus online investment service. The centralized operation of the process refers to the creation of a centralized business processing center and a centralized operation management platform.

At the end of 2014, Wanda Group established Wanda Finance by establishing a third-party transaction payment platform and began to use internet finance.[12] Subsequently, it launched two phases of internet financial products to support its light asset strategy, including a combination of internet finance and real estate. This has helped spur the development of real estate companies.

Traditional Online Investment

China Merchants Bank uses Machine Gene Investment to advise its customers on how to grow their wealth. China Merchants Bank has launched a money market fund, Yiyibao, which can be used to redeem funds at a later time. If the purchaser of Yiyibao sold by Minsheng Bank is a Minsheng Bank customer, the current deposits in its account can be used to directly purchase the product, and major banks are launching similar network wealth management products.

Ping An Life Insurance offers an online wealth management platform called Safe Fortune, which integrates investment and finance, using advanced technology such as artificial intelligence and big data to assist a variety of customers. Safe Fortune offers products such as Live Profit that has a seven-day annualized return of more than 5 percent. As of May 2017, Ping An Safe Fortune had more than seven million registered users and more than one million actively trading users. Per capita investment assets amounted to 390,000 RMB.

In the era of internet finance, commercial banks' wealth management business has become increasingly diverse. For example, China Commercial Bank has a mobile phone app that allows customers to see links to financial products, as well as an e-link that provides customers with comprehensive financial management.[13]

Online investment still has far to go in China, because the investment industry is immature. According to a 2017 white paper published by Ping An Finance, online wealth management needs to develop in several important areas.[14]

First, the internet wealth management industry should improve business standards and human resources, as well as management and risk control capabilities.

Second, the industry must better understand customer needs and effectively classify them to meet their individualized and diverse needs. Chinese investors have high levels of demand, but this is a relatively unexplored area by the financial industry because of a lack of overall financial deepening. As the economy has developed, many individuals have become wealthy, and others have moved into the middle class. Allowing investors to purchase products with a variety of risks and returns would satisfy growing investment needs.

Third, the industry needs to expand available product types and quantities and establish customer-centric products and service systems. Fintech firms should not emulate wealth management products that were offered through the shadow banking system in recent years, which were filled with risky underlying products. Products should be created with a consideration for both returns and risks.

Fourth, the internet wealth management industry must market to customers based on their preferences to improve service satisfaction and customer loyalty. Consumers are becoming increasingly sophisticated and selective and are demanding better customer service.

Fifth, the industry needs to enhance the online user experience; create contact points at the presale, sale, and postsale stages; and generate a positive feeling that matches the promise of the brand.

Sixth, the industry must improve its risk management system and level of transparency. A strong risk management system and appropriate disclosure of information can help attract and retain customers. Companies that survive have strong risk assessment tools and controls. Explaining these controls and why they are important to consumers is essential in educating investors.

New Developments in Wealth Management and Intelligent Investment

In the latest developments in wealth management and intelligent investment, Yirendai has launched a Financial Health Checkup tool and a one-stop shop for innovative asset allocation. The health checkup tool is aimed at customers who wish to assess their understanding of their current wealth status. The innovative asset allocation tool benefits customers who need to better understand what products are available to meet their needs. This allows customers to create customized wealth management solutions.[15]

Everbright Bank has released a Wealth Checkup in its mobile banking app, which uses historical data to assess the wealth status of customers. Customers are able to understand their wealth and risk status and obtain personalized advice about how to improve their wealth health through online and offline services.[16]

Tencent's wealth management vehicle Tencent Licaitong has seen an increase in its funds to 500 billion yuan.[17] Tencent Licaitong introduced its Salary Wealth Management Plan in January 2016. In September 2018, Tencent Licaitong also introduced China's first two online pension funds. Fund products included share funds, mixed funds, bond funds, and indexed funds. In total, the company has introduced nearly three hundred funds.

The Chinese firm CSCI offered a credit risk management product, called CreditMaster, for bond markets.[18] The software includes a variety of information, such as financial data, legal information, operating statistics, administrative and shareholding structure, and algorithms based on the combination of data and rating professionals' experience. This information helps investors determine whether a potential bond investment creates a good balance between risk and reward. Information is rated in terms of risks, and warnings are sent to investors when information arises that could change the credit level of the bond or bond issuer. As a result of using CSCI, credit risk is lowered, and the credit asset turnover rate can be increased.

Online Investment Regulation

As China's internet finance industry has grown, regulations have continued to develop. Not only does regulation apply to internet-based companies but also to products sold by the firms. Firms have been regulated to ensure that they are properly licensed to sell investment products. The individual products, some of which could be sold by banks or other financial institutions and not just by internet-only firms, also have faced stricter regulation as risks mounted.

The Guiding Opinions on Promoting the Healthy Development of Internet Finance, as noted earlier, laid out the role of regulators in creating guidelines and encouraging innovation for internet finance. The Notice on Strengthening Rectification of Internet-Based Asset Management Operations and Carrying Out Inspection and Acceptance (Document No. 29) issued in April 2018 laid out license requirements for internet wealth management firms, stating that the unlicensed sale of asset management products was illegal. Any such unlicensed business would have to cease operations by June 2018. This requirement ensured that remaining businesses were licensed and controlled by the CSIRC.

Some products, namely, wealth management products or asset management products, also required regulation. Wealth management consists of several underlying assets, such as stocks, bonds, and other types of financial assets. The products are securitized and sold to mainly retail investors. Wealth management products were sold by online and traditional financial institutions and became increasingly risky over time.

One major problem with such products is that many retail investors were assured that the products would not fail—they were given an explicit or implicit guarantee. The implicit guarantee, which meant that the bank or government would bail out a wealth management product that failed, resulted in mispricing of risk and increased risk throughout the financial industry. Many customers believed that the reputation of the selling institution was more important than the quality of the assets they purchased. The problem was widespread, as many people purchased such products and many institutions sold the products.

The Guiding Opinions Concerning Standardization of Asset Management Operations by Financial Institutions, released in April 2018, raised the standards for accredited investors, increased supervision of financial institutions, and removed implicit guarantees. The latter requirement indeed emphasized the fact that financial institutions should not bail out the borrower if the fund could not make redemption payments. As in other industries, removing the implicit guarantee marked a big step toward creating a more market-based financial system. As a result, investors understand that the government will not bail out poor investments, which holds the investor accountable for their decisions.

Online Insurance

China's insurance industry is lagging, having achieved a penetration rate of only 3.6 percent by 2015.[19] Per capita holdings of insurance policies are 0.13, compared with 3.5 in the United States and 8 in Japan. According to the 2016 Oliver Wyman report, "China Insuretech: Industry Report," in recent years, the scale of internet premiums has increased by about sixty-nine times, and the proportion of total insurance premiums has increased from 0.2 percent to 9.2 percent.[20] According to statistics, in 2015, 33 percent of internet premium income was obtained through the insurance company's own platform, and 67 percent was brought in by third-party network platforms.

Most sales are made to young customers, such as millennials and generation Y consumers. In China, however, overall, both online and offline insurance penetration is low. Therefore, the market potential among many types of customers is significant. The health-care insurance sector in particular has a large projected expansion. This market is expected to grow to $1 trillion by 2020.

The development of insurance e-commerce in China has gone through ten years of development in the new century.[21] After the early stage of exploration and downswing, especially after 2005, more insurance companies have begun to pay attention to the role of e-commerce. Many large and midsize insurance companies have successively entered the e-commerce field, established their own e-commerce websites, and realized online sales and claims through networking with banks. Consumers are slowly accepting the development of insurance e-commerce. The online insurance premiums and number of people have doubled year by year, and the domestic insurance e-commerce development environment also has improved.

Online insurance has both penetrated the traditional financial system as well as created a new space for innovative insurance products. The traditional insurance industry struggles with proper risk pricing, high sales costs, and customer service in dealing with claims. Insurance companies often lack sufficient data and data-modeling programs. Traditional insurance firms pay agents to sell the insurance in an extremely competitive environment, which is costly. Finally, customers have made many complaints about dealing with claims, which have adversely affected the industry's reputation.[22] Online insurance can provide a greater amount of data, data analysis models, automatic customer service, and a streamlined claims process.

Distribution Models

The insurance industry follows four main online distribution models. First, insurance companies may sell insurance through their own online platforms, such as their websites. Second, insurance companies can sell through a broker platform. Third-party broker platforms like Ubao or Zhongmin sell a variety of insurance types. Third, an insurer can sell through other e-commerce websites. For example, Ctrip, a travel website, may offer travel insurance. Fourth, the insurer may be an online-only insurer, such as Zhong An Insurance.[23]

In general, digital functionality has focused on online distribution, market analysis, and data analysis to reach customers at lower costs. Traditional insurance was first upgraded through the use of digital distribution and improved operational efficiency. Traditional insurance has taken advantage of internet channels to boost its existing products and processes. This reduces costs, as selling products offline usually requires a large sales team. Some traditional firms have built up new internet distribution capacity, whereas others have formed partnerships with new internet-based firms. Both China Life and Ping An Insurance have invested billions of renminbi to improve online sales through the development of online and artificial intelligence technologies.

The insurance industry has evolved toward an online system by using a digital platform to identify consumers' insurance needs. Higher levels of integration between insurance companies and the online ecosystem have resulted in more customized insurance products and automated data gathering and data analysis.

At this time, insurance is becoming further integrated into online systems to potentially gather additional data and improve customer service. This integration could lead to the creation of a larger fintech system to serve a wider range of customer needs, providing consumer loans, wealth management services, and other services.

Online-Only Insurance Companies

Online-only insurance companies include Zhong An Online Property and Casualty Insurance, Tk.cn insurance, TongJuBao, 1 An, and

Answern Property and Casualty Insurance. Zhong An is the biggest and most well-known company, having been founded by major internet firms. Zhong An offers auto insurance, consumer finance insurance, travel insurance, and specialized illness insurance.

Tk.cn is a subsidiary of Taikang Insurance Group, offering online property and casualty protection. The company was formerly part of Taikang Life's e-commerce department, which started in 2000. The firm integrates online and traditional platforms, and it had reached 675 million RMB in premiums in 2016. Products offered include shipping return insurance, auto insurance, travel insurance, property and freight insurance, and critical illness insurance.[24] Its partners include CITIC Credit Card Center, DX Clinics, Yihao Pharmacy, Xinjingbao, Baoduoduo Insurance Broker, Didi Chuxing, Trip.com (formerly Ctrip), and Tuniu Corporation. Tk.cn cooperates with nursing homes and hospitals to provide health-care insurance.

TongJuBao uses a different business model to provide peer-to-peer insurance. Community members can pay into an insurance pool and draw from it in the case of a claim. Products include marriage safety insurance, child safety insurance, and insurance for a host of emerging social risks, including income protection. 1 An began in February 2016 and brought in 224 million RMB in premiums that year. The company specializes in property and casualty insurance. Answern started in June 2015 and specializes in online payment safety, auto insurance, ski and travel accident insurance, and bank card safety. The company had 75.3 million RMB in premiums in 2016. Answern offers, among other products, a unique type of insurance called love insurance, which pays customers a congratulatory payment if they marry their current partner within a ten-year period that begins three years after purchase. Its online and offline partners include Bailian Insurance Platform, Qing Song Chou, Jupaopen, Xiaomi, Bundwealth, Shuidihuzhu, Zhongmin Insurance, OK Bao, Shang Cheng, Shijilongteng, eLong, and Suning Insurance.

Officially launched in 2012, P Insurance is an online mall platform offering a range of insurance services.[25] The structure of the online mall has become inevitable in the development of insurance industry marketing.

P insurance's mall system includes a basic operating platform and an external interface. After customers order insurance through the online shopping mall, they obtain certification, purchase the policy, and communicate with network service personnel to obtain detailed service information of the policy. P insurance companies can use the platform for marketing and promotion. As of December 2016, through continuous online marketing, P Insurance's online mall had realized a substantial increase in business.

Agricultural insurance has become an important type of coverage for farmers. PICC Property and Casualty Company provides agricultural insurance that uses innovations like remote-sensing technology and mobile investigation, which incorporates satellites and drones to provide information to insurers. This allows for more accurate underwriting and claims settlement processes.[26]

Figure 5.3 shows the internet premium income and penetration rate in China by year.[27]

The penetration rate of internet insurance has experienced positive growth since its inception. Some internet insurance companies, however, have done better than others. Figure 5.4 shows the four major internet insurance companies' premium incomes.[28]

In terms of premiums, Zhong An preformed the best, followed by Taikang, Yian, and Anxin Agricultural Insurance (figure 5.5).

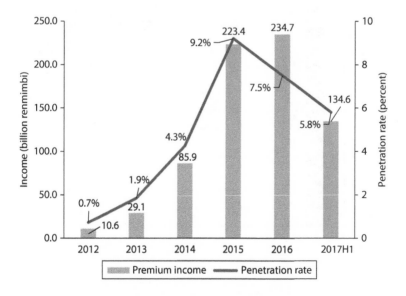

Figure 5.3 Internet premium income and penetration rate. *Source*: Xiao Yang, "Internet Insurance Market Analysis Report for the First Half of 2017" (in Chinese), csai.cn, August 25, 2017, https://www.csai.cn/baoxian/1247123.html.

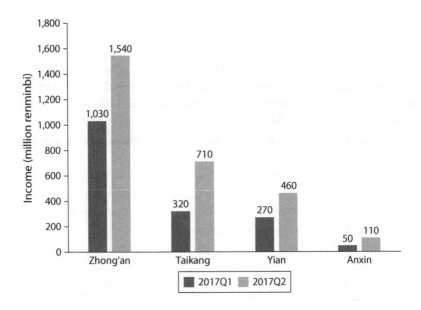

Figure 5.4 Four major Internet insurance companies' premium income. *Source*: Xiao Yang, "Internet Insurance Market Analysis Report for the First Half of 2017" (in Chinese), csai.cn, August 25, 2017, https://www.csai.cn/baoxian/1247123 .html.

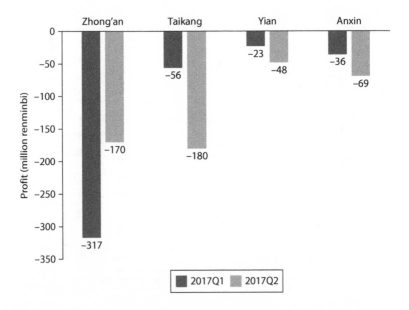

Figure 5.5 Net profit of the four major Internet insurance companies. *Source*: Xiao Yang, "Internet Insurance Market Analysis Report for the First Half of 2017" (in Chinese), csai.cn, August 25, 2017, https://www.csai.cn/baoxian/1247123 .html.

We can see that Zhong An is the least profitable, followed by Tai-kan, Anxin, and Yian.[29]

Problems with Online Insurance

The online insurance industry (insuretech) also has encountered problems.[30] The website construction of online insurance companies, the use of online sales platforms, and the processing of internal policies not only require computer knowledge but also involve a large amount of e-commerce application knowledge, insurance business development knowledge, customer service experience, and marketing skills. As far as the people engaged in insurance services are concerned, most of them are professional sales associates under the traditional sales model. Many do not know how to sell insurance products online, let alone maintain and manage a website.

Many online insurance websites are not fully functional (e.g., many of the usual online insurance functions are not available), and insurance professional websites may contain too many ads, resulting in a website that appears to lack authenticity. Consumers may question whether or not products are authentic. In addition, insurance websites now have a twenty-four-hour consultation platform; however, when customers use the consultation services, they find that it gives a machine response. Many responses are mechanically repeated answers, which reduces consumer satisfaction.

Internet insurance lacks a uniform standard. To attract customer traffic, the industry has gone so far as to develop products that provide coverage for half a year, three months, or even shorter periods. To ensure an income stream, insurance companies have made large-scale investments, mainly in the stock market. Because China's capital market is still not perfect and investment channels are limited, the entrance of large-scale funds into the market has caused fierce turmoil in the stock market.

Moral hazard is another issue associated with online insurance. A high degree of identity recognition is required. In addition to setting the required frame of the webpage to allow the insured to provide required information, customer service personnel can use electronic cameras to make video inquiries with the insured and use mobile apps to collect and insure. Fingerprints can be compared with the household registration information of the government security department to complete the authenticity verification of the insured or their agent.

Issues also are associated with internet insurance wealth management products. Internet insurance wealth management products have been popular because of their low threshold, high flexibility, low and medium risk levels, and convenient purchasing. The current yields of these insurance wealth management products, which currently are sold on the four major internet financial platforms of WeChat Richcom, Alipay Wealth, Jingdong Finance, and Weizhong Bank, range from 4.5 percent to 5 percent. This return is higher than that of money funds and is basically the same as the rate of return on bank financing. This rate of return is unstable, however, and these products present a risk to the health of the insurance industry.

Innovations

Cybersecurity insurance first arose in the 1990s. In areas where the internet is relatively developed, such as North America, this market is growing quickly. At present, in the United States, about fifty insurance companies provide specialized cyberattack insurance, including many giants in the insurance industry such as AIG, ACE, and Chubb. China's network insurance development is slightly inferior to that of industrial countries. At the beginning of 2016, Zhong An Insurance launched data security insurance, but the products were available only to Alibaba Cloud users. If the data on the user's cloud server is hacked and causes economic losses, Zhong An Insurance will provide the insured user with a high level of compensation of 1 million yuan. In general, cybersecurity insurance has been developed abroad, but domestically, not many insurance companies carry out insurance programs in this area, particularly as demand for such products is low.

Network security insurance is also a new phenomenon.[31] When a computer is experiencing a virus attack and network security is out of control, network security insurance can reduce recovery costs. The coverage provided by an insurance product may reduce the risks incurred by either or both parties. The policy for the first party covers the company's own assets, including digital assets, business interruption caused by the network, online fraud, reputation loss, cyber theft, and so on; policies for third parties include customer assets that have been placed at risk because of security and privacy breaches, multiple media responsibilities, and loss of third-party data.

Big data analysis can greatly assist the insuretech industry in reducing the incidence of fraud. An insurance fraud identification model, as well as outlier detection, can enable insurers to identify such risks. Insurers can make use of customer driving and health data to monitor changes in a customer's risk status.

The current domestic market, mainly Ping An Property Insurance and AIU Insurance, provide comprehensive network security insurance. From the product side, in 2015, AIU launched safety insurance for the enterprise market in the Chinese market. The business is divided into three layers. In the first layer, the insurance compensates the enterprise during a period of system security failure, minus normal operating expenses. The second layer includes service identification and data recovery. The third layer helps companies bear legal costs as well as the costs and expenses incurred by the data owner as a result of disclosure of personal information or data security incidents. The types of customers served by AIU Insurance include manufacturing companies, public transportation companies, IT companies, and cloud storage companies. Ping An Property and Casualty launched Ping An Comprehensive Insurance in early 2017, targeting the insured's own losses resulting from cybersecurity incidents and information security incidents (i.e., first-party losses, including business interruptions, network extortion, and incident handling costs) and third-party liability (i.e., third-party losses, such as information disclosure) up to 150 million yuan.

Online Insurance Regulation

The State Council issued the *Guidelines on Speeding Up the Development of Modern Insurance Service Industry* in 2014 to boost reforms that increase insurance market access. Internet firms are but one component of improving access. In 2014, the China Insurance Regulatory Commission issued the *Notice on the Relevant Matters Concerning the Regulation of High Cash Value Products* to supervise such products. In October 2016, the China Insurance Regulatory Commission issued the *Implementation Plan for Special Remediation of Internet Insurance Risks* to strengthen the supervision of the internet insurance industry.

In June 2018, the CSRC laid out the notice Regarding Further Regulation of Money Market Fund Internet Sales, which stated that money market internet sales business must be carried out by licensed businesses that engage in fair competition, prevent the misappropriation of sales settlement funds, and transfer the funds. The notice included rules regarding redemption and withdrawal.

According to the Interim Measures for the Supervision of Internet Insurance Business, three parties may be involved in the internet insurance business: insurance institutions, insurance intermediaries, and third-party network platforms.[32] The provisions of Articles 68 to 70 of the Insurance Law state that an insurance company must meet the minimum registered capital conditions in addition to the requirements for the establishment of a general company. The establishment of the company must be approved. According to the Insurance Professional Agency Regulations (2015), in addition to the special provisions on registered capital, staff qualifications, and office equipment, the approval system is required to pass the approval of the China Insurance Regulatory Commission. At the same time, according to Article 119 of the Insurance Law, insurance brokers need to pass the license exam of the China Insurance Regulatory Commission to earn the right to operate an insurance business within the statutory scope. The current e-commerce platforms do not possess relevant insurance agency and brokerage qualifications, and as such, they do not belong to the category of insurance institutions and intermediaries. These companies therefore act as third-party network platforms.

Online-only insurance licenses continue to be approved, as the China Insurance Regulatory Commission has encouraged innovation in the industry. Mature products, such as auto insurance, are already heavily regulated and may be less amenable to innovation, whereas newer products, like flight insurance, have fewer regulatory requirements in terms of pricing and underwriting and thus are easier to innovate. Property and casualty insurance companies have performed well in online sales, collecting $12 billion in premiums in 2015. Local governments also have supported the use of agricultural insurance.

Zhong An Insurance Profile

Zhong An Online Property and Casualty Insurance was launched in 2013 by Ping An, Tencent, and Alibaba to become China's first fully online insurer. Zhong An has specialized in property, travel, and health insurance. Zhong An Insurance does not have a branch office in China, outside of its registered location in Shanghai. Its business model is purely online. The company aims to improve risk management and efficiency through its product design and usage as well as through the claims process.

Zhong An Insurance obtained a high valuation and high level of financing in less than one and a half years after its establishment, and the company has raised 10 billion RMB in the four years since its establishment. The company earned strong revenue for three consecutive years.[33] In its first year of operation, Zhong An underwrote more than 630 million insurance policies and served 150 million clients.

Zhong An experienced a growth rate in premiums in 2014–2016 of 107 percent compound annual growth rate (CAGR) and a further 80 percent year over year in the first half of 2017, which was much higher than that of the rest of the industry. Zhong An then launched a $1.5 billion initial public offering (IPO) in Hong Kong in September 2017, attracting many investors for the world's first insuretech listing. The company has spent much time and money building brand awareness.

Zhong An has a flat management structure, which allows the company to operate in a decentralized fashion. Teams are product oriented, which has shortened the product time to market. At present, it takes only fifteen days to launch a new product.[34]

For Zhong An, new product development begins with product developers creating the business specifications for the new product and sending them to the information technology staff, who create the products. Priority is placed on expediting product rollout. Insurance products are created to be embedded into partner services.[35] The company has a tech subsidiary, Zhong An Information Technology Service, which allows Zhong An as well as other companies to use available tech components to embed their insurance services.

Products are made to meet specific consumer needs. Zhong An uses big data and cloud computing to calculate risks, providing dynamic pricing to consumers depending on their individual risk profiles. For example, one product covers visitors to Disneyland in Shanghai for high levels of rain or heat. Using real-time government reports, the insurance product pays compensation to customers directly to their bank account if adverse weather is encountered.[36]

Zhong An uses artificial intelligence and big data to properly price in risk and distribute goods accurately online. Chatbots built upon artificial intelligence are used to communicate with customers. Its business model relies on selling high volumes of insurance through large internet partners. Online and offline partners include Taobao, Chuchujie, Weidian, Xiaomi, WeChat, Fenqile, Aiyoumi, CYDC.com, Didi, Alitrip, Ctrip, Qunar, LY.com, Ping An, Chang An Auto, China Eastern Airline, and Air China.

Zhong An's first insurance product was called Zhonglebao, designed to insure Taobao retailers in the case of a dispute with a customer, allowing retailers to use deposit funds for daily operations.[37] In 2015, Zhong An launched the Bao Biao Car Insurance in partnership with Ping An Insurance, combining several businesses on its online platform, including carmakers, dealers, after-sales service companies, car driver service providers, and consumer lending institutions.[38] The insurance product covers vehicle damages caused by collision, fire, theft, and natural disasters. Policyholders can photograph their damaged car and upload the images to the system to begin the damage assessment process for claims.

In 2015, Zhong An partnered with Ctrip, China's largest online travel company, to sell flight delay insurance. This allows customers to insure against late flights. If travelers cancel a trip or their flight is delayed and they miss another flight, they often must pay a large penalty. Travel insurance guards against those costs. The flight insurance can be purchased when the ticket is bought. By 2016, Zhong An's travel insurance had reached a scale of 1.1 billion RMB.[39]

Zhong An has worked with wearable tech device manufacturers, including Mi Ban, Ledongli, and Meizu, to provide a health insurance policy. Customers' exercise data is coupled with insurance products that cover major chronic diseases, and those who exercise more frequently can receive a lower premium. Similarly, the company's Diabetes Policy sends frontend blood glucose monitoring data to backend medical tracking management services. In January 2018, Zhong An partnered with UnionPay to provide more comprehensive financial services to UnionPay customers.

Other online insurance companies have arisen, including Taikang Online, Yi'an Insurance, and Peace Insurance. This growth has increased the level of competition in the industry. Because it is necessary to constantly meet the special needs of customers, these companies must avoid creating homogenized products and improve personalized services. As a result, Zhong An creates custom products for consumers, taking complex risks and splitting them up so that customers can choose products that suit their specific risk level.

Hong Kong Online Investment

Hong Kong is a sophisticated financial center, so investors have been using online platforms for stock trading for years. One study showed that 55 percent of investors trade online most often, as opposed to using traditional channels. Investors also purchase funds online, although some also consult with traditional intermediaries to better understand the features and risks of funds.[40]

Hong Kong is home to a number of up-and-coming online investment startups, also known as wealthtech. These companies are fairly international in scope. For example, Aidyia is a hedge fund that uses artificial general intelligence to closely predict price movements in financial markets. The company has a fund of U.S. equities that makes all trades using artificial intelligence. 8 Securities is an online investment service with offices in Hong Kong and Tokyo that includes a robo-advisory service and a stock trading app. Quantifeed provides an investment platform to financial institutions across Asia, allowing brokers to offer online investment solutions.[41] Chong Sing Fintech is a Hong Kong–based company that provides online services to SMEs, merchants, and individuals throughout Asia. Services include supply chain financing and online investment.

China's Place in Global Online Investment and Insurance Development

Although China is a global leader in the digital payments industry, it is a laggard in global online investment and insurance. Although these sectors are relatively new, even offline, both areas are growing. Fintech firms are educating consumers about how to invest and insure themselves and are learning how to create products to meet China's unique demand and financial regulatory characteristics.

Because this sector is underdeveloped, China likely will continue to suffer somewhat in the medium term from its lack of diverse investment products offered through wealthtech. The stock and bond markets do not fully reflect risks and rewards, and at least partial government ownership remains in many of the listed companies, which means that listed companies in China may be less efficient than listed

TABLE 5.1
China Mutual Fund Assets Under Management (RMB)

Category	December 2016	December 2017
Money market	4.32 trillion	6.74 trillion
Allocation (mixed asset)	1.65 trillion	1.76 trillion
Fixed income	1.24 trillion	1.31 trillion
Equity	440 billion	540 billion
Other	397 billion	316 billion

Data source: Piotr Zembrowski, "China's Mutual Funds: Two Charts," Fund Selector Asia, February 8, 2018, https://fundselectorasia.com/chinas-mutual-funds-two-charts/.

companies in the Western hemisphere. China's domestic mutual funds market is dominated by money market funds and other fixed income assets. This reflects the inadequacy of the equity market in meeting investor demands (table 5.1).

China needs to improve investment outlets in several key areas:

1. Equities. China's stock market is dominated by retail, rather than institutional, investors. This makes the stock markets rather volatile, and the investment horizon is often more short term. For firms, it can take a long time to be listed on the stock market because the government seeks to control listings to maintain market stability. As a result, investment opportunities are dampened, and potentially profitable firms are withheld from the market. Some of the best firms seek to list overseas. China had planned to implement a registration-based listing system that would speed up the listing process, but this has been prolonged until February 29, 2020. In contrast, less profitable companies are often not forced to delist.

2. Bonds. Bond market pricing for risk and returns needs to be improved, especially for corporate bonds, some of which are junk bonds that are misclassified as less risky. In addition, China needs to break the relationship between the government and institutional investors, namely banks. The government has been known to ask banks to hold certain bonds, such as municipal bonds, that may be undesirable. If this continues to happen,

bonds will be mispriced and demand for particular bonds will be greatly overstated, failing to reflect true market conditions. China needs to improve liquidity in its secondary bond market, increasing trading transactions among institutional investors. This can be aided with the creation of a classic repo market with more stable repo rates and the complementary development of derivatives. A liquid bond futures market would improve the bond and derivatives markets.

3. Fixed income derivatives. China has been developing interest rate swaps based on benchmark interest rates, which do not play a key role in determining corporate funding costs. Products need to be based on deposit and loan rates to properly hedge corporate assets and liabilities. Credit risk derivatives are being developed but continue to require clarity to reduce counterparty risk, for example.

4. Asset-backed securities. China's asset-backed securities market has grown rapidly, which has helped to provide liquidity to financial institutions and local governments. Assets that are securitized may include loans to households for consumption of automobiles or real estate, or loans to companies for infrastructure construction, for example. Some of the underlying assets are risky because of a lack of cash flow.

Only when these investment outlets are improved can online investment truly develop. Certainly, wealthtech can help middle-class and other individuals gain access to investment more easily and increase investment in existing channels. This explains the surge in investment in money market funds. Wealthtech, however, is mainly a tool to reach these products, which require a great deal of shaping.

Insuretech suffers from some of the same issues as wealthtech. The insurance market is underdeveloped in China. Outside of health insurance, much of which is provided by the state, few people have insurance. For those who do have insurance, the main providers of life insurance are China Life, Ping An, and Anbang. The top property and casualty insurers are PICC P&C, Ping An P&C, and CPIC P&C.

Insurance product returns are regulated to some extent, as are insurance investments. The China Insurance Regulatory Commission specified a cap on the guaranteed rate of return to 3.5 percent, although it allowed insurers to provide a higher guaranteed rate with approval.

Auto insurance premiums also fall under certain pricing restrictions. Asset management rules prevent insurers from investing more than 20 percent of assets in stocks or corporate bonds and 10 percent in real estate and mortgages. This has restrained profitability and therefore expansion in the insurance market.

Furthermore, the shortage of long-duration assets has resulted in a maturity mismatch for insurance companies. The average asset duration for insurers is six years, whereas the average liability duration is almost thirteen years.[42] In an interest rate downcycle, insurers must take somewhat more risk to earn higher returns. Here again, as in the wealthtech market, China's financial markets face problems of insufficient diversity in assets in terms of risk and returns as well as in maturity, which has an impact on other financial subsectors.

CHAPTER SIX

Blockchain Finance and Virtual Currencies

CHINA IS POISED to become a major global leader in the application of blockchain in finance. Blockchain represents both a technology and a burgeoning industry, which is providing services to financial and nonfinancial firms as well as to government institutions. Blockchain technology has the potential to revolutionize the financial sector, because the blockchain, or digital ledger on which transactions are recorded, reduces or eliminates the need for intermediaries. The blockchain can directly digitize assets and transfer value from one party to another. Use of the blockchain enhances trust between the parties and allows for interinstitutional data sharing. This technology enables individuals to share their data securely and directly when applying for a loan, making a cross-border payment, or executing a contract, for example. Therefore, blockchain can greatly reduce the costs of carrying out financial transactions.

Figure 6.1 shows how a blockchain uses a distributed ledger technology. Copies of the ledger are shared among members of a decentralized network. Transactions are recorded among the participants of the network. The blockchain is a chain of blocks that contain encrypted

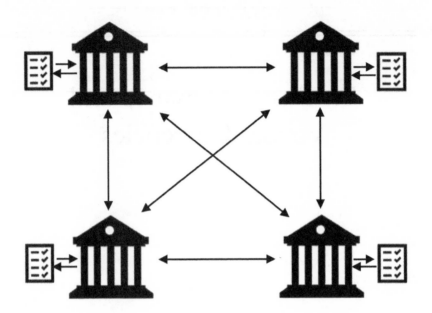

Figure 6.1 Blockchain's distributed ledger technology. *Source*: Courtesy of the authors.

transaction information as well as timestamps to prevent data tampering. A majority of nodes, or members of the network, must check the validity of the transaction for it to be approved.

The technology can be applied to many areas, including banking systems, payment transactions, and the stock market. The secure nature of the blockchain can make financial transactions safer and keep costs down, particularly as it reduces the number of necessary intermediaries to verify or connect transactions. The industry is, at present, in its early stages, and blockchain is not yet widely used. This chapter discusses the development of the industry as applied to fintech in China.

China has played an important role in mining, purchasing, and selling virtual currencies like Bitcoin and is considering adopting a sovereign digital currency. First, we discuss the application of blockchain to fintech.

Background

China is in the process of gradually adopting blockchain, in both the private and public spheres. In 2017, China already had more than

430 blockchain companies, which mainly were used in the real economy and financial sectors. China also had 930 blockchain-related apps. These apps were used for various activities, including mining, currency trading, infrastructure, platform technology, and related services. Many entrepreneurs are dedicated to building businesses out of this new technology.

Most blockchain companies are located in Beijing, Shanghai, Guangdong, and Zhejiang, where capital resources and education levels are higher than in other areas of the country. Beijing has 175 blockchain companies, Shanghai has 95 companies, Guangdong Province has 71 companies, and Zhejiang Province has 36 companies.[1] Figure 6.2 shows the number of blockchain companies in China between 2013 and 2017. The trend is clearly upward.[2]

China's government backs the use of blockchain and currently is piloting a blockchain-based sovereign digital currency. Large internet firms like Ant Financial and Tencent Holdings Limited are incorporating the technology into their businesses. Some Chinese technology firms also are investing in blockchain startups around the world. Blockchain alliances, such as the Financial Blockchain Shenzhen Consortium

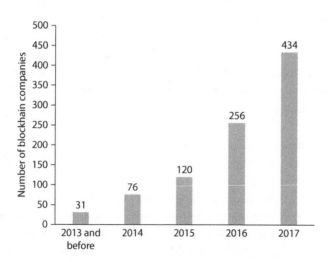

Figure 6.2 Number of China's blockchain companies. *Source*: China Industry Information Network, "Analysis of the Development Status and Industry Development Trend of China's Blockchain Industry in 2018" (in Chinese), China Industry Information Network, June 14, 2018, http://www.chyxx.com/industry/201806/649549.html.

(FISCO) and Qianhai International Blockchain Ecosphere Consortium (IBEC), have welcomed Chinese researchers in the development of blockchain projects. FISCO and IBEC build research collaboration under the backdrop of government policy support.

China's largest fintech companies have become increasingly involved in blockchain development after 2015. For example, Baidu Finance announced that it would issue the first blockchain-based asset-backed security backed by personal car leases worth 424 million RMB.[3] Tencent released a blockchain consortium platform, TrustSQL, and JD Finance has tested a blockchain consortium with UnionPay. The ChinaLedger Alliance of eleven regional commodity exchanges, equity exchanges, and financial asset exchanges led by Wanxiang Blockchain Lab is attempting to develop an open-source blockchain protocol. The goal is to develop blockchain technology that meets the needs of Chinese businesses and creates regulatory standards.

Hangzhou Qulian Technology Co., created in 2016, provides a blockchain platform called Hyperchain, used in medium and large-size financial institutions. The platform was one of the first to pass the Blockchain Standard Test of the China Electronics Standardization Institute and the China Academy of Information and Communications Technology. The company supports such applications as digital bills, asset-backed securities, accounts receivable, data transactions, equity, bonds, and supply chain finance, and it helps firms and institutions implement blockchain networks on the cloud. The company received 1.5 billion RMB in Series B financing in June 2018. Financial institutions that use the products include China Zheshang Bank, Shanghai Stock Exchange, China UnionPay, China Everbright Bank, Agricultural Bank of China, China Zheshang Bank, Tebon (for asset-backed securities management), Industrial and Commercial Bank of China (ICBC), Medical Finance Service supply chain finance, Bank of China, and Bank of Beijing.

A major reason the technology is so popular is that it is viewed as tamper resistant by many Chinese firms, according to a survey conducted by PricewaterhouseCoopers.[4] The same survey found that the three application fields in which blockchain is viewed as most useful include the logistics, government, and medical industries. Security traceability and distributed data storage are viewed as major beneficial features. All over the world and particularly in China, firms are closely watching policy normalization, which, if put into place by the government, would allow blockchain to become a more mainstream technology. This means that companies already using the technology potentially would be able to reap great benefits.

Smart contracts are another area on which many Chinese innovators have pinned their hopes. Smart contracts are user-defined programs running on the blockchain that contain contract information, enforce those contracts, and help businesses and individuals exchange money or property, potentially without an intermediary. Smart contracts assume the responsibility of a trusted third party that allows people to exchange goods safely, with proper enforcement and auditable history.

Banks Using Blockchain

Several banks are using blockchain platforms. In August 2018, the Bank of China signed a strategic cooperation agreement with China UnionPay to create a blockchain-backed payment system. This system will provide the framework for a cross-border payments system, improving banking services. The system would enable cardholders to make transfers and trades using a QR code.

China Zheshang Bank, a private bank, issued $66 million in securities using its own blockchain platform in August 2018.[5] The securities are backed by a loan portfolio and are broadcast through the blockchain platform, called Lianrong. The bank is one of the first in China to issue blockchain securities. China Zheshang Bank joined JD Finance, a subsidiary of JD.com, to launch a similar product in partnership with another commercial bank.

China Minsheng Bank has been in cooperation with China CITIC Bank to launch the first domestic letter-of-credit blockchain application. Ping An Insurance's asset trading and credit application scenarios also use the technology.

China Merchants Bank implemented the first blockchain cross-border payment application in China. China CITIC Bank has a blockchain letter-of-credit business, Bank of Jiangsu uses a blockchain bill business, Suning Financial Services uses a blockchain blacklist sharing platform, and Bank of Nanjing has a blockchain clearing system.

Weizhong Bank has invested in research on blockchain technology since 2015. In May 2016, Weizhong Bank, along with the Shenzhen Financial Technology Company and Shenzhen Stock Exchange, led the establishment of the Financial Blockchain Cooperation Alliance (Shenzhen) called the Gold Chain Alliance. The alliance has more than one hundred members, including banks, funds, securities, insurance, local equity exchanges, and technology companies. The members of the Golden Chain Alliance conduct research and apply financial blockchain technology and also perform research in the areas of cloud services, digital assets, credit, over-the-counter (OTC) equity market, wealth management products, insurance, and bill payments.

Weizhong Bank has developed two major blockchain open-source platforms. One platform involved a joint launch of Blockchain Open Source (BCOS), the underlying platform for the enterprise-level blockchain, which was completely open source as of July 2017. Several institutions belonging to the Golden Chain Alliance Open Source Working Group then developed and opened up the financial branch version of BCOS, called the Financial Blockchain Shenzhen Consortium (FISCO) BCOS. Now, dozens of companies are using FISCO BCOS for supply chain, bills, data sharing, asset securitization, credit reporting, and off-market equity activities.

BLOCKCHAIN TRADING AND SETTLEMENT

The Shanghai Stock Exchange, Digital Money Research Institute, and Hangzhou Bank Blockchain Technology Research Institute completed a test run of a digital block trading platform based on blockchain technology developed by four commercial banks (i.e., ICBC, Bank of China, Shanghai Pudong Development Bank, and Hangzhou Bank) on January 25, 2018. The group issued the first digital ticket on the Shanghai Stock Exchange with a face value of 160,000 RMB. The platform uses blockchain technology, and the central bank, digital bill exchange, commercial banks, and other participating institutions are licensed to access the digital ticket network through blockchain nodes. After the digital notes are issued, they are registered in the blockchain as smart contracts and traded on the chain.

The Shenzhen Stock Exchange has created an interbank equity trading platform based on blockchain to provide intermediary information and credit lines for regional equity markets. Blockchain is used to verify intermediary data to provide interconnectedness for regional equity markets.

In July 2016, China's monetary authorities began work on the development of the digital bill trading platform, which was launched in 2017. Several banks, including the Bank of China, started pilot work in this area as well. On March 15, 2017, China officially established the National Monitoring and Operation Management Center for Blockchain Notes. Digital bills using blockchain technology can help address the chaos of the bill industry, which suffered from cases of fraud, including the 2016 incident involving the illegal discounted bills for Jiaozuo's retired staff. In this case, a bill issuance defrauded the public of more than 1 billion RMB. In 2016 alone, the volume of risk-related bill incidents exceeded 10 billion RMB.[6]

Zhongan Technology uses blockchain for settlement between merchants and their suppliers. China UnionPay uses IBM blockchain technology to create a cross-banking card loyalty exchange platform. In August 2017, Shinmei Life Insurance Co., Ltd., implemented blockchain technology to improve transparency in accounts.

GOVERNMENT USE OF BLOCKCHAIN

Even though Bitcoin has been banned by the Chinese government, blockchain has received government endorsement. The People's Bank of China has created a system that digitizes checks issued by Chinese businesses. China's central bank has also piloted a sovereign blockchain digital currency.

Blockchain was integrated into the Thirteenth Five-Year Plan in 2016, and projects involving use of the blockchain in social security funds management and mortgage valuations were announced in 2016. The Supreme People's Court has released rules that support the use of blockchain to store digital evidence. President Xi Jinping has even referred to blockchain as a "breakthrough" technology.[7]

In December 2016, the State Council mentioned the blockchain in the Notice on Printing and Distributing the National Informationization Plan of the Thirteenth Five-Year Plan, as it related to other cutting-edge technologies, such as quantum communication, artificial intelligence, virtual reality, and big data analysis. China's Ministry of Industry and Information Technology (MIIT), working closely with the International Organization for Standardization and the International Telecommunication Union, established a National Blockchain and Distributed Accounting Technology Standardization Committee in 2018 to create an international blockchain standard. The committee will recommend standards for blockchain reference architectures, data format specifications, smart contracts, and interoperability. The government also established a Blockchain Registry Open Platform in 2018, which is responsible for registering intellectual property rights on the blockchain.

In 2017, the State Council issued a document to promote the application of new technologies like blockchain and artificial intelligence to establish a credit evaluation mechanism based on the supply chain. The rule encouraged the development of open-source software in finance and other sectors.[8]

Central government research documents also support this technology. For example, a 2016 white paper issued by the China Blockchain Technology and Industry Development Forum for the MIIT states that blockchain can be used to reduce financial transactions costs and lower the incidence of financial fraud.[9] Costs associated with collecting information as well as resolving disputes can be cut significantly by using the blockchain. The paper finds that digitizing financial infrastructure would improve efficiency in asset trading.

Blockchain has been promoted at the local government level as well, as can be seen in figure 6.3. Blockchain development has been particularly active on the eastern coast. For example, in March 2018, the Hebei Provincial Government issued the Guiding Opinions on Accelerating Industrial Transformation and Upgrading to Build a Modern Industrial System to cultivate high-technology industries, including blockchain. In April 2018, the State Council approved the Planning Outline of Hebei Xiong'an New District, which focused on building up the information technology industry, including the use of blockchain. In Guizhou Province, the Guiyang municipal government has stated that it plans to construct a demonstration zone for the use of sovereign blockchains.

In December 2017, Guangzhou issued a government support policy on the blockchain industry, with the aim for the Guangzhou Development Zone's Measures for Promoting the Development of Blockchain to expand finance by about 200 million RMB per year. In February 2017, the Nanjing Municipal People's Government issued the Notice of the General Office of the Municipal Government on Printing and Distributing the Thirteenth Five-Year Wisdom Development Plan of Nanjing to put forward new technologies, such as blockchain.

Figure 6.3 Areas of blockchain development. *Source*: Courtesy of the authors.

Later, Nanjing established a $1.48 billion blockchain fund as well as the first Industrial Public Chain Summit (IPCS) on May 23, 2018. The fund was set up along with Yuandao Capital and Jolmo investment management to provide funds for blockchain startups and university innovation projects, traditional firms that wish to adopt blockchain technologies, and cryptocurrency projects.

In May 2017, the Wuxi Software Industry Association's Blockchain Industry Committee and the Joint Laboratory of Internet of Things and Blockchain were established. As of December 2017, Suzhou High Speed Rail New City had created fifteen blockchain application scenarios and issued several support policies to attract blockchain companies. In June 2017, the People's Government of Shibei District of Shandong Province issued the Opinions on Accelerating the Development of Blockchain Industry to cultivate blockchain innovation firms. Qingdao announced plans to establish a global blockchain center in September 2017 with the Taishan Sandbox in Laoshan District. In July 2017, Zhangzhou District established a blockchain financial industry sandbox park. As of September 2017, Jiangxi Provincial People's Government issued the Notice on Printing and Distributing the Plan for the Construction of the Green Finance System in Jiangxi Province during the Thirteenth Five-Year Plan, which promoted development of blockchain technology, trusted timestamp identification, and other internet financial security technologies.

In November 2017, the Chongqing Municipal Commission of Economics and Information Technology issued the Opinions on Accelerating the Cultivation and Innovation of Blockchain Industry to construct two to five blockchain industrial bases in the city by 2020. In April 2018, the Chengdu Big Data Association Blockchain Professional Committee was established. In December 2017, the General Office of the People's Government of Guangxi Zhuang Autonomous Region issued the Opinions on the Further Expansion of Guangxi's Development (Implementation), to cultivate blockchain innovation firms.

In 2016, Chancheng District in Foshan City, Guangdong Province, launched a project called the Comprehensive Experimental Area of Big Data in Guangdong Province.[10] The city launched this program to test the usefulness of blockchain in public services. An intelligent multifunctional identity feature is used to authenticate identities and complete forms.

Also in Guangdong Province, the Guangzhou Huangpu District People's Government and Guangzhou Development Zone Management Committee implemented the Guangzhou Huangpu District Guangzhou Development Zone Promotion Blockchain Industry Development Measures to create incentives for the blockchain industry. The Huangpu District government will contribute 200 million RMB ($32 million) annually to promote the development of the blockchain industry. Blockchain startups may receive a talent subsidy each year, and the blockchain technology lab may receive an award if they meet certain criteria.

In 2016, the Beijing Financial Work Bureau established the Zhongguancun blockchain alliance to promote the application of financial technologies, including the development of blockchain technology, trusted timestamp identification, and other internet financial security technologies that protect consumer rights and improve the security of digital finance. In addition, the Zhongguancun Science Park Management Committee has introduced measures to support high-tech fintech firms that provide services for financial regulatory agencies and financial institutions. In Xiong'an New Area, near Beijing, the city has made several agreements with Chinese technology companies for blockchain integration. Xiong'an is also slated to use a blockchain-powered fund management platform to guard against fund misappropriation.

In Shanghai, the Shanghai Baoshan District Development and Reform Commission set up the Miaoxing blockchain incubation base and Weinan Shanghai Internet Finance Evaluation Center in 2017. Both of these groups were established to expand the use of fintech and blockchain. In April 2017, the Technical Committee of the Internet Finance Industry Association of Shanghai laid out the first self-discipline rules for blockchain in the fintech industry. These rules required fintech companies to apply blockchain technology with a focus on innovation, regulation, and safety.

In Shenzhen, the Thirteenth Five-Year Plan for the Development of Shenzhen Financial Industry, written in November 2016 by the Shenzhen Municipal People's Government, encourages financial institutions to strengthen research and development in technologies such as blockchain and digital currency.

Suzhou's city government and Tongji University formed a partnership in November 2016 to set up a blockchain training base to educate hundreds of blockchain technicians. Suzhou also earmarked funds to build a Digital Economic Application Demonstration City to create a Blockchain Valley.[11] This Blockchain Valley is attracting blockchain firms to use the technology in public service.

In April 2018, Hangzhou in Zhejiang Province set up the first city-level blockchain fund in China, the Xiong'An Global Blockchain Innovation Fund (worth $1.6 billion). Hangzhou also created a blockchain industrial park for research and development of blockchain applications. The first central bank blockchain platform in China was launched at the Zhongchao Blockchain Research Institute in Hangzhou.

Descriptive Statistics and Characteristics

Figure 6.4 highlights some descriptive statistics. The figure shows China's blockchain technology income, estimated through 2020, in millions of renminbi.[12]

Blockchain technology income is predicted to rise at an increasing rate. This increase is due to the growing use of the technology in the

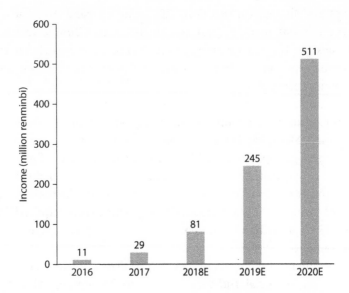

Figure 6.4 China Blockchain technology income. *Source*: China Industry Information Network, "Analysis of the Development Status and Industry Development Trend of China's Blockchain Industry in 2018" (in Chinese), China Industry Information Network, June 14, 2018, http://www.chyxx.com/industry/201806 /649549.html.

Asian nation. By 2020, industry income is expected to reach 511 million RMB, up from 11 million RMB in 2016.

Figure 6.5 shows the distribution of blockchain companies and their financing events in China. The figure shows that the number of blockchain companies obtaining financing is relatively high, revealing the enthusiasm of investors for this burgeoning industry. Much of the financing is going toward the application of blockchain in the real economy and financial industry, with sixty-five and forty-eight financing events, respectively.

Risks and Rewards

Companies that use the blockchain face many risks as well as potential rewards. These are not unique to China. The blockchain has the potential to revolutionize finance and other industries by increasing

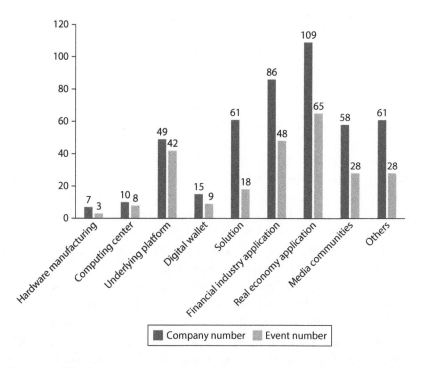

Figure 6.5 Distribution of companies and financing events in China's blockchain industry segment. *Source*: Ministry of Industry and Information Technology, *2018 China Blockchain Industry White Paper* (in Chinese) (Beijing, China: Ministry of Industry and Information Technology Information Center, May 2018), http://www.miit.gov.cn/n1146290/n1146402/n1146445/c6180238/part/6180297.pdf.

trust among parties to a transaction. This trust will greatly reduce the need for third-party verification of transactions and, as a result, bring down transaction costs. Blockchain can reduce fraud, speed up claims processing, improve know your customer (KYC) compliance administration, reduce costs associated with making payments, and speed up asset management processes, particularly for cross-border transactions. When the potential for fraud is reduced, this can speed up money transfers, insurance claims processing, and KYC compliance, as the validity of each party can be ensured through proof of identification. Eliminating third parties can improve the efficiency of making payments. Improved transparency and automation through the use of the blockchain also simplifies asset management.

These are the potential rewards of a well-developed blockchain, but blockchain technology remains in its early stages. Some serious risks also are associated with use of this technology, and blockchain firms must guard against these issues.

For one, the area of smart contracts poses legal risks, as the liability for enforcing contracts falls to the blockchain rather than to a third-party law firm. Smart contracts can be hacked—for example, in 2016, one hacker stole $55 million from a smart contract on the Ethereum network called the DAO (decentralized autonomous organization). Second, implementation risks are inherent, as participants may delay the creation of blockchain consensus, and the blockchain faces the heavy challenge of integrating with legacy systems. Such delays cost time and money and result in inefficiencies.

Third, additional risks, such as key management risk, are associated with securing a digital signature as well as coding and cryptography risk. These issues can create security risks, even though the blockchain is supposed to be more secure than other types of technologies. For example, vulnerabilities in the code or improper encryption can enable hackers to take advantage of the exposure to exploit the system. In several cases, the blockchain has been exploited to steal funds from cryptocurrency exchanges. In one of many examples, the cryptocurrency Verge was hacked in April 2018 by mining fraudulent new blocks on the blockchain.[13] Weaknesses in the blockchain code allowed the hacker to penetrate the system and he obtained two hundred and fifty thousand coins. Coinbase, a cryptocurrency platform based in the United States, stopped trading Ethereum Classic in January 2019 after it was discovered that the blockchain platform had been subject to a 51 percent attack, a situation in which some blockchain miners control over 50 percent of the hashrate to compromise the blockchain.[14]

Standards can combat some of these security and professional weaknesses. According to Li Lihui in a 2018 *China News Weekly* article, it is necessary to develop standards and professional verification when the blockchain expands to cover a range of applications.[15] Li notes that, currently, no authoritative third-party professional certification institution has been established in China or outside of China, which is a major shortcoming. The National Internet Finance Association in China has stated, however, that it will issue blockchain technical standards. To this end, the Internet Finance Association has set up the Internet Finance Standards Institute to improve standardization of the industry. Already, the Shanghai Internet Finance Association has released its first set of rules pertaining to blockchain in China, called the *Internet Finance Practitioners Blockchain Technology Application Self-Regulation Rules.*

China's Place in Global Blockchain Development

Several Chinese firms have focused on building blockchain innovations. Major internet companies such as Baidu, Alibaba Group Holding Limited, and Tencent have invested strongly in this area. Alibaba, for example, uses blockchain in the areas of public welfare, food, and health care. Tencent worked with the Shenzhen tax bureau to issue the first blockchain electronic invoice in China. Baidu issued China's first blockchain-backed asset-backed securities on the Shanghai Stock Exchange. The government also voiced its support for this technology, approving the creation of the first national standard for blockchain technology. The Chinese Communist Party website released a primer that even states, "We call on the industry peers to continue to look at the blockchain technology with a development perspective."[16]

At the same time, some uncertainty remains in terms of China's regulation of blockchain. Even though blockchain cannot be equated with Bitcoin, some blockchain advocates were intimidated by China's Bitcoin ban. At the time, it was unclear whether China would ban other areas of new technology. As the number of regulations increased regarding cryptocurrencies and initial coin offerings (ICOs), technology entrepreneurs became nervous about what might come next. Now, although the message is somewhat muddy—given that China has rejected cryptocurrencies in general but embraced the idea of a sovereign digital currency—it seems blockchain is here to stay in some form or another.

China has become a major player in the global development of blockchain technologies. North America and Europe are home to most distributed ledger startups, but in terms of individual countries, China follows behind only the United States and the United Kingdom.[17] China is a global leader in patents, having filed 32 percent of all global patents for blockchain technology in 2017, with the

United States in second place. Many observers expect China to over-take the United States as a global blockchain leader in the next three to five years.[18]

Figure 6.6 shows the global blockchain patents distribution.[19] China is in the lead, by far, over the United States. Blockchain in China has been applied to an ever-growing number of industries, including finance, energy, medical, the Internet of Things, entertainment, social media, medical, legal service, and agriculture industries.

A major reason that China is moving ahead of other countries in blockchain development is that Chinese regulators have a better understanding of the technology than regulators in countries like the United States. In addition, China's legal system is more conducive to promoting new technologies, by contrast with the United States, where complications arise because state and federal laws are divided. Chinese government support for blockchain technologies has given a strong signal to firms to invest in the sector.

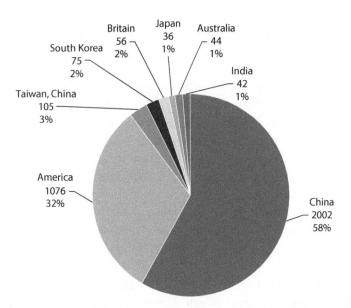

Figure 6.6 Global blockchain patents distribution. *Source*: China Institute of Information and Communications (CAICT), *Internet Investment and Financing in the Second Quarter of 2018* (in Chinese) (CAICT, 2018), http://www.caict .ac.cn/kxyj/qwfb/qwsj/201807/P020180720343745695019.pdf.

Virtual Currencies

Virtual currencies, digital currencies, and cryptocurrencies all describe the same thing—nonphysical currencies that can be traded on decentralized exchanges. Bitcoin and Ether are the two major cryptocurrencies globally that use blockchain to record transactions. These two cryptocurrencies are mined using computers to process transactions for the blockchain. Other cryptocurrencies include Ripple, Litecoin, and Dogecoin. Some digital currencies also have been issued by federal governments, and China has proposed doing just that.

The use of digital currency originated from the first Bitcoin blockchain established in 2009.[20] In May 2010, U.S. programmers used ten thousand Bitcoins to exchange $25 pizza coupons to initiate the digital currency trading process. During the development period (July 2010 to May 2013) of digital currencies, Bitcoin formed a complete industrial chain. A bubble period began in November 2013 when Bitcoin rose to more than 8,000 yuan, and on June 19, 2017, Bitcoin reached 20,000 yuan. On December 17, 2017, Bitcoin reached an all-time high of 138,800 yuan.

Bitcoin and Cryptocurrencies

China has had an uneasy relationship with digital cryptocurrencies, especially Bitcoin. Initially, Bitcoin became wildly popular in China as investors sought a potentially lucrative investment outlet. A number of exchanges arose starting in 2011, with a significant amount of competition. Some initial regulations were implemented in 2013 in response to an attempted theft by Chinese Bitcoin trading platform GBL's chair in October of that year. The trading platform was the fifth largest in the world in market size, and the scandal resulted in losses of more than 30 million RMB. As a result, the central bank, along with other ministries, issued a notice in December 2013 called the Prevention of Risks Associated with Bitcoin. The central bank clarified that Bitcoin should not be used as a currency and directed financial institutions to refuse to provide any services associated with Bitcoin.

This regulation did not entirely deter people's participation in the Bitcoin market. After this period, China's vast interior spaces and access to cheap electricity gave rise to a whole industry engaged in Bitcoin mining. Chinese mining pools controlled more than 70 percent of Bitcoin's hash rate at one point, having most of the world's Bitcoin mining pools. By late 2016, the Chinese Bitcoin market accounted for more than 95 percent of the global trading volume.

BTCC, Huobi, and OKCoin, the three largest Bitcoin exchanges in China, provided margin trading services starting in 2014, but these services were halted in January 2017. Over the course of the year, the Chinese government would crack down on the virtual token. The government shut down cryptocurrency exchanges and banned ICOs, which many fintech companies had become dependent on for fundraising. China came to view ICOs as enabling fraudulent funding. ICOs had been a means for startups to raise funds, allowing innovators to raise money from around the globe. According to a white paper published by the central bank, 90 percent of ICOs were used for fraud or illegal fundraising, and were quashed by Circular 99, which called ICOs "a non-approved illegal open financing behavior."[21] ICOs were far less regulated than other fundraising channels.

Bitcoin and other virtual currency traders were forced to use OTC and foreign exchanges. Regulators blocked access to exchanges that continued to operate illegally and blocked connections to 124 offshore exchanges. WeChat, Tencent, and Ant Financial also blocked cryptocurrency trading on their platforms. China's two largest cryptocurrency exchanges, Binance and OKEx, moved to Malta to avert the crackdown.[22]

China also initiated a crackdown on Bitcoin mining in 2018, forcing mining operations to close. A government task force instructed local governments to "actively guide" Bitcoin mining companies to close. As with Bitcoin exchanges, Bitcoin mining companies were forced to close or move overseas. China's central bank issued a report in July 2018 stating that the cryptocurrency ban had succeeded in virtually eliminating cryptocurrency trading activity carried out in renminbi, which declined from 90 percent to less than 1 percent.

China's Digital Currency

Perhaps surprisingly, China is not opposed to the idea of digital currencies, just to the idea of private digital currencies as they have arisen. Bitcoin has experienced problems with volatility, lack of widespread usage, and fraud. Sovereign digital currencies may be better equipped to handle these issues. In August 2016, the vice president of the central bank, Yifei Fan, released a proposal outlining a framework for an official Chinese digital currency. Yao Qian, director of the central bank's Digital Currency Research Lab, has stated in a March 2018 op-ed that "the dream of turning physical money into digital currency has been pioneered and tested in the private sector. As a monetary authority, the central bank has been catching up and is of great significance."[23]

China's aim is to create a digital currency, called digital currency electronic payment (DCEP), to replace physical currency, or cash, at least at the outset. The central bank would issue digital currency to commercial banks, which then would issue the currency to the public. Yifei Fan refers to this as a "double-layered delivery," which would take advantage of the existing bank infrastructure to issue currency, rather than creating a new structure to bring currency directly to the public. The digital currency could be managed alongside electronic money in customer bank accounts; the digital currency does not necessarily rely on the bank account but can also be managed by the customer's digital currency wallet in peer-to-peer transactions.

The traditional currency banknotes we use now have many drawbacks.[24] First, the cost of issuance and use of currency is high. Printing, recycling, and ensuring traceability are costly. Second, the life of banknotes (relative to other forms of currency) is short because notes can wear out or become torn. Furthermore, carrying a large amount of banknotes is a significant safety hazard. Compared with traditional currencies, digital currency is more convenient to use and has an indefinite useful life. Because digital currency is registered on the blockchain and has no physical carrier, it is inexpensive. In recent years, the popularity of mobile terminals and the rapid development of mobile payment also have provided conditions for the issuance and circulation of legal digital currency in China.

Digital currency offers several advantages in future economic and social development.[25] Because information cannot be falsified, it has the ability to solve existing financial transaction security issues. When a transaction is verified and added to the blockchain, it is permanently stored. Digital currency can prevent economic crimes and is tamper resistant. In addition, the issuance of digital currency would allow the central bank to introduce a more accurate monetary policy by building a big data system based on transaction information. A sovereign digital currency can strengthen supervision of digital currency transactions.

At present, the digital currency represented by Bitcoin has an anonymous, unregulated nature, and the transaction party can trade without public identity. Criminals use this regulatory blind spot to conduct money laundering and speculation activities. In contrast, after the digital currency is issued by the central bank of China, the supervisory authority will be able to record each transaction's information, track the flow of each fund, and establish a sound monitoring system to reduce economic crimes.

A sovereign digital currency also offers economic benefits. Central bank issuance of digital currency can effectively reduce the incidence of inflation.[26] Digital currency can replace cash with other financial assets, which can reduce the transaction costs of traditional currencies (e.g., transfer fees), so people are more likely to exchange interest-earning financial assets. This will increase the proportion of interest-earning assets and people's sensitivity to interest rates will rise, which is conducive to increasing the effectiveness of price-based instruments such as interest rates.

Finally, a sovereign digital currency can boost China's position in the international monetary system. Issuance of digital currency can improve the control over cross-border renminbi circulation and control the inflow and outflow of domestic and foreign currencies. The application of digital currency issued by China for cross-border payment will enhance China's financial strength in the world, boost the internationalization of the renminbi, generate dividends from global financial markets, and even reorganize the current international monetary system.

Research on Digital Currency

Intense research is being conducted to set up China's own digital currency. China currently has a digital currency research lab that is exploring how to implement such a currency. Use of digital currency would help the central bank bring down the costs associated with traditional banknote issuance and circulation, increase transaction transparency, reduce the incidence of money laundering and other criminal activities, and improve control over the money supply. A digital currency would help China improve the overall efficiency of payment and settlement. As of June 2018, the Digital Currency Research Lab at People's Bank of China had filed forty-one patent applications to create a technology that issued digital currency.

One patent issued in June 2018 describes how the proposed digital wallet coordinates with the central digital currency issue registration authority to track transaction data using a private key.[27] Other patent applications include a query system for digital currency trading information; a method of synchronizing digital currency wallets, terminals, and systems; a digital currency exchange system; and a means of querying associated accounts based on digital currency wallets. The lab is attempting to include encryption characteristics in its digital currency that are better suited for the financial sector and to make the cryptocurrency as money-like as possible under the current financial structure.

Scholarly thought regarding the structure of digital currency has grown in China. Jinfu Du asserts that digital currency has two levels: a broad digital currency and a narrow digital currency.[28] Generalized digital currencies include virtual currency and electronic money; narrowly defined digital currencies are indexed virtual currencies, including private cryptocurrencies. The legal digital currency, also known as the central bank digital currency, is the digital currency issued by the central bank. This is the digital form of the base currency, which belongs to the central bank's liabilities. The base currency includes two forms of currency and deposit reserve, which can be transformed from one to the other. Among these forms of currency, the deposit reserve has already been digitized. Many countries, including the Central Bank of China, currently are studying the technical feasibility of the digitalization of currency, and some research studies refer to the currency in such research and development as the central bank cryptocurrency.

Chen and Zeqing state that the inherent contradiction of the modern credit currency system reduces the quality of money as a value scale altering the generation of the currency anchor.[29] Monetary anchors have three inherent rules, including that they vary in quantity and value, reflect the total value of goods, and require the support of state power. The current credit monetary system based on state power does not guarantee the quality of money. The maintenance of monetary quality depends on the establishment of an effective monetary anchoring mechanism. The legal digital currency can rebuild the current credit system to maintain the quality of money through new digital technologies, such as big data and blockchain, and thus improve anchoring resources.

The central bank has only the monopoly power of money and does not have effective control of the currency. Private bankers have control over the currency. An analysis of the development of monetary anchors shows that monetary anchors should follow four rules: First, monetary anchors cannot be valued by anchoring themselves. Second, the amount of money anchors and their value can change with changes in social production conditions or production efficiency; otherwise, it will undermine the monetary anchor as the basis for the value scale. Third, the currency anchor must be able to reflect the total value of the commodity at the stage of the currency; otherwise, the currency will not accurately reflect the value of other commodities after anchoring it. Fourth, currency anchors need the support of state power. Because credit money can reflect the nature of capital by purchasing labor commodities, that money can be created by private individuals. Therefore, to realize the sociality of money, it is necessary for state power to support these money anchors.

China's Place in Global Virtual Currencies

China has been at the forefront of the creation of global virtual currencies. China is in the process of developing its own sovereign digital currency, and it is among a small number of countries that have embraced this idea. Other central banks have carried out digital currency experiments based on distributed ledger technology, including the Bank of Canada's Jasper project, the Singapore Monetary Authority's Ubin project, and the Hong Kong Monetary Authority's Lion Project.

In terms of its position in the world of cryptocurrencies, China has played a major role, although that role has declined because of regulations. China had been a major center for cryptocurrency mining that has utilized China's cheap electricity intensively, supplying cryptocurrencies to the rest of the world, but it has also provided a large percentage of global demand for cryptocurrencies.

For years, China mined Bitcoin in remote areas of the country, taking advantage of rock-bottom electricity prices. Bitcoin mines promised big returns in provinces that held fewer job opportunities. Bitcoin mining went under heavy scrutiny in 2017 and was added to a draft list of industries to eliminate in April 2019. The draft list also contains Bitcoin as an industry to be eliminated. The nation already has forced many cryptocurrency mining firms to relocate to other countries.

When China's Bitcoin mining sector was in its heyday, global concerns were raised about China's dominance of the Bitcoin mining industry. Well over half of the hash power was located in China. Because of the Chinese government's strong control of networks (and potentially its control over mining institutions), there was concern that the government could take control of hash power and end or take over the firms. In addition, the great firewall of China could slow Bitcoin traffic because of technical interference.[30] Therefore, Bitcoin would not be released or exchanged in a timely fashion.

China not only was a strong supplier of cryptocurrencies but also provided a strong demand force. China's demand for cryptocurrencies has been so strong, at one time holding as much as 90 percent of the world's trading volume, that it has had the power to influence global prices of cryptocurrencies. All of this changed by 2018, when China's share of global trading in cryptocurrencies dropped to 1 percent because of its ban on cryptocurrency trading. China's sudden ban resulted in sharp declines in the price of Bitcoin through the first half of 2018, as evident in figure 6.7.[31]

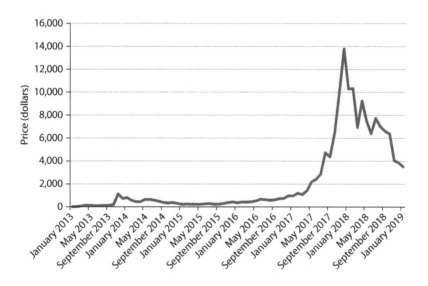

Figure 6.7 Price of Bitcoin by month, 2013–2019. *Source*: "BTC/USD—Bitcoin US Dollar," Investing.com, 2019, https://www.investing.com/crypto/bitcoin/btc -usd-historical-data (accessed February 2, 2019).

China was one of the first countries to implement strong regulation on cryptocurrencies. Other countries have little to no regulation in this area. Chinese regulation quashed the Bitcoin bubble, forcing Bitcoin prices to deflate by more than 50 percent in 2018. Therefore, China has again led the way in terms of cryptocurrencies, as other countries have been slow to shape the industry by setting their own rules.

CHAPTER SEVEN

Disruption of Traditional Banking

FINTECH HAS DISRUPTED the traditional banking system in China in two major ways. First, it has created strong market competition for banks and provided nonbank financial services with a powerful edge over traditional banking models. Second, it has brought about major changes in the types of services provided by traditional banks.

Banks have found that some of their business is being transferred to online banks, so they must remain competitive. Narrowing interest rate spreads has forced commercial banks to seek other sources of profit. This has occurred with the gradual relaxation of interest rate controls, the intensification of market competition, the expansion of corporate financing channels, and the scarcity of good assets outside of real estate, reducing net interest margins of commercial banks from 2.7 percent in 2011 to 2.27 percent in the first half of 2016.[1] At the same time, fintech fund products like Ant Financial's Yu'ebao have a substitution effect on traditional bank deposits, so that banks' capital bases also are reduced. Moreover, each loan issued by digital lending platforms creates a deposit for the borrowers, similar to deposits created by commercial banks.[2]

Banks can add a fintech component in several ways. First, they can use internal research and development to do so. Second, they can acquire or invest in another firm's technology. Third, they can cooperate with other firms to use their technologies.[3] The first option provides banks with better control over the technology but can come at a high cost. The second choice can help to overcome a lack of internal innovation, but control of the product and of the data may present a challenge. The third option, cooperation with another firm, has the lowest associated investment cost, but may result in cultural conflicts between the two firms. About half of Chinese financial institutions are buying services from fintech companies, and financial institutions are willing to invest up to a third of their resources in fintech projects.

Banks also provide wealth management services using fintech. Just as with fintech firms, banks can offer customers intelligent investment recommendations based on customer risk preferences and revenue targets.

At present, the Chinese financial sector is in the stage of smart banking. The fintech structure at this level has three layers: the management (control), delivery, and interface layers. The management or control layer is the infrastructure of the system based on cloud computing (90 percent of financial institutions have or are planning to obtain cloud computing technology). The delivery layer is where back-office activities are conducted and the interface layer interacts directly with the customer. Several components permeate these layers, including precision and personalized marketing, antifraud modeling, data mining and auditing modeling, customer analysis and asset allocation, and intelligent recommendations.

Competition with Traditional Banks

Traditional banks in China must add a digital component or stand to lose profit, as much consumer financial activity is increasingly conducted outside of physical banks. For example, customers can transfer money to Alipay or WeChat Pay to shop online or at brick-and-mortar stores or to send money to family and friends. They do not have to go through a physical bank, as customers in other countries do. Fintech firms attract business away from traditional banks by accepting deposits for digital wallets or wealth management products. Wealth management products like Yu'ebao provide customers with a higher interest rate than do normal deposit accounts.

IMPACT OF FINTECH ON TRADITIONAL BANKS

Competition from the fintech sector has had several impacts on traditional commercial banks. First, competition requires greater investment from commercial banks in financial technology and personnel, which small and midsize banks in particular lack. This has reduced the ability of small banks to keep up with fintech innovations. In addition, the main customers of small banking services are small and midsize customer groups that are ignored by the larger banks, and this part of the population happens to be the target market of internet finance. Fintech companies can carry out the transactions at lower costs. Higher costs of technology and personnel will put downward pressure on the market share and profits of small banks, and this reduction in profits further restricts the innovation capacity of small banks. Therefore, internet finance may put small banks out of business, creating greater risks.[4] Yu and Zhou examine sixty-one commercial banks in China to study the impact of internet finance on bank risks.[5] Their results show that internet finance has significantly increased the risk of midsize commercial banks in particular.

Qian examines the impact of internet finance on small and midsize local banks, using Hangzhou as an example.[6] In 2013, the scale of internet payments in Hangzhou reached 2,666.38 billion RMB, a year-on-year increase of 71 percent, and the volume of mobile payments reached 924.47 billion yuan, a year-on-year increase of 1,238.4 percent. In 2016, Hangzhou reached a per capita payment of 180,000 RMB through Alipay, ranking first in the national cities. Hangzhou has many peer-to-peer (P2P) financing institutions, compared with Beijing and Shenzhen, but the number of larger platforms with greater influence is relatively small. In 2016, a total of 24,015 transactions were facilitated, with a turnover of 1.728 billion RMB.

The field of crowdfunding investment and financing also is growing. On May 24, 2014, the Zhe Li Investment equity crowdfunding platform initiated by the Zhejiang Equity Exchange Center was officially launched. With the help of the internet crowdfunding model, various micro-, small-, and medium-size enterprise financing projects were promoted. WeChat banks, mobile banking, digital wealth management, smart accounts, and other innovative products have challenged the position of smaller banks.

Second, commission income from the sales of funds and insurance going to banks has also declined because of competition from fintech firms. Banks account for between 60 percent and 80 percent of the fund's sales market share, and fund companies' direct-sales ratio is 10 percent to 20 percent. With the current boom in internet finance, customers' reliance on physical outlets and salespeople has steadily weakened. As customers have begun to switch to third-party platforms to purchase funds, insurance, and other products, commission income for bank sales funds and insurance has declined. The commission for online products is only 0.5–1.2 percent compared with banks in the traditional case.

Third, fintech has reduced the share of loans made by traditional banks. For example, the Fast Loan program launched by the China Construction Bank (CCB) is an online self-service loan for individual customers. Customers can complete loan applications online through CCB electronic channels, with real-time application and loan approval. Customers can use this self-service through CCB Mobile Banking, online banking, and smart teller machines for repayment. Loans are connected to debit cards, so that customers can complete payment, consumption, inquiry, and return tasks anytime. The Bank of China's BOC E-loan (Personal Network Consumer Loan) uses the internet and big data technology to provide high-quality customers with full-process online credit consumer loans.

Li discusses the fact that with the rise of the P2P network loan industry in online finance, Minsheng Bank's share in the loan market has gradually declined.[7] In 2015, the growth rate of Minsheng Bank's net interest margin was only 0.24 percent, declining further in recent years. Loan and deposit income have been reduced by online finance.

Zhao and Xiaotian use panel data of ninety-four commercial banks in China from 2011 to 2015 to show that the development of internet finance reduces the overall noninterest income level of commercial banks.[8] The main reason for this reduction is that the competitive effect brought by the development of internet finance somewhat exceeds the technology spillover effect. This impact is especially large for local commercial banks.

At the beginning of 2016, the five major banks of China announced the cancelation of the handling fees for mobile banking interbank and off-site transfers. This resulted in a reduction of the fee income of the five major banks by several billion renminbi per year. This has had a large impact on the intermediary business income of commercial banks. In this transaction, the issuing bank can receive 70 percent of the handling fee, the bank that installs the point-of-sale (POS) machine for the merchant receives 20 percent, and the remaining 10 percent is used for the transfer of UnionPay. If the two banks are the same, then the bank can obtain a 90 percent commission. At the same time, however, banks have had to lower their fees to compete with Alipay. For Alipay, for example, the handling fee is only 0.4 percent of the transaction amount. Although the issuing bank can still receive 70 percent of the handling fee, the handling fee is only 28 percent. This can reduce banks' fee income by 42 to 62 percent.

Fourth, in the face of internet companies, commercial banks have started to fight for deposits.[9] The competition between fintech and traditional banks is fierce. The interest rate of demand deposits of major banks is between 0.35 percent and 0.385 percent, and the interest rate for five years or more is between 3.75 percent and 4.8 percent, whereas the annualized rate of return of online finance is generally between 5 percent and 10 percent. In the financial business, the previously mentioned internet companies have diverted the funds originally belonging to commercial bank demand deposits and time deposits, forcing commercial banks to make corresponding business innovations. To compensate for this issue, the Industrial and Commercial Bank of China (ICBC) and CCB launched "balance management" and "speed surplus" features, respectively, in their mobile apps. These features are linked to funds owned by the bank, which is equivalent to leaving a deposit in the bank. In addition, many joint-stock commercial banks have launched online direct-selling banks, thus expanding customers through internet channels, featuring simple products and convenient channels. For example, China Minsheng Bank's savings products and balance wealth management products attract funds through higher interest income and money funds

Fifth, in addition, the increasing use of third-party intermediaries has reduced the amount of transaction data that large banks previously could access. Now, fintech firms may hold this information, which reduces the ability of traditional banks to market specifically to them. Many banks have invested in improving their data and information technology centers.[10]

Traditional banks, however, may have an advantage in competition with fintech firms because many of them have a well-established reputation and history. In finance, trust is everything. Although consumers have been quick to embrace the Alipay and WeChat Pay payment systems because of their preexisting relationships with Alibaba's marketplaces and WeChat, they may be less confident in new fintech applications. Established banks do not have this problem, and customers may be more likely to believe that their funds deposited in traditional banks are better protected by the government, particularly since the implementation of deposit insurance in 2015.

For this reason, the traditional banking industry should attach great importance to the experience of the customer base, fully draw on the business model of internet finance with customers as its core, create its own set of models, and advance the development of financial products.[11]

Innovations

Some traditional banks have remained at the forefront of technology to compete with fintech firms. CCB has even set up its own unmanned bank in Shanghai. The branch uses self-service machines to handle all customer transactions. The intelligent service robot acts as the manager of the lobby and answers questions through voice recognition. The unmanned branch has several smart automated tellers that can carry out a variety of transactions, including account opening, money transfer, foreign exchange, gold investment, and the issuance of wealth management products.[12] A growing trend since 2015, intelligent robots are now commonplace at China's bank branches.

Yufeng Dong examines the Postal Savings Bank's use of internet finance to improve inclusive finance, accelerate the pace of innovation, and establish an internet financial laboratory.[13] The Postal Savings Bank has designed targeted mobile financial products, such as mobile intelligent terminals, to meet the needs of urban and rural areas as well as migrants. To improve the rural payment environment, the Postal Savings Bank also improved the rural payment network through such channels as personal online banking, mobile banking, television banking, telephone banking, self-service equipment, and POS and has solved the problems of farmers' difficulty in withdrawal and settlement to serve last-mile customers.

In addition, the Postal Savings Bank uses internet information technology to explore the financial needs of long-tail customers, such as farmers, agriculture-related enterprises, individual entrepreneurial groups, and high-tech small and midsize enterprises. In terms of online credit, for the personal business loan customers, the Postal Savings Bank has launched E-Jet products, which do not require review and allow for real-time lending. In March 2014, the Postal Savings Bank and the No. 1 store (an online shopping platform) reached a strategic cooperation, jointly launched e-commerce supply chain financial products, and built several small microloan products, credit loan products, and financial groups.

Lipeng He writes about CCB e-banking, which was established in 1999.[14] Since its development, it has formed a modern e-banking service system consisting of online banking, self-service banking, mobile banking, and electronic payment. In recent years, CCB has made e-banking development a strategic goal and has increased its investment in this area. It has been replaced by the construction and expansion of intelligent networks. CCB has increased the transformation of personal payment and settlement business and has built an ecosystem based on payment and settlement finance. In 2016, CCB launched the "Dragon Payment" business for the first time. This business is the first payment product in the industry to combine near-field communication, QR codes, and facial recognition technology to cover all the scenes online and offline. This product has combined eight core functions—namely, CCB wallet, full card payment, CCB QR code, Longkayun flash payment, free pick, friend payment, AA collection, and Dragon merchant to meet mobile payment trends. As a result, small and medium-size enterprises (SMEs) have obtained more ideal microfinance channels, paving the way for further expansion of SME financing needs in the future.

China Guangfa Bank has understood that application and lending efficiency are key factors in customer financing. In July 2015, Guangfa Bank launched its internet loan product, E-second loan, which can accept individual customers' credit applications. Customers apply for loans online and the bank uses big data to complete online preapproval, so that customers can know their loan quota in as few as three seconds. The system can synchronize with offline banking professionals to bring about efficient signing. Since its launch, it has provided services to nearly 140,000 customers in 2015, with loans exceeding 600 million RMB.[15]

The Agricultural Bank of China (ABC) is the first Chinese bank to use facial recognition to verify the identities of its customers. ABC started this practice in 2013, and the process takes less than a second to complete. This technology is also used at the bank's automated teller machines (ATMs).[16] China Merchants Bank also uses biometrics, including facial and fingerprint recognition, to verify customers' identities in its retail and wealth management units. The bank incorporates artificial intelligence (AI) technologies into business functions in the areas of risk management and compliance. Biometric technology is considered superior because biological information is hard to forge and use of the technology can shorten customer authentication time.

The ICBC introduced an internet-based finance development strategy in 2015. As noted earlier, it began cooperation with JD.com in 2017. The e-ICBC business line has three platforms and one center. The business allows customers to communicate easily with ICBC staff and to obtain financial products. ICBC also has an e-Payment tool to permit small payments online and e-Link to allow customers to invest and manage funds online.[17]

According to Xugang Yu, China Merchants Bank was one of the earliest internet finance companies in the Chinese banking circle and became the early leader of internet finance business.[18] In 2013, China Merchants Bank established the first WeChat Bank in China. This channel allows users to make credit card payments, apply for loans, and pay utility bills. A robot customer service representative can answer questions.

Cooperation with Traditional Banks

Banks have attempted to embrace innovations in financial technology. To a large extent, such innovations can improve the operation and viability of banks, reducing costs, improving efficiency, and providing convenience to customers. Li Yunze, vice president of ICBC, has previously noted that fintech has generated a lot of innovation on the part of commercial banks. Zhang Dongning, chair of the Bank of Beijing, has stated that "banks need to actively embrace financial innovation and change that was born in the era of big data, and use financial technology innovation to improve the quality and efficiency of financial services."[19] Improving the efficiency of these big commercial banks is greatly needed, as a large body of research has shown that these banks lag behind their private (i.e., joint stock or private) counterparts.

New applications require nontraditional marketing mechanisms as well. Wei Sun asserts that to promote the multichannel layout of e-banking, one cannot rely solely on traditional physical banking marketing methods.[20] Traditional ATM management costs are high, and the use of electronic channels can expand marketing channels, while also reducing operational pressures, thereby increasing customer volume. Service functions can be extended over traditional ATM outlets by providing e-banking channels to bring down costs, particularly for low-margin business and standardized business operations.

Because internet finance has increased service and marketing channels and reduced costs, it has had little adverse impact on the asset business of commercial banks. The cooperation between traditional banks and fintech firms may bring to commercial banks the expansion of credit business and larger amounts of data. This allows banks to evaluate the repayment ability of merchants and issue more loans, thereby expanding the credit of commercial banks.

Several examples of fintech–bank cooperation stand out. A number of smaller fintech firms have formed partnerships with traditional banks to provide fintech services, including Hundsun, CraiditX, Birdpush.com, Eyecool, and TD Fintech, among many others. These partnerships help banks to attract retail customers, particularly since regulations have reduced the income that banks receive from wealth management sales. Fintech firms provide banks with the technology they need to create new sales and marketing channels. Some examples of this type of cooperation follow.

Beijing Bank and the Netherlands ING Group launched a direct-sales banking service model in September 2013. This was the first domestic direct-sales banking service in China. Over the past five years, direct banking has grown. According to the 2017 China Electronic Banking Survey Report released by the China Financial Certification Authority as of November 2017, there were 114 direct-sales banks in China.

China Merchants Bank worked with SAS in 2015 to improve its marketing capabilities. The result was the China Merchants Bank Smart Marketing Platform Project to improve the marketing business precision of China Merchants Bank. The project won the Best CRM Project award from the Asian Banker in 2017.

China CITIC Bank founded Baixin Bank or aiBank (as in AI) with internet search engine giant Baidu to offer deposits and loans to individuals and small businesses, and the Bank of Beijing is collaborating with Tencent in the areas of Beijing Medical Link Project, WeChat Payment, Group Cash Management, and Retail Finance. In these latter platforms, patients can pay at any time and place and receive medical advice through the collaborative app.

Several banks have initiated smart investment businesses using fintech, including ICBC, China Merchants Bank, Shanghai Pudong Development Bank, and Industrial Bank. These services are provided mainly by third-party fintech firms. The four largest internet firms, Baidu, Alibaba, Tencent, and JD (BATJ), have all gotten into the business of providing fintech for big banks. In March 2017, Alibaba and Ant Financial signed a strategic cooperation agreement with CCB. This cooperation allows Ant Financial to offer the bank's wealth management products on its digital platforms. In June of that same year, JD announced that it would cooperate with ICBC to meet its fintech and retail financing needs. That same month, Baidu and ABC also announced a cooperation. Bank of China and Tencent set up a joint fintech laboratory to bring about financial innovations in cloud computing, big data, blockchain, and AI.

Banks may be lacking in sufficient research services, and information may be scattered across different departments. For this reason, an interactive search engine was launched by the Ping An Bank Innovation Committee and Wenin Internet to improve employee productivity through intelligent search, financial question and answer, and report generation.

To standardize the digital payment process, the People's Bank of China issued the Payment Measures for the Payment of Clients' Payments in June 2013. The measures state that in the reserve fund bank, "the non-current deposit deposited by the payment institution through the reserve payment account shall not be stored for more than one month." Therefore, the provision of the third-party payment institutions is converted into a time deposit within one year. The personal demand deposits originally stored in commercial banks have been converted into time deposits as a result of these third-party payment institutions. Since the interest rate of demand deposits is lower than that of time deposits, third-party payment institutions have improved banks' competitiveness to some extent.

An empirical study has classified banks' efficiency according to their use of fintech. Qin, Wang, and Huang examine data from sixty listed banks using a data envelope analysis model to determine banks' efficiency, comparing those using internet banking to those which do not or who use it inefficiently.[21] Although data are from 2014, the results remain interesting. The authors identify four groups of banks. The first group includes the Banks of Ningbo, Nanjing, and Huaxia, all of which have a high overall performance using internet finance. The second group includes the Agricultural Bank of China, Bank of China, Bank of Communications, and China Everbright Bank, which emphasize both traditional and internet finance but are overburdened by traditional business. As such, that overall performance is relatively low. The third group includes ICBC, Industrial Bank, Ping An Bank, Minsheng Bank, Pudong Development Bank, and the Construction Bank, which have a strong traditional business but inefficient internet business. As a result, overall operating efficiency is in the middle. The fourth group includes Merchant Bank, CITIC Bank, and Bank of Beijing, which operate in both the internet business and traditional business, and as such, their performance also falls in the middle.

Newer data rank China's top-twenty direct-sales banks as shown in table 7.1. These are the top banks out of a total of 114 direct-sales banks in China. Banks are ranked based on financial products, user behavior, system performance, security compliance, user experience, and innovative services.[22] Minsheng Bank Direct Bank, Jiangsu Bank Direct Bank, Hui Wealth, Xingye Bank Direct Bank, and Societe Generale Bank are in the top five.

Regional Banks in Digital Finance

The rise of internet finance has had regional impacts. City commercial banks are still unable to open outlets throughout the country, and as a result, e-banking is particularly important.[23] Local banks have focused on the development of online banking and mobile banking to make the operation of mobile banking and online banking simple and convenient. Accelerating the construction of electronic banking can make up for the shortage of the number of outlets within a city. A city commercial bank that is opening up a new network needs to consider myriad aspects, such as population density in the region and economic development level, to avoid opening unnecessary outlets. For existing

TABLE 7.1

Top-Twenty Direct Sales (Online) Banks, First Half of 2018

Bank	Direct Sales Arm
1 Minsheng Bank	Minsheng Bank Direct Bank
2 Jiangsu Bank	Jiangsu Bank Direct Bank
3 Huizhou Merchants Bank	Hui Wealth
4 Xingye Bank	Xingye Bank Direct Bank
5 Societe Generale Bank	Societe Generale Bank
6 Ping An Bank	Ping An Direct Bank
7 Hangzhou Bank	Hangzhou Silver Direct Bank
8 Guangdong Development Bank	Guangdong Development Bank Direct Selling Bank
9 Beijing Bank	Beijing Bank Direct Selling Bank
10 Gansu Bank	Gansu Bank Direct Selling Bank
11 Ningbo Bank	Ningbo Bank Direct Selling Bank
12 Nanjing Bank	Hello Bank
13 Hengfeng Bank	Yi Guan
14 Qingdao Bank	Qingdao Bank Direct Selling Bank
15 Kunlun Bank	Kunlun Bank Direct Selling Bank
16 Zhejiang Commercial Bank	Zhejiang + Bank
17 Shanghai Bank	Uplink Express
18 Zhejiang Tailong Commercial Bank	Xiaoyu Bank
19 Guangzhou Bank	Guangzhou Direct Bank
20 Huarun Bank	Huarun Direct Bank

Source: Bing Yang, "List of Direct Selling Banks in China in the First Half of 2018" (in Chinese), *Internet Weekly*, August 5, 2018, 38–39.

outlets, city commercial banks should strengthen management and improve the service level and operational efficiency of outlets. If some outlets are unnecessary, city commercial banks can close or change locations. In addition, city commercial banks can set up community banks to bring finance into the community, making service more convenient for customers.

In addition to receiving competition from fintech firms, rural commercial banks are confronted with a great deal of competition from online services provided by urban banks.[24] These urban commercial banks that create online competition with rural banks include China Merchants Bank, Minsheng Bank, and Guangfa Bank. These banks have reached rural customers by developing new financial products.

This has forced rural commercial banks to compete more fiercely. Both state-owned and commercial banks have started to enter into and compete within the rural market. ABC, CCB, and the Postal Savings Bank have set up small sites in rural areas as well as self-service terminals for farmers. It remains a fact, however, that rural financial institutions have a solid local advantage of knowing their customers.

This competition and deepening of internet finance are changing the rural financial environment. Traditionally, rural finance has been relatively straightforward, dealing with deposits and withdrawals, transfers, remittances, and loans. Farmers' financial needs have become more complex over time, however, as they require funds for leasing land to start businesses, for example. Rural financial institutions have not necessarily adapted to these changing needs and have continued to focus only on traditional needs. These institutions must change to meet the requirements of a changing countryside.

Auditing Risks of Traditional Banks with Fintech

As the internet has brought an increased use of big data and has expanded the potential for data risks, fintech has brought with it another set of risks—auditing risks.[25] Commercial banks are attempting to adapt; they have gradually shifted from the traditional extensive mode of pursuing profits to the refined management model that matches risks and benefits. Traditionally, financial auditing tended to be manual, but auditing in the fintech era has become highly informatized, automated, and networked. With increasing numbers of commercial banks launching internet products and the number of direct banking platforms increasing as well, accounting firms must audit these network platforms as well as traditional channels of finance. These audits must examine network traffic as well, including network chat records, e-mails, and file transfers.

Growth of Traditional Banks in Fintech

Traditional banks have ample room to grow into the fintech space. At present, Yiou Think Tank estimates the application market for banks' financial technology will reach 11.6 billion RMB in 2018, and that by

2020, the annual market size will reach 24.5 billion RMB. Many banks are investing in new technologies to increase their fintech capabilities.

Because different fintech firms have specific areas of expertise, banks often contract with a variety of fintech service vendors rather than a single company. In addition, banks may use their fintech services to solve inefficiencies in other sectors. For example, CCB has created an app to connect builders, apartment owners, and tenants in the Greater Bay Area. The app offers clients loans for long-term leasing.[26]

ICBC Profile

ICBC incorporated fintech into its business model. The company has an online interface, mobile WeChat platform, digital bank, and new technologies.

According to an ICBC disclosure, the proportion of customers in 2013 using traditional banking was 73.6 percent, which fell to 68.2 percent in 2014.[27] The proportion of business conducted through internet finance rose from 4 percent in 2013 to 8 percent in 2014, which increased in 2015 with the introduction of e-ICBC, an online banking environment.

ICBC began moving toward online finance in 2014.[28] The construction of the internet finance component involved setting up functions for making payments, obtaining finance, carrying out financial transactions, conducting business, and obtaining information. ICBC also set up an agency, the Internet Finance Marketing Center, to run the internet finance business component.

e-ICBC incorporated the goals of creating three platforms, establishing three product lines, setting up an online and offline financial system, and building up big data applications. Within the platforms, finance was the core business, reaching customers through the internet. These platforms provide banking services to hundreds of millions of users. The e-purchase internet platform allows transactions to be conducted between online vendors and users. Between 2014 and 2016, the total trading volume grew to more than 1 trillion RMB.

To properly manage this new channel, ICBC established a group that would be responsible for the internet finance business. The group included the chair and president of the company, along with seventeen traditional bank departments, to establish the Internet Finance Marketing Center and a data analysis team.

As a result of its successful internet finance business, ICBC quickly built up its three product lines (i.e., payment services, financial services, and investment and financial management). Payment services can be made through ICBC e-pay, an online payment service for individuals, online POS for interbank payment, and financial e-payment for firms and other institutions. Investment services are accessed through e-investment transactions. Financing services include Easy Loan and Online Loan Helper.

ICBC internet banking launched an open platform for the bank to directly sell money market funds and bank wealth management products through the internet. Among them, the most frequently purchased product is Yinruixin Tianyi Express. Yinruixin Tianyi Express is like Yu'ebao in terms of its purchase and redemption characteristics. It requires a one-time purchase and the income is stable, but it is safer and more reliable than Yu'ebao.

The mobile finance platform, which includes an instant messaging platform (i.e., ICBC WeChat), provides customer service to clients with the added benefit of information security. This service has reduced the cost of text notifications. This platform also includes several services, such as Pay Someone and Payment in Person. In addition, ICBC features an app called Financial e-Direct that ICBC and non-ICBC customers can use to purchase products and services. The service is provided through both online and offline channels.

According to Jingjing Zhang, online products on ICBC's online financial system have faced challenges in attracting new customers.[29] Compared with the accessible interface and operability offered by Alipay, for example, the service has a big gap. This gap demonstrates the need for ICBC and other commercial banks to learn from existing internet companies when trying to create a rich application environment. ICBC should monitor local consumption and collect information on local leisure travel, catering, beauty, and health care and should actively promote e-payments and other services to provide real benefits to customers. Zhang recommends that ICBC also improve marketing and evaluation incentives of its online products.

ICBC's Xiaobai digital bank was launched in cooperation with JD.com and allows customers to open an electronic account online, deposit proof of distribution, and purchase financial products and other services twenty-four hours a day.[30] After one month of operation, the total number of customers had reached five million.

ICBC engaged in the uptake of new technology early on. ICBC characterizes customers using big data analysis. The bank subdivides customers into specific groups and formulates exclusive financial service plans. Financial portfolio products are based on customer behavior information, making marketing more accurate and effective. Smart monitoring continuously promotes customer service evaluation, analyzes customer satisfaction evaluation data in real time, and highlights advantages and areas of improvement. ICBC also uses AI Investment to construct customer portraits, recommend professional products, and adjust product offerings according to market conditions. Smart Guardian, another ICBC innovation, is an account security service provided to customers through intelligent risk control, enhancing account security detection.

Although internet finance generally has reduced the monopoly power of banks, including ICBC, it also has improved bank efficiency. For ICBC, the incorporation of fintech has helped the bank remain competitive in a rapidly changing financial marketplace.

ABC Profile

ABC has used technology to a limited extent but could go further in incorporating technology into its business model. At present, it can be said that the ABC faces some challenges to improving its digital service offerings. The bank struggles to serve many of its customers through physical outlets. Examining the Xinjiekou branch of the ABC, Ning Jiang finds that about 80 percent of the counter business can be handled by the Agricultural Bank Super Counter and Super Cabinet.[31] This, however, takes a lot of time. Many elderly customers must deal with the counter, as they are concerned about fraud in using electronic transactions. Double-recording requirements for the business of free banking and card opening has further extended the processing time of the super-counter. This has resulted in counter queuing with an average waiting time of twenty minutes, creating low levels of efficiency. As a result, many customers have complained because they are not satisfied with the service of the outlets.

Although ABC does offer online or direct banking, this service needs to be a bigger focus for the bank. Direct banking relies on internet platforms and mobile terminals rather than offline physical outlets, thus greatly reducing operating expenses. As home prices are skyrocketing, the fixed cost of opening physical outlets is also rising, and the cost of establishing ordinary outlets is now more than 2 million RMB. Direct sales can eliminate the need for a physical place to operate, reducing daily expenses. Operations also can be scaled up easily as more customers are obtained. Fewer employees are necessary than are required to set up physical banking outlets. Looking at Minsheng Bank as an example, we see that after the introduction of direct-selling banks in 2014, the level of assets rose significantly without requiring much additional labor. Physical branches would have required Minsheng Bank to pay an additional labor cost of 1.6 billion RMB to create the same amount of assets.

According to a special 2016 research report on China's direct-sales banks, the main income of direct-sales banks is derived from wealth management business and online lending business. Many banks have launched a credit loan business online. For its part, ABC has launched NetEase Lending. Still, ABC's direct banking services can do more. ABC has a large customer base, and it must analyze and study the behavioral characteristics of customers in the selection of financial products to launch better products. When building an online platform, it is necessary to focus on the construction of customer databases and to better apply technology to the platform. Online services can offer a wider variety of wealth management products and provide better service. Even though ABC does engage in direct banking, many of its products continue to be somewhat homogeneous.

Finally, ABC must go further in terms of marketing its online services. As of now, the two most important marketing platforms for ABC are Weibo and WeChat. WeChat and Weibo's large user bases make them the most popular marketing platforms. ABC has many WeChat public accounts, such as Jiangsu Jinsui Pilot and Nanjing Agricultural Bank Micro Service. This service allows the bank to establish a close communication and interaction platform between enterprises and users through text, voice, video, and other communication methods and to further deepen the connection between enterprises and users. Although some attention has been given to ABC's WeChat and Weibo, they have not attracted much attention, in terms of both the number of responses and the number of forwarded messages. Taking Weibo of Jiangsu Agricultural Bank as an example, its users number 320,000, but Weibo replies and forwards are only in the single digits. Most of these comments are about ABC's employees and cannot be used for advertising. To create good publicity, advertising must be able to quickly attract people's attention in a short period of time, and with a certain topicality.

CHAPTER EIGHT

Risks of Fintech and Regulatory Technology

Overview

Many risks are associated with fintech, particularly risks related to fraud and security. Regulators must pay attention to these risks as well as to business compliance. Although use of technology increases the spectrum of risks it also can help to reduce and control risks.

Just as fintech firms have had to cope with risks, the fintech industry has presented a serious challenge to Chinese regulators. Most of the existing regulations pertain to the traditional financial industry rather than to fintech per se. Many of the characteristics of these new fintech firms are unprecedented and thus are not covered by current rules.[1] Before 2015, regulators allowed the fintech industry to develop without substantial regulation; however, because of the growing size of the industry, this is no longer possible. Therefore, additional regulations have been made, as laid out in the previous chapters.

Compliance with regulations can be costly, but regulatory technology (regtech) reduces these costs and ensures that complex regulations are fully implemented and also can be applied in real time to financial market changes. Using the definition of the UK Financial Conduct Authority (FCA), regtech refers to the adoption of new technology to serve financial regulation and business compliance, and regtech is an important part of fintech. The technology can boost consumer protection and enhance business insight.

Currently, the global regtech industry is only in its beginning stages. An increasing number of firms, however, are aimed at improving the process of regulatory reporting, risk management, compliance, transaction monitoring, due diligence tools, and financial crime control.

Risks of Fintech

Fintech has raised several challenges to regulation, including mixed industry operation risks, compliance risks, associated risks, volatility and procyclicality risks, and technology risks. We discuss these challenges in the following sections.

Mixed Industry Operation Risks

Financial technology has broken through the boundaries of traditional financial industries. Cross-industry, cross-institutional, and cross-sector financial products have emerged in an endless stream, breaking the time and space restrictions of risks and increasing the possibility of the rapid spread of financial risks and cross-border contagion. In addition, innovative products often run through multiple levels of financial markets, blurring the underlying assets and ultimate investors, increasing the concealment of risks, and making it difficult to identify and measure risk. These risks place higher demands on the technical level of financial supervision.

Compliance Risks

Fintech has reconstructed many of its financial trading habits and methods. The emerging financial formats and new financial trading behaviors are difficult to effectively regulate within the existing legal framework, and compliance risks are prevalent. For example, the current legal rules cannot clearly define the legal nature of smart contracts in which blockchain is applied. Whether the existing legal norms, such as the Contract Law, are applicable to smart contracts remains unclear, and the disputes that arise are difficult to accurately characterize and regulate.

Associated Risks

The development of financial technology links financial institutions at home and abroad. This had led to a sharp increase in the incidence and spread of financial risks.

Volatility and Procyclicality Risks

Although financial technology is improving the efficiency of financial services, the risk transmission speed is becoming faster and faster. As the behavior of participants in the financial market converges, financial market volatility is amplified. Financial institutions now use intelligent systems to provide customers with programmatic asset management recommendations. In the case of these smart investment consultants, when similar risk indicators and trading strategies are adopted across investors, they may lead to overall riskier behavior in purchases and sales in the market, since this phenomenon will aggravate market volatility.

Technology Risks

At present, financial business increasingly relies on technological innovation, and technology risks inevitably will spread to the financial sector and evolve into financial risks. Some organizations have weak security awareness, and the safety of the production system is not standardized. Additionally, some criminals may take advantage of the system to exploit fraud.

Big data can be used to combat fraud in online banking.[2] As internet banking has expanded, this has facilitated the innovation of bank financial services. The use of internet technology in banks, however, also has provided lawless elements with new opportunities to commit fraud. Third-party payment, peer-to-peer (P2P), and crowdfunding apps have introduced great challenges to traditional banking services, as banks must continuously improve their service quality to meet the development needs of modern society. Although people have become increasingly accustomed to the convenience of online services, internet financial fraud continues to threaten the safety of online property and thus has received a lot of attention. Relevant fraud departments should increase the attention given to targeted attacks, as criminals increasingly use big data as a tool for committing online fraud. Through such attacks, criminals can obtain information from unsuspecting victims, including their names, consumption habits, and so on. Criminals may design appropriate fraudulent links according to the purchase habits of the victims to commit illegal and criminal activities. Therefore, fintech firms must use various means and technologies to establish a safety shield for consumers to prevent internet fraud and better protect people's property.

Common forms of fraud include customer identity theft, transaction fraud, and mobile terminal fraud. Identity theft occurs through two primary methods. The first is to make fraudulent applications— that is, to obtain customer information through the network and apply for the financial business using someone else's customer information. The second is account theft. This theft includes the illegal acquisition of a customer's account information through a Trojan virus or other means and the use of the customer's account to conduct fraudulent transactions to obtain financial or material benefits. This transaction fraud also has two types: (1) the pseudo-card transaction, in which the criminal copies the card through illegal channels and makes transactions using the copied card; and (2) the fraudster obtains customer cards through illegal channels and conducts transactions through online payment and other noncard transactions.

Fraud may occur through mobile banking or personal computer clients through the webpage login. It is easy to affect transaction security by pushing computer and mobile phone viruses, causing loopholes in transactions. In recent years, as smartphones are updated rapidly, the frequency of customers changing mobile phones has increased, and the use of mobile banking has become more frequent. These trends have combined to provide an important channel for fraudsters. Compared with the risk defense line of traditional bank offline business, internet finance business has added many more risks, including both network risks and traditional risks.

Security risks brought about by banks' emerging internet business applications also have risen in recent years.[3] The emergence of new applications, such as mobile finance, network finance, third-party payment, corporate network financing, and direct banking, has extended banks' online business chain. The hidden dangers have increased, not only introducing technical security problems but also creating potential security risks. The most significant security vulnerabilities of a bank's internet financial system include business design flaws, cross-site scripting attacks, mobile phone SMS verification defects, login function defects, SQL injection attacks, and sensitive information disclosure. In addition to the traditional vulnerability scanning, SQL injection attacks, web backdoors, false webpages, unauthorized access, and brute force attacks, internet financial platforms face the prospect of false registration and malicious swipes. Security risks for fintech also include collision attacks, in which an attacker repeatedly tries to log in to the website through an automated tool. To accomplish this, a large number of valid usernames and passwords are collected or illegally purchased, and automated tools are used for continuous login attempts. Customers often use the same username and password combination on different websites, which makes it easier for an attacker to impersonate the user to log onto an internet financial platform for illegal activities, resulting in extensive economic losses.

Although the bank currently deploys firewalls, intrusion protection and intrusion detection systems, web application framework application firewalls, anti–distributed denial of service (DDoS), and malware protection, traditional security technologies, whether based on signatures or rules, can combat known malicious behavior. Applications can analyze and write behavior rules for protection. Automated attacks that simulate legitimate operations, such as collision-causing attacks, however, may not be identified as malicious attacks under the existing security software. If system usernames and passwords are leaked online, attackers can easily access accounts in other systems as well. Therefore, new security protection technologies are needed for these new types of security threats. To combat these threats, new security technologies have been created. These include camouflage technology and remote-browser technology. The essence of camouflage technology is to target the attacker's network, application, terminal, and data to make the hacker's tools invalid and disrupt the attacker, thus creating the need for Remote-browser technology addresses the fact that browsers are gateways to attacks, some people use a remote browser server pool. Users access the web using these remote browsers, which means that the servers on which these browsers reside are isolated from the terminals and networks in the user's environment.

Yao Junxian proposes a dynamic method of interrupting hackers' intrusions.[4] These include dynamic encapsulation, dynamic verification, dynamic confusion, and dynamic tokens. Dynamic encapsulation encapsulates the underlying code of a web page. It encapsulates sensitive portals, URLs, and online forms that may be attacked on a web page, thereby hiding the entrance to the attack and preventing the attacker from predicting server behavior. Dynamic verification prevents dynamic terminals from being accessed through dynamic two-way authentication of the client and server. This form of verification randomly selects the detected items and quantities each time to increase the unpredictability of the application and greatly increase the attack cost. Dynamic confusion obscures sensitive data transmission on web pages, including cookies, post data, and URLs, to prevent forgery requests, malicious code injection, eavesdropping, or tampering with transaction content. Dynamic tokens grant one-time tokens for legitimate requests, ensuring the appropriate execution of business logic and effectively defending against automated attacks, such as web content search, web backdoors, advanced persistent threat attacks, and application-layer DDoS. Compared with the traditional security protection technology, dynamic camouflage security protection technology uses the concept of dynamic protection as its guiding ideology.

Dynamic security protection systems prevent the abuse of normal functions, such as account access, and can prevent malicious hacking, false registration, and bulk account opening using automated tools. These systems can address the defects that are difficult to identify using traditional security methods. This type of security also can prevent users from experiencing cross-site forgery attacks, fraudulent transactions, and business fraud. In this way, sensitive information can be protected from attacks such as SQL or command injection, effectively preventing attackers from accessing sensitive data.

Regulatory Technology

In 2014, the UK FCA first proposed the concept of regtech, which was defined as "using new technologies to promote financial institutions to achieve regulatory requirements more effectively."[5] Since then, the International Finance Association has defined regtech as "a new technology that can efficiently and effectively address regulatory and compliance requirements."[6] These new technologies include machine learning, artificial intelligence, blockchain, biometrics, digital encryption technology, and cloud computing.

The international mainly examines regtech from the perspective of financial institutions. The Chinese government attaches great importance to the application of regtech, and defines regtech from a broader perspective, combining it with prevention and control of financial risks. The People's Bank of China's Financial Science and Technology Committee has proposed "to strengthen RegTech and actively use big data, artificial intelligence, cloud computing and other technologies to enrich financial supervision methods and improve the ability to identify, prevent and resolve financial risks across industries and markets."[7]

Guofeng Sun, director of the People's Bank of China Financial Research Institute, wrote in *Contemporary Financiers* magazine in April 2018 that regtech is an emerging technology represented by big data, cloud computing, artificial intelligence, blockchain, and other technologies.[8] Regtech is used to maintain the security and stability of the financial system, to achieve the stable operation of financial institutions, and to protect the rights of financial consumers. From the perspective of the body applying such technology, regtech includes both "compliance" and "regulation." On the one hand, financial institutions use regtech as an important tool to reduce compliance costs and adapt to regulation. From this dimension, regtech can be understood as compliance technology (comptech). On the other hand, regtech can help financial regulators to enrich regulatory tools, improve regulatory efficiency, and reduce regulatory pressure. This is an important way to maintain the security and stability of the financial system, prevent systemic financial risks, and protect the rights of financial consumers. In this way, regtech can be understood as supervised technology (suptech)—that is, regtech = suptech + comptech.[9]

From a regulator's perspective, regtech applies technology to carry out regulatory duties. The rapid development of financial technology has introduced changes in the existing financial business, and financial industry risks have revealed characteristics that are reflected primarily in the reduction of financial entry barriers, the high frequency of financial transactions and big data, and ongoing emergence of cross-industry financial products that break through the boundaries of traditional financial industries. Thus, the prediction and identification of financial risks have become increasingly difficult. Although the application of financial technology brings a wide range of financial service innovations, it also generates a series of new risks, which introduce new challenges to the supervision of the financial industry. Financial regulators urgently need to improve their regulatory capabilities and reduce regulatory costs. With the development of new technologies, such as big data, cloud computing, blockchain, and artificial intelligence, conditions have been created to improve regulatory measures and reduce compliance costs.

From the perspective of financial regulatory reform, the rapid rise of regtech is a rational response to lowering the compliance costs of financial institutions and addressing the latest round of financial regulatory reforms. Since the international financial crisis in 2008, the regulatory systems of major global economies have undergone profound changes, regulatory requirements have escalated, and regulatory measures have become more complicated. The cost of regulatory compliance to meet requirements has increased, leading to the further development of regtech.

According to a study by the Boston Consulting Group, global financial institutions suffered fines of $321 billion between 2009 and 2016 because of regulatory noncompliance.[10] At the same time, the rapid development of financial technology has led to an increase in the relevance of financial services worldwide, and the differences in financial regulatory frameworks across countries also have increased the compliance costs of multinational financial institutions. The principle of unification and standardization of regtech as an emerging technology framework can resolve financial regulatory differences and conflicts between countries.

Relationship Between Regtech and Fintech

The Financial Stability Board defines financial technology as "a financial innovation brought about by technology that creates new business models, applications, processes or products. This has a major impact on the way financial markets, financial institutions, or financial services are provided."[11] The essence of financial technology is to use emerging information technology to transform and innovate financial products and services. It is to optimize, upgrade, and reshape the financial industry from the perspective of technology research and development and application.

Financial technology has brought about financial innovation and injected new vitality into the financial industry. At the same time, it has ushered in new challenges to financial security. To better prevent and respond to financial technology risks, regtech has emerged. Because of the increasingly virtual service mode of fintech, along with blurred business boundaries and the continuous opening of the business environment, the financial risk situation is becoming increasingly complicated. Although the application of financial technology introduces a wide range of financial service innovations, it also generates a series of new risks, which in turn raise difficulties to supervise the financial industry.

First, cross-border financial services across industries and markets are increasingly enriched. Different businesses are becoming interrelated. Financial risks are complex and potentially contagious. Second, financial technology uses information technology to transform business flow into information flow. Although improving the efficiency of capital financing, it breaks the time and space restrictions of risk transmission, making the risk spread faster. Third, the correlation of financial products is increasing, risks are difficult to identify and measure, and risks are more concealed. Traditional regulatory measures are difficult to work. In this context, the financial management department builds a modern financial regulatory framework through regtech and develops financial regulatory platforms as well as tools based on artificial intelligence, big data, and application programming interfaces (APIs). Regtech thereby effectively enhances the accuracy, traceability, and nonrepudiation of financial regulatory information, identifying and defusing financial risks and rectifying financial chaos.

In contrast, in the context of financial technology, the financial industry, as a typical data-intensive industry, generates and processes massive amounts of data resources every day. The huge amount of financial data with scattered sources and diverse formats exceeds the processing power of traditional regulatory methods. In the face of the massive data submitted by financial institutions, the regulatory authorities need to use technology to improve processing efficiency and regulatory effectiveness. The China Finance and Technology Commission noted the necessity to strengthen regtech and proposed the use of financial technologies such as big data, artificial intelligence, and cloud computing to enrich financial supervision. Financial regulators and financial institutions are aware of the important driving role of technology, thus accelerating the emergence and development of regtech.

Regtech has emerged in recent years to cope with the challenges brought about by the development of financial technology. It has become an important research field to improve the technical level and regulatory efficiency of the regulatory system and to build a new paradigm of technology-driven regulation.

Regtech is used to regulate the entire financial industry, including traditional financial and financial technology, rather than being limited to regulating the financial technology industry. That is, regtech is not just the application regulation in the fintech field but rather encompasses a comprehensive technology of regulation. The effective use of technology in the financial sector and the risks exposed by financial technology have made financial regulators and financial institutions aware of the important driving role of technology, thus accelerating the emergence and development of regtech.

Fintech promotes the development of regtech. Financial institutions use financial technology to meet compliance requirements. The UK FCA considers regtech to be a part of financial technology and has proposed that regulatory technology can ensure that regulatory requirements are met in an efficient way. The concept is narrowly defined as regtech (compliance technology), in which financial institutions use new technologies to more effectively meet regulatory compliance issues and reduce rising compliance costs. After the 2008 financial crisis, the need for financial regulation was elevated to unprecedented heights. Regulators are eager to obtain more comprehensive and accurate data. The increasingly strict supervision and intensive laws and regulations have increased the compliance costs of financial institutions. In response, the development of financial technology has enabled financial institutions to use new technologies to save compliance costs, meet regulatory requirements, and promote the development of regtech.

Regtech is used not only in the financial industry but also in all industries that are involved in compliance, especially in highly regulated industries, such as medical and health, food safety, environmental monitoring, and safe production. Therefore, the regtech industry is not limited to the financial industry but will also expand horizontally to other industries.

Operation Mechanism of Regtech

Compared with European and American countries, China's regtech started relatively late, and the gap remains. Table 8.1 shows that no major Chinese companies currently rank among the global regtech firms. The recent development of China's regtech, however, has been highly motivated, and the application needs are quite broad.

At the policy level, the state gives strong support to the development of regulatory science and technology. In May 2017, the People's Bank of China established the Financial Science and Technology Committee and proposed to strengthen the supervision and application of science and technology as an important means to enrich financial supervision. In June 2017, the People's Bank of China issued the Thirteenth Five-Year Development Plan for China's Financial Industry Information Technology, proposing to strengthen the research and application of fintech and regtech. In May 2018, the China Securities and Regulatory Commission (CSRC) Science and Technology Supervision Expert Advisory Committee, composed of academicians from the two academies, university scholars, and experts from the business community, was established. In August 2018, the CSRC issued the China Securities Regulatory Commission to Supervise the Overall Construction of Science and Technology notice, marking the completion of the top-level design of the supervision of science and technology construction work and the start of the full implementation stage.

Table 8.1 shows the distribution by country of major regtech companies in 2017.[12] The table shows that the United Kingdom and United States lead the world in the number of large regtech companies,

TABLE 8.1
National Distribution of Major Global Regulatory Technology Companies in 2017 (percent)

Country	United Kingdom	United States	Ireland	Luxembourg	Australia	Israel	China
Number	42	41	13	12	6	6	0

Source: China Institute of Information and Communications (CAICT), *Internet Investment and Financing in the Second Quarter of 2018* (in Chinese), CAICT, 2018, http://www.caict.ac.cn/kxyj/qwfb/qwsj/201807/P020180720343745695019.pdf.

whereas China had none. This likely will become an area of intense focus in the coming years.

Specific Application of Compliance Technology

Regtech can help to ensure compliance with regulations. It also acts as an early warning system for fintech companies. Dagong Credit Data Co., for example, has a list of indicators used at the provincial level to screen online loan platforms for risks and fraud. This technology was applied early on, in 2014, and found that nearly half of the 1,395 companies screened did not meet basic viability standards. Warnings arose because of a lack of information disclosure, insufficient cash flow to cover costs, situations in which a promised rate of return was higher than the actual rate of return, fraud involving false guarantees, and the possibility for other credit risk events to emerge.[13]

Specific Regtech Applications

Government Applications

Chinese financial regulators are constantly exploring the application of regtech. The Anti-Money Laundering Monitoring Center of the People's Bank of China is building a comprehensive analysis platform for the second generation of anti-money-laundering monitoring and analysis; the China Banking and Insurance Regulatory Commission will apply the distributed architecture to EAST data, combining on-site inspection programs with big data.

In August 2018, the CSRC issued the China Securities Regulatory Commission RegTech Overall Construction Plan, marking the completion of the regtech top-level design by the CSRC and entering the full implementation stage. This plan clearly defines the needs and work contents of various informatization construction work for supervising Regtech 1.0, 2.0, and 3.0. The main content of Regtech 1.0 is designed to improve the digitalization, electronification, automation, and standardization of supervision work by purchasing or developing mature and efficient software and hardware tools or facilities to meet the information needs of the basic office and specific work of the departments and agencies. The content of Regtech 2.0 is to continuously enrich and improve the functions of the central regulatory information platform, optimize the construction of business systems, and realize the online operation of the entire process of cross-departmental supervision services. This will establish a good foundation for the application of technologies, such as big data, cloud computing, and artificial intelligence in Regtech 3.0.

The core of Regtech 3.0 is to build a highly efficient and effective big data supervision platform and to comprehensively use electronic evidence, statistical analysis, data mining, and other technologies to conduct comprehensive monitoring and data analysis around the main business activities of the capital market. This will enable supervisors to discover insider trading, market operations, and other violations in a timely manner.

In December 2018, the CSRC issued the Measures for the Management of Information Technology of Securities Fund Operating Agencies to guide the securities fund–operating institutions, to continuously strengthen the supporting role of modern information technology in their business activities, and to improve legal compliance and prevent risks. The management approach comprehensively covers all types of entities; clarifies the three main lines of governance, security, and compliance; strengthens the main responsibility of information technology management; and supports the application of information technology to improve service efficiency. The measures also clarify the corresponding penalties for various market entities that fail to fulfil their information technology management responsibilities.

In October 2018, the first phase of the Corporate Portrait project, which was independently developed by the Shenzhen Stock Exchange, was officially launched. The project application functions include locating information about a company's quick view, company label, equity shareholder, restructuring review assistance, and relationship map. By using text mining, cloud computing, and other information technologies, it is possible to automatically extract and intelligently prompt different means of monitoring high-frequency information, thereby effectively helping first-line supervisors to improve the ability to detect illegal activities and prevent and resolve risks.

In 2016, the Beijing Financial Work Bureau began to build a network loan risk monitoring system based on the blockchain as the underlying technology, which enables the regulatory authorities to record the data reported by all online lending platforms and quickly identify and respond to abnormal transactions.

Corporate Applications

Typical corporate applications in China include the Risk Brain System of Ant Financial, the financial risk monitoring platform of Tencent Financial, and the Rubik's Cube security products of Jingdong Financial.

THE RISK BRAIN SYSTEM OF ANT FINANCIAL PROFILE

The Ant Risk Brain System has four core segments: risk detection warning, risk identification decision, risk intelligence optimization, and risk analysis insight. These four parts work together to make up a comprehensive risk control system.[14]

The risk warning system is equivalent to the eyes of the risk control system and is used to sense and predict risks. Risk groups are identified through risk anomaly identification, which are presented graphically and visually, and risk experts are used to judge risks and anomalies. This process will push the necessary model and strategy adjustments in real time to form a closed-loop optimization of the risk control system.

The risk identification system is at the core of risk prevention and control. The process must be comprehensive and three-dimensional. This means that it is necessary to build a comprehensive risk-scanning system based on people, environment, network, equipment, blacklists, and conflicts. The most worrying aspect of risk prevention and control is that the system will default when one layer is broken. To address this issue, the Ant Risk Brain presents a three-dimensional risk control system with five layers. If a single layer is broken, the next layer will take over, which is more secure and reliable than the traditional risk prevention and control system.

Behind the risk identification is a security policy model. If a customer is identified as posing a risk, the final judgment needs to be intelligently analyzed from multiple dimensions, considering the availability and applicability of the actual environment and risk preferences to make intelligent and personalized decisions based on risk control and user experience.

Ant Financial also practices faster and more effective control of risks through human-computer collaboration. It does so in three main ways. First, it analyzes user tags based on a single case and connects time, space, and behavior to restore the whole process of a case, locating missing points (such as missing customer income) and risk points in the risk control system. Second, it analyzes the knowledge map and uncovers fraudulent rings and their characteristics. Third, it makes a strategically intelligent recommendation, combining intelligent algorithms and expert experience and using it to adjust the risk prevention and control system. In addition, Ant Financial's risk control system can self-optimize and self-evolve, making timely and effective adjustments and optimizations for new risk situations.

The Ant Risk Brain System has extended its risk security capabilities to three areas. The first is in the field of government and people's livelihood, including areas of aviation, taxation, and railway. Ant Financial offers six core competencies: account protection, marketing protection, channel protection, transaction protection, mobile protection, and content protection. Taking the Eastern Airlines app as an example, the Ant Risk Brain provides China Eastern Airlines with a full risk control solution to prevent user points from being stolen and to prevent mistakes in customer seating.

The second area of security capabilities is applied to the banking sector. Under the background of digital banking transformation, Ant Financial has exported risk prevention and control programs and infrastructure for banks to help banks transform. On April 9, 2018, Ant Financial Services Group signed a cooperation agreement with Chongqing Three Gorges Bank Co., Ltd. The two parties will establish a joint venture innovation laboratory for financial technology to explore and practice the implementation of new financial technology in the banking business. The Ant Risk Brain will help construct the Three Gorges Bank's risk control system and enhance the ability of the Three Gorges Bank to prevent and control risks and serve the real economy.

The third field of risk security capability is in regtech. The Ant Risk Brain uses advanced technologies such as big data, cloud computing, blockchain, and artificial intelligence to build a more efficient intelligent monitoring system. The system enables financial regulators to realize real-time, intelligent, and visualized financial risk monitoring. The Ant Risk Brain can help local regulatory authorities conduct multidimensional risk investigations of financial institutions and achieve dynamic scanning of all risk areas, including stakeholder, operational, and compliance risks. Through knowledge map mining, regulatory authorities can identify potential risks among affiliates in a timely manner and identify suspected financial fraud rings at their root. It also helps regulators build regional and industry-wide risk indices, quickly identify regional and industry risks, and detect macrofinancial risk trends.

Regtech Core Technologies

The core technologies of regtech are cloud computing, big data, artificial intelligence, blockchain, and API. Cloud computing provides low-cost computing and storage resources for regtech and provides large-scale data resources through centralized data aggregation to enhance the sharing of regulatory tools. Big data enables large-scale data mining and analysis capabilities as well as efficient real-time processing capabilities. Artificial intelligence further enhances the intelligent analysis capabilities of data and enhances customer interaction capabilities. The blockchain guarantees the authenticity and efficiency of the acquired basic information, ensures business compliance, and improves the efficiency of business processing. The API helps to effectively enforce regulatory policies and compliance guidelines, improve the regulatory nature of regulation, and conduct supervision in a minimally disruptive manner.

Regtech Application Scenarios

To date, regtech's basic application has been to electronically report paper regulatory processes, reduce regulatory human resource costs, and effectively reduce compliance costs. The high-level regtech application utilizes advanced technologies to program regulatory policies and directives, embed them in various business systems, and verify and alert to risks in a timely manner. The five main applications for the use of regtech are data processing and reporting, customer identification, financial institution stress testing, market behavior monitoring, and legal and regulatory information tracking.

The first application is in the field of compliance data processing and reporting. After the financial crisis, the requirements of regulatory agencies for the reporting of financial institutions' data were constantly increasing. Financial institutions needed to submit data of different structures and different statistical dimensions to multiple regulatory agencies, which greatly increased the compliance costs of financial institutions. Financial institutions can improve compliance data-reporting capabilities through data asset management and reduced compliance costs. The underlying technologies involved in this area include big data, cloud computing, and digital encryption technologies. Compliance data reporting is achieved mainly by acquiring and processing a large amount of structured data, establishing standardized data reports, improving the convenience of data sharing, and achieving rapid generation of compliance data reports. With this encryption technology, the security of data sharing is improved simultaneously and data integrity and privacy are guaranteed.

The second application is in the field of customer identification. Regulators have clear regulatory requirements for financial institutions to "know your customers" (KYC) to avoid illegal business practices that are not operated by customers, such as credit card theft and opening of accounts with false documents. The process uses intelligent biometric technology and big data comparison technology to automate the KYC procedure and integrate multiple KYC data sources into one application through an API to improve customer identification ability and intercept abnormal account operations.

The third application is in the field of stress testing for financial institutions, to simulate real trading scenarios in a virtual environment and to test the stability and security of financial institutions. This application mainly uses technologies such as big data, artificial intelligence, and cloud computing to quickly process large amounts of data, analyze many data variables, reduce scene distortion, improve the accuracy of scenario testing, realize the dynamics of stress testing, and help financial institutions maintain stability. Timely discovery of risks and related measures are used to effectively prevent risk accumulation. It also is possible to reduce the cost of stress testing through cloud computing and to help financial institutions achieve self-compliance.

The fourth application is in the field of market behavior monitoring. Regulators and financial institutions need to take effective measures to identify violations of internal transactions, money laundering, fraud, illegal fundraising, and multiaccount manipulation. Monitoring is mainly applied to big data processing, artificial intelligence, and machine learning and is accomplished through the multidimensional, high-frequency, full-dynamic real-time analysis of transaction data, mining the subject relationship and deep information from large amounts of information on trading behavior.

The fifth application is in the field of legal and regulatory information tracking. With the continuous tightening of financial supervision and the intensive introduction of regulatory laws and regulations, financial institutions need to keep track of current rules every day and compare the similarities and differences between old and new documents. This application primarily uses artificial intelligence technology to quickly identify and learn the latest laws and regulations, promptly remind the financial institutions of relevant regulatory changes, and reduce the legal compliance risks of financial institutions. It also analyzes and compares the similarities and differences between regulatory documents in different countries, helps to achieve global requirements, conducts risk assessment, and provides guarantees for financial institutions to achieve legal cross-border business.

Regulatory Sandbox

Some experts have recommended a regulatory sandbox, which would allow small-scale, live testing by small firms under government supervision. This is in use in many industrial countries, including the United States, Canada, Thailand, Australia, and the United Kingdom.

In the United Kingdom, a regtech sandbox has enabled startup fintech firms to create applications for compliance, data analysis, and risk evaluation. The UK's regtech sandbox is for institutions engaged in financial innovation, under the premise of ensuring consumer rights, following the FCA's simplified approval procedures, submitting applications and obtaining limited authorizations, and conducting financial product or service innovation tests within the scope of application. The FCA monitors the testing process and evaluates the situation to determine whether formal regulatory authority is granted and can be promoted outside of the sandbox.

Other economies, such as Abu Dhabi, Singapore, Australia, Hong Kong, China, and Taiwan, also have implemented a regulatory sandbox plan or proposed similar regulatory measures. The regulatory sandbox has relaxed regulatory restrictions for financial technology innovation, will not have an impact on the current legal framework, and also can serve as a decision-making system in which the legal regulation may be difficult to adjust quickly during the rapid emergence of innovation.[15]

The regulatory sandbox concept is similar in its implementation to China's regional financial reform pilots. Both concepts reflect the fact that in the process of reform, the government allows local areas to take the first step, carry out institutional innovations, summarize the pilot experience and lessons learned, and then push the new system to the greater economy. Therefore, from the perspective of the financial reform in mainland China, a basis already exists for adopting a regulatory sandbox for financial technology supervision.

As the wave of financial technology sweeps around the globe, increasing numbers of countries and regions have joined the ranks of regulatory sandboxes. Compared with other countries and regions, the regulatory sandbox is still in the conceptual stage in China. Chinese regulators can learn from the practices followed in the United Kingdom, Singapore, and other countries: adjust regulatory objectives and responsibilities in a timely manner; enhance forward-looking thinking; and study the applicability to China. Regulators also can explore the creation of a regulatory tool that applies financial innovation in order to reduce risks.

Fintech incubators and accelerators have been set up to test the risk properties of innovative firms. China's city of Ganzhou in Jiangxi Province, as well as the National Internet Emergency Center and Xinhua Net, already have set up the first regulatory sandbox. This sandbox is exploring the role of regtech in the fintech industry and aims to identify and resolve financial risks of internet finance companies operating in the sandbox to improve risk control technology and further develop the regtech industry.

CHAPTER NINE

Credit Reporting and Key Financial Technologies

CREDIT REPORTING in China is experiencing rapid development. Much of this development is dependent on key financial technologies. In this chapter, we first discuss China's credit system, and then we describe key financial technologies, including big data, cloud computing, biometric technologies, blockchain, artificial intelligence (AI), Internet of Things, smart machines, augmented and virtual reality, application programming interface (API) platforms, quantum computing, robotic process automation, and instant payments. We close with a brief description of e-commerce and social media platforms that have facilitated the rise of fintech.

Big Data and Credit Reporting

Background

The experience of countries such as Europe, America, and Japan show that use of the internet has greatly promoted the development of the credit-reporting industry. China's credit system construction started late, but in recent years, with the development and application of mobile internet, big data, cloud computing, data mining, and other information technologies, the source of credit data has become more diversified, and the data processing capability has been vastly improved. Credit-reporting agencies can now more fully explore and analyze the data resources they have mastered and develop products and services with higher technology to meet the multilevel and professional credit-reporting needs of society. The credit industry has expanded demand and potential.

At the same time, the development of financial technology has deepened the development of online credit business. The explosive growth of consumer finance and online lending has brought about massive expansion of long-tailed user data. Internet agencies are increasingly demanding personal credit data. However, the existing People's Bank of China (PBC) credit-reporting system has not been able to provide a strong guarantee for the healthy development of internet finance because of low coverage and high query costs.

According to the *China Social Credit System Development Report 2017*, as of September 2016, 899 million people were included in the People's Bank Credit Information System, but only 412 million people had credit business records, which represented less than one-third of the country's total population.[1] Similarly, 18.28 million enterprises were included in the system, but only 4.2 million of these enterprises had credit records. Most of the enterprises that do have credit records are large state-owned enterprises, and many small and midsize private enterprises are not covered. Furthermore, most residents and enterprises have not been able to incorporate credit information into the credit information system.

Market-based credit-reporting agencies can further develop the central bank database. Big data credit companies use big data, cloud computing, and other technologies to redesign credit evaluation models and algorithms to achieve wide coverage and real-time updates of credit data, which largely fills in the blanks left within traditional credit investigations.

Big data credit refers to the application of new generation information network technologies, such as big data and cloud computing, to the data collection and credit evaluation of the credit-reporting system. Through deep and comprehensive credit information collection, firms can obtain diversified data resources and redesign the credit evaluation algorithms and models to analyze the data. Therefore, the credit characteristics of the subject are sorted out, and finally a more accurate credit evaluation result for individuals, enterprises, and social groups is formed.

Data sources for big data credit analysis include diversified data, such as daily life information (e.g., traffic, travel, utilities, gas), social data (e.g., Weibo, WeChat, QQ), social behavior data (e.g., tourism accommodation, online shopping, online loans), and government-related data (e.g., taxation, passport, and visas).

The Reason for the Rapid Rise of the Big Data Credit Industry in China

The rapid growth of consumer credit has become an important impetus for the development of China's credit-reporting industry. Credit reporting and consumer finance are complementary. The rise of consumer credit has prompted credit institutions to generate huge demand for personal information screening and has become an important driving force for the development of China's credit-reporting industry. The existence of the credit inquiry industry is to reduce the transaction cost of consumer credit as well as potential credit risk. It is the most important link in the process of consumer credit transactions.

In recent years, consumption upgrades, policies, and financial technologies have worked to promote the development of China's consumer credit market. China's internet consumer finance industry exploded in 2016–2017. In 2017, China's internet consumer finance scale reached 4.38 trillion RMB, an increase of 904 percent compared with 2016. In 2017, the balance of consumer credit (excluding mortgages) reached 9.8 trillion RMB, a growth rate of 66 percent, and consumer credit accounted for 12 percent of gross domestic product (GDP). Although a big gap exists between China and the United States (20 percent), the growth rate has been quite fast in recent years, and the future development potential for consumer credit is huge.

Figure 9.1 shows changes in China's internet consumer finance scale. The scale is growing rapidly, from 6 billion RMB in 2013 to 9.7 trillion RMB in 2018.

Data sources are now mobile and enriched. Data provide the foundation of the credit-reporting industry, and all of the business of a

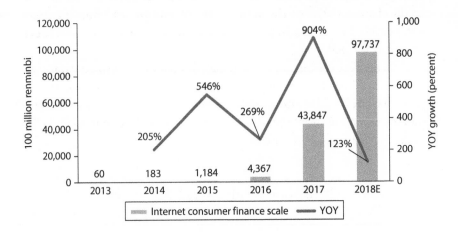

Figure 9.1 China internet consumer finance scale statistics, 2011–2017. *Source*: Qianzhan Intelligence Co.

credit agency is centered around data. Credit investigation agencies can build models and provide specific credit information services after integrating multidimensional data sources. Therefore, data sources are critical to every credit agency. In recent years, the popularity of the internet and smartphones has spawned real-time dynamic data for e-commerce, mobile payment, online to offline (O2O), and other scenarios. Credit-reporting products, services, and application scenarios are also accelerating the transfer to mobile terminals.

In addition, through machine learning and AI methods, credit data mining and risk analysis can be carried out in depth, and the convenience of credit information services can be improved through cloud computing and mobile internet. Emerging technologies represented by big data have injected new vitality into the credit industry chain.

The rapid development of financial technology has spawned new credit demand. Taking the peer-to-peer (P2P) industry as an example, P2P services have been highly sought after in recent years because of its low threshold, convenience, and improved capital utilization. The industry is part of the inclusive financial field distinct from traditional banks. The number of P2P platforms in China reached a peak of three thousand five hundred in 2015. With the emergence of problems in recent years, however, the total number of platforms has been declining year by year.

The main reason hindering the healthy development of China's P2P industry is that the country does not have a well-developed credit-reporting system, whereas countries like the United States have a complete system. At present, China's personal credit-reporting system is weak, and the data range is limited. As a result, many domestic P2P platforms are working with third-party guarantee companies and offline small loan firms in cases in which they cannot implement user risk analysis and control. Improvements in China's credit investigation system will greatly reduce the repayment risk of the P2P platform and directly reduce the operational pressure of the P2P platform. This can further help to develop the market space.

The Development Level of China's Credit-Reporting Industry

China's credit-reporting industry began in the 1990s. With the deepening of market-oriented reforms, China has now formed a credit-reporting system in which public credit and commercial credit coexist and public credit is the mainstay. Credit reporting can be divided into three categories: personal credit, corporate credit, and capital market credit. Personal credit is used for individuals, primarily for financial credit risk assessment. Corporate credit is targeted at small and medium-size enterprises, mainly for lending and commercial cooperation purposes. Capital market credit-reporting targets include bonds, infrastructure projects, and international sovereign ratings, which are used mainly for credit registration, credit investigation, and credit rating. China's credit investigation system is illustrated in figure 9.2.[2]

China has two main forms of public credit reporting. The first is the financial credit system led by the People's Bank Credit Information Center. The *Regulations on the Administration of Credit Reporting Industry*, promulgated by the State Council, have given the PBC the responsibility of supervision and management of the credit-reporting industry. The financial credit information basic database, which is under construction, operation, and maintenance by the People's Bank Credit Information Center, plays an essential role in building the financial infrastructure and is the most important component of the social credit system.

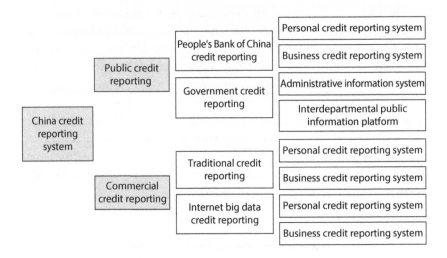

Figure 9.2 China credit investigation system. *Source*: "China Social Credit System Development Report 2017," *Liaowang Institute and China Financial Weekly*, 2017.

Second, government credit is promoted by the National Development and Reform Commission as well as by other ministries and local governments. For example, government credit also includes the credit information exchange platform led by the National Development and Reform Commission and the industrial credit system promoted by government functions, including industry and commerce, taxation, and customs. The government credit information shared by these departments is an important part of the Chinese credit-reporting market.

In addition, the credit-reporting institutions established by the internet, e-commerce platforms, and financial enterprises constitute the market-based credit model in China. The credit-reporting institution in the background of an internet enterprise or an e-commerce enterprise has the advantage of containing user behavior information, and the credit-reporting agency provides the credit information service by using the obtained user data. Most of the credit-reporting institutions in the financial enterprise background rely on their comprehensive financial licenses and risk control advantages to concentrate transaction data and control risk.

In January 2015, the PBC issued the Notice on Doing a Good Job in the Preparation of Personal Credit Reporting Business, clearly requiring eight institutions to prepare for the personal credit information business. The eight institutions include Sesame Credit Management, Tencent Credit Reporting, Shenzhen Qianhai Credit Reporting Center, Koala Credit Reporting, Pengyuan Credit Reporting, China Chengxin Reporting, Zhongzhicheng Credit Reporting, and Beijing Huadao Credit Reporting. These eight credit-reporting agencies can be grouped into three categories.

The first category consists of big data credit-reporting agencies, including Sesame Credit, Tencent Credit, and Qianhai Credit Information. In addition to external access to traditional credit data, big data credit-reporting agencies also have massive payment, internet e-commerce, and social media data. From the perspective of the technology used in the credit-reporting system, these three companies have supplemented and improved the classic credit investigation model by using innovative technologies. Big data credit-reporting agencies paid more attention to the development of nonfinancial product applications from the outset.

The second category includes the traditional credit-reporting agencies, which are China Credit Rating, Pengyuan Credit, and Zhongzhicheng Credit. These three traditional credit bureaus collect traditional credit data, as well as industry or regional data, and have adopted a mature credit information model for the financial service field. Its completely independent third-party position, however, also leads to a lack of direct and extensive data sources, and the coverage of the population is limited. Compared with other practitioners, although these organizations have not used multidimensional data and innovative technologies on a large scale, they are all conducting research and exploration in a positive and open manner.

The third category is based on the credit agency model established by financial giants, including Qianhai Credit Reporting, Koala Credit Reporting, and Huadao Credit Reporting. Shenzhen Qianhai Credit Reporting Center is a wholly owned subsidiary of China Ping An Insurance Group. The rich financial data, as well as the great risk management and modeling capabilities of Ping An, give Qianhai Credit Rating's credit-scoring system higher credibility. Qianhai Credit Reporting is rooted in Ping An Group, covering the entire financial product line. The company has distinct advantages, including an in-depth understanding of financial behavior risk management, and it actively explores diversified and innovative data collection, storage, processing, and analysis methods. The 100 percent controlling share-holder of Koala Credit Information is Lakala Credit Management Co., Ltd. which is involved in personal and corporate electronic payments, small loans, factoring, P2P trading platforms, and O2O community e-commerce platforms.

Notably, none of the eight companies falling under the central bank's notice was able to meet the requirements of the PBC. Wan Cunzhi, director of the PBC's Credit Information System Bureau, stated in April 2017 that "the preparation the eight companies have made for running the personal credit reporting business is far below market demand and regulatory standards. . . . It's fallen short of our expectations that none of them has made it yet."[3]

In response to this gap, in November 2017, Baihang Credit Reporting was set up under the supervision of the government. In February 2018, it obtained the first personal credit business license in China. It officially opened in May and was led by the China Internet Finance Association. The China Internet Finance Association accounted for 36 percent of the shares, and each of the eight credit-reporting companies held 8 percent of the shares. Baihang focused on collecting data from nonbank sources, such as consumer finance firms, online lenders, and P2P platforms. The data supplemented the central bank's credit-reporting database. Baihang thus formed a national financial credit investigation database with the People's Bank Credit Reporting Center. The market structure of dislocation development and complementary functions aimed to include long-tail customers who lacked bank credit records to bring them into the scope of credit information services and to expand the coverage of credit information.

The establishment of Baihang Credit Reporting attempted to establish a comprehensive information-sharing network to break the "data island" phenomenon that existed in the credit information market. Third-party credit-reporting agencies can connect scenarios, technologies, and risk management to achieve effective integration of credit information and improve the industry's risk pricing ability. This integration can enhance the industry's risk prevention and control level, reducing the financing cost of the whole society. To date, Baihang Credit has signed credit information cooperation and sharing agreements with more than 120 internet finance and consumer financial institutions and has reached cooperation intentions with more than 50 institutions.

Regulations

The Chinese credit system began in the early 1990s. Compared with industrial countries, China's credit-reporting system is still in the initial stage of industry development. Legal norms, data processing, and information sharing are in urgent need of improvement. In addition, authoritative and internationally influential credit-reporting agencies are lacking, which further restricts the development of the Chinese credit system. In recent years, the state has begun to attach importance to the status of credit-reporting activities in the economic system and to vigorously promote the creation of a social credit system. Since 2013, China has successively issued a series of policies aimed at providing institutional guarantees for the development of credit reporting.

In March 2013, the State Council promulgated the first Chinese credit-reporting industry regulation, the Regulations on the Management of Credit Reporting Industry, clarifying that the credit-reporting industry was open to third-party institutions and that the door to the private credit-reporting market was officially opened. This was an important milestone in the development of China's credit-reporting system.

In December 2013, the PBC issued the Measures for the Administration of Credit Reporting Agencies, which clearly established the requirement for corporate credit-reporting agencies to adopt the filing system for supervision. The measures refined the conditions, application procedures, and management norms for the establishment of individual credit-reporting agencies. Separate supervision and different entry barriers have been established for corporate and individual credit-reporting agencies. These measures laid the foundation for the marketization of China's credit-reporting industry.

In June 2014, the State Council promulgated the Outline of Social Credit System Construction Plan (2014–2020), which clarified the main objectives of China's social credit system. These objectives state that by 2020, the government should establish basic social credit laws, regulations, and standards. A credit-reporting system covering the entire society based on the sharing of credit-reporting resources has been established. This is the first special plan for the creation of a national-level social credit system, marking a new stage in the development of the Chinese credit-reporting system.

In January 2015, the PBC issued the Notice of the People's Bank of China on Preparing for Personal Credit Investigation Business (described earlier), requiring eight credit-reporting agencies to prepare for the personal credit-reporting business, with a preparation time of six months. In October 2015, the PBC issued the Guidelines for the Supervision of Credit Reporting Agencies to further clarify the operational norms of credit-reporting agencies.

As of April 2017, according to the network exposure policy, none of the eight credit-reporting agencies approved for construction had passed the qualification. After two and a half years, the license was repeatedly postponed. In June 2017, the Network Security Law of the People's Republic of China improved the rules for the protection of personal information and established a system for the protection of critical information infrastructure.

Big Data Financial Security Platform: Lingkun Business Study

Launched in 2017, Lingkun, a big data financial security platform, is a financial security product developed by Tencent's Security Antifraud Lab. Lingkun is positioned as a financial supervision technology platform based on Tencent's nearly twenty years of experience in the area of security and AI technology. It has the world's largest fraud database and big data security team, and it has successfully solved the problem of insufficient data, algorithms, and computing power in the existing regulatory industry. Combined with the local data of the regulatory authorities, Lingkun conducts machine learning on specific financial cases and generates risk quantification indicators to help banks, internet finance groups, and other financial institutions intercept and protect against hackers in the financial industry in real time. At the same time, it can export the risk prediction ability and assist the government regulatory authorities in warning against financial crimes, such as illegal fundraising and financial pyramid sales.

The AI Big Data Engine Lingkun Box is the core of the Lingkun platform. It can realize accurate warning and insight into perceived risks through cloud data, online and offline data, and AI algorithms. This engine covers a comprehensive range of eight dimensions and contains more than one hundred features. It can visualize the risk status of financial companies. The more prominent each index is, the higher the financial risk of the company; the accuracy of its financial risk prediction reaches 99.9 percent.

At present, the Lingkun Platform has served the State Administration for Industry and Commerce, Beijing Financial Bureau, Guangzhou Financial Bureau, and Shenzhen Financial Office, and it has access to more than one hundred banks and payment institutions, including the Bank of China, China Merchants Bank, China CITIC Bank, and JD Finance. Cooperation with payment institutions, mutual fund institutions, e-commerce, and O2O platforms has achieved remarkable results in financial risk prevention. Millions of fraud incidents occur every day, involving more than 1 billion yuan in funds.

The most representative structure is the cooperation with Shenzhen Financial Office. In this case, Tencent's self-developed Lingkun Platform is combined with the government data of more than forty administrative units in Shenzhen. Using AI-based platform identification, multidimensional information association based on data mining, platform risk index calculation based on knowledge mapping, and warnings of abnormal population size increases, the system can identify, monitor, and correct financial risks and assist with local financial regulation. During the platform's trial operation, Lingkun made a preliminary analysis of more than 250,000 enterprises engaged in financial business in Shenzhen and has since made a key analysis of 11,354 of these enterprises, identifying 790 risky enterprises and handing over 19 companies to the police.

PBC Credit-Reporting System Profile

China's personal credit-reporting industry originated in early 2004 when the PBC organized commercial banks to build a nationwide centralized personal credit-reporting system. In 2006, the central bank's personal credit-reporting database was officially put into operation, and the credit-reporting service was provided nationwide. The database is updated annually. According to the China Social Credit System Development Report 2017, as of the beginning of September 2016, there were 2,927 access agencies in the personal credit-reporting system, with a natural population of 899 million, of which 412 million had credit business records.

The information collected by the central bank's personal credit-reporting system includes personal loans, credit cards, guarantees, personal housing provident fund deposit information, social insurance deposit and release information, vehicle transaction and mortgage information, court judgment and enforcement information, tax information, telecommunications information, personal subsistence information, practice qualifications, and rewards and punishment information. A total of eight types of public information is collected, covering more than eighty topics. The personal credit report is the core product provided by the personal credit-reporting system.

The Chinese corporate credit-reporting system originated from the bank credit registration consultation system established by the PBC in 1997. In 2002, the bank credit registration consultation system for the three-level network of prefectures, cities, and head offices was implemented. In 2004, the bank credit registration and consultation systems were upgraded to the enterprise credit-reporting system. In 2006, the national centralized and unified enterprise credit-reporting system was established. As of the beginning of September 2016, the enterprise credit-reporting system includes 2,823 access institutions and a total of 18.28 million households, of which 4.203 million had credit business records.

The information collected by the enterprise credit-reporting system covers the public credit business operated by financial institutions. More than two hundred types of information are collected, including loans, factoring, bill discounting, trade financing, letters of credit, letters of guarantee, bank acceptance bills, public credit, and other credit business as well as related guarantees, advances, interest payments, asset interventions and asset disposal, pension information, and housing provident fund contributions.

In early 2013, the PBC began piloting an online inquiry service for personal credit reports. On October 27, 2013, the personal credit-reporting service platform of the PBC Credit Reporting Center was launched. The platform provides three types of information services, including personal credit-reporting tips, personal credit-reporting summaries, and personal credit reports. The following sections explore the PBC credit service's transition from offline to online.

The PBC collects information from banks and other institutions, including social security payments, housing provident fund payments, tax arrears, and court judgments. Financial institutions may obtain information from or submit information to banks, rural credit cooperatives, trust companies, consumer finance companies, auto finance companies, and microfinance institutions.

Zhima Credit Profile

Basic Information

Zhima Credit Co., Ltd., known as Zhima Credit Management Co., Ltd., was established in January 2015. It is an independent credit evaluation and management organization and an important part of the Ant Financial System. Zhima Credit uses cloud computing, machine learning, and other technologies, through logistic regression, decision tree, random forest and other model algorithms, and comprehensive processing and evaluation of each data dimension to objectively present the business credit status of individuals and enterprises. The company created the Zhima Credit Score, credit life, corporate credit score, corporate credit report, enterprise risk cloud map, corporate attention list, and enterprise risk-monitoring system.

In terms of personal credit, Zhima's personal credit-scoring model is based on the FICO credit-rating model. The Zhima Credit Score is based on a user's various consumption and behavioral data available online combined with internet financial lending information. The system uses cloud computing and machine learning as well as other technologies, to present five dimensions: user credit history, behavior preference, performance ability, identity traits, and personal relationships. This data provides a comprehensive score of the individual's credit status.

Zhima's credit scores range from 350 to 950. The higher the score, the better the personal credit status, and the lower the corresponding default rate. Scores are divided into five personal credit status grades: 350 to 550 points (poor); 550 to 600 points (medium); 600 to 650 points (good); 650 points to 700 points (very good); and 700 points to 950 points (excellent). Higher Zhima scores can help users obtain more efficient and better service. Zhima Credit is updated on the sixth day of every month, conveniently showing the user's real-time health status by credit report score.

In the corporate credit-reporting field, Zhima Enterprise Credit has committed to cooperating and co-creating with the partners in the credit industry in an open and innovative way. On the basis of massive data sources, using cloud computing and machine learning, credit data insight, credit value link, credit risk model construction, and other experience, Zhima presents the objective credit status of small and medium-size enterprises, enabling trustworthy enterprises to reduce transaction costs and conveniently access financial services. The credit service promotes inclusive finance and lets small enterprises know that credit is equal to wealth. Zhima Credit possesses the Corporate Credit Reporting Business Operation Record Certificate in order to act as a credit reporting company. Zhima Credit's corporate credit products include corporate credit scores, corporate credit reports, corporate risk cloud maps, corporate attention lists, and corporate risk monitoring.

Business Model

The basis of the credit information is the data. As an important part of the Ant Financial Services ecosystem, Zhima Credit has a rich source of data. In addition to working with the e-commerce platforms of Alibaba Group, Ant Financial Services Group, Alibaba Cloud Service, and other Alibaba investment services, the data group also cooperates with external banks, credit institutions, and other business units to form an independent credit information database.

For example, some government departments provide public information to Zhima Credit. At the beginning of 2017, China Construction Bank also provided financial information related to financial credit and personal investment for Zhima Credit. These channels provide a huge data source for the credit provider. Zhima Credit integrates big data technology into a data information resource pool, and it applies cloud computing, AI, and other unique or emerging technologies to establish an evaluation model that reflects the basic credit situation of each user. From credit cards, consumer finance, financial leasing, and mortgage loans to hotels, car rentals, weddings, classified information, student services, and public services, Zhima Credit conveniently provides a wide range of credit services to users and merchants in hundreds of business scenarios.

Risks and Regulation

Although Zhima Credit successfully established a credit industry, the development of Zhima Credit still faces some problems. Two common problems in the big data credit industry are credit evaluation risks and challenges in the protection of personal privacy.

Credit evaluation risk poses a significant challenge. Zhima Credit uses a large amount of internet behavior data as the main source of credit information, lacking the support of traditional financial institutions' credit data. Whether a large amount of noncredit data can truly reflect the credit status of an individual remains to be tested. Zhima Credit also faces challenges in conducting a comprehensive and objective credit evaluation for those who do not often shop on Taobao or use Alipay.

The protection of personal privacy is another notable challenge. Compared with industrial countries in Europe and America, China's current privacy protection has not yet received widespread attention. In May 2018, the EU General Data Protection Regulation (GDPR) came into effect. These regulations stipulate that any internet platform providing services in the European region must obtain the consent of each user when utilizing the user's data, and the user may revoke consent at any time. Offending companies will face a maximum of 20 million euros or a 4 percent annual global turnover. Personal data belong to users, which is a core principal of the development of financial technology enterprises. If Chinese regulators increase the protection of personal information, it undoubtedly will affect the development of credit information.

To address the issue of data privacy, Zhima Credit attempted to establish a user information security protection mechanism. Real-name verification is performed for all users, and a dedicated information database has been established to protect the security of user information. At the same time, Zhima Credit provides protection measures such as device locks and security passwords, and strictly confirms whether it is operated internally to prevent leakage of information. User information is strictly contained unless the user grants permission and is never provided to third-party organizations.

Innovations

Zhima Credit has remained competitive by constantly innovating products that meet customers' needs. Taking corporate credit as an example, a distinctive feature of China's credit risk is that it is highly correlated with related entities. When one enterprise has problems, risks, or crises, those will be transmitted to related enterprises along a continuum until it spreads to the entire group, causing a domino effect. To combat this problem, Zhima Credit created an infectious disease transmission model, which uses a risk-related cloud map to examine investment, management, debt, and other relationships and to assess enterprises, individuals, enterprise groups, industries, and regions to reveal complex business relationships and risks.

Zhima Credit has established an enterprise credit score through advanced technology using a risk model that categorizes companies into different dimensions for more accurate risk measurement and characterization. The score has three characteristics: data collection is broad, the evaluation method is advanced, and the results are widely applied. The performance is scored on a range of 1000–2000 points. The higher the score is, the lower the credit risk. Corporate credit scoring can help financial institutions and enterprises stratify and differentiate customers and partners and use quantitative evaluation indicators to establish corresponding risk strategies.

The system includes an enterprise list of concerns that helps customers filter out bad companies and build risk firewalls. This list includes bad records of various types of enterprises from government, public utilities, industry alliances, and partners. Zhima Credit discloses negative information from government departments, such as administrative penalties and abnormal operations, on this list of concerns. By indirectly restricting the use of credit services in financial, commercial, and life scenarios, the company can increase the cost of untrustworthiness and promote the development of a healthy social credit system.

The enterprise risk-monitoring service can monitor and immediately forecast the indicators affecting the enterprise credit risk in real time. Zhima Credit relies on cutting-edge tools, such as AI and machine learning, applying it to massive structured and unstructured data collections, processing and analyzing to help customers quickly judge risks, ensuring capital security, and supporting customers. The firm addresses the need for high-speed operations of the business in a highly competitive environment.

Data Issues

Zhima has faced issues related to data, including issues regarding the authenticity of data, the siloing of individual credit data, and the lack of social data. In terms of data authenticity, a wide range of sources of information provides Zhima Credit with the information of hundreds of millions of users, so it is difficult to ensure that all the information is true. Some users may make up some basic information, and internal staff negligence may lead to data errors, which will affect data authenticity. Because the Zhima Credit Score is based on the user's consumption data on Alibaba or specific data on other websites and platforms, this may result in one-dimensional data being obtained, which is not conducive to obtaining accurate results.

Another issue stems from the siloing of credit data. The source of personal credit data of Zhima Credit is based primarily on the businesses within the Alibaba Group. Although Alibaba Group continues to acquire and invest in other companies, companies that already dominate their industry have a large amount of personal credit data and use it to make a profit. Therefore, they are unlikely to sell these economic resources to Alibaba Group. The isolation of Zhima Credit's individual credit data acts as a bottleneck, restricting Zhima Credit's scale of development.

Finally, social data are lacking. Alibaba's products are mostly used in e-commerce and its derivative entertainment ecosystem. They lack large-scale social applications like Tencent's WeChat and do not result in high-quality social data.

From the perspective of the entire credit-reporting industry, China's personal credit information is in its infancy, and the development of personal credit databases lacks uniform standards. In addition, imperfect laws and regulations have rendered the data quality of different credit-reporting agencies uneven. Individual credit-reporting agencies are constantly strengthening cooperation with other institutions to expand sources of information while also realizing partial industry data sharing to promote the development of the entire credit-reporting industry. At the same time, this sharing of information between such institutions may violate the provisions of the General Data Protection Regulation, which require the personal information provided by the credit reporting agency to be approved in writing by the information subject.

To overcome these data issues, Zhima Credit has worked to improve the quality of its data collection. The company has attempted to obtain unprocessed first-hand data directly from the data source, which not only ensures the integrity and accuracy of the data but also establishes its advantages as a data source. In addition, small, low-quality data should be detected and eliminated to improve data quality. The new data should be optimized and validated in conjunction with the credit model to ensure that it can be widely used. Strengthening cooperation with other institutions, especially with influential state-owned holding companies and large private companies that have large user traffic, can increase the number of users and enrich the data source, thus establishing an authority.

Key Technologies

We have discussed key technologies in other chapters, but here we focus on how these technologies are changing the face of finance. We look at big data, cloud computing (including hybrid clouds), biometric data, blockchain, AI, Internet of Things, smart machines, augmented and virtual reality, API platforms, quantum computing (including prescriptive security), robotic process automation, instant payments, and e-commerce and social media platforms.

Big Data

Big data includes larger data, variation in data types, and data that flows much more rapidly. Hence it is "big" in every way. Big data was popularized with the growth of the internet and was made easier to manage with the emergence of a software framework that could handle structured and unstructured data, Hadoop. Hadoop uses the Hadoop Distributed File System and Yet Another Resource Negotiator as its two main components. Several other processing frameworks are now available for big data.

To carry out sufficient credit risk assessment, fintech companies needed to access better and different data than banks. Many of these companies did not have long records of credit histories to use to understand customer creditworthiness. Therefore, the advent of big data allowed such fintech companies to operate while also minimizing risks. Alipay was the first company in China to use big data, relying on data collected on Alibaba's Taobao and Tmall marketplaces as well as historical data from its own payment history. Ant Financial's Sesame Credit scored customer data to make up for China's lack of credit scoring. Tencent also developed its own scores based on five indices (as discussed earlier).

Other fintech companies developed credit-scoring mechanisms based on different types of data, such as phone payment history or social media. A boom in credit-scoring capabilities allowed many fintech companies to move from low-tech, high-risk intermediaries to viable lenders. For many small borrowers in China who previously had little access to financing, the ability to obtain funds through fintech companies that could properly assess their credit risk made a significant impact in raising China's level of inclusive finance.

Because traditional antifraud measures have been insufficient in dealing with internet finance fraud, big data also is now being used to combat fraud. Traditional antifraud measures have included the use of a blacklist, a rules-based prevention mechanism, and internal data analysis for risk prevention. These applications have issues, however. First, a time lag exists when placing users on a blacklist, as some may be real users. The rules-based prevention mechanism may create additional rules and investment thresholds that users are required to meet but that may result in the setting of overly rigid rules. Without the use of big data, internal data analysis for risk prevention also has had an insufficient impact. Big data companies such as Sesame Credit, Tencent Credit, TalkingData, Bairong Jinfu, and Aurora Big Data can reduce this kind of risk.

Cloud Computing

The use of big data also has made it necessary to use more flexible infrastructure technology, which is available through cloud computing. Use of the cloud allows customers to access big data processing without investing in large-scale big data resources. Cloud computing arose as computing became more complex, particularly with the rise of resource-intensive interactive services.

For fintech firms, use of cloud computing helps them innovate more quickly and flexibly, thus allowing firms to cater more easily to the needs of customers.[4] Technology can be scaled up or down depending on a firm's requirements. Use of cloud computing also improves risk mitigation, providing fintech firms with the latest types of security methods. The cloud can keep costs lower, as firms pay per use.

Although cloud technology was developed in the United States, it is rapidly being adopted in China. Alibaba dominates cloud computing in the Asian nation, and foreign companies that want to operate in the cloud computing space must partner with domestic Chinese firms. For example, Amazon.com has cooperated with Beijing Sinnet Technology Co. and IBM has worked with an affiliate of the Wanda Group to provide cloud computing services. Legally, companies are not allowed to transfer data abroad. Cloud computing in China is restricted for foreign firms, as it is considered to be a telecom service, which means that Chinese domestic firms have a huge market potential.

Cloud computing makes use of remote servers to process and store information. They possess five basic characteristics: on-demand self-service, allowing users to obtain computing resources as needed without human assistance; broad network access, providing users with access across networks and devices; rapid elasticity, permitting firms to scale usage up or down as needed; resource pooling, sharing information technology (IT) resources across multiple applications and users; and measured service, allowing use to be tracked by application and firm user.[5]

Clouds may be public, operated by third-party cloud service providers, or private, often operated on site. Public clouds use common physical resources for data transfers, storage, and processing across several organizations, although individual customers have private visualized computing environments and isolated storage. A private cloud is operated by one organization, but it can be offered in-house or externally. Private clouds meet the requirements for separation of a firm's data storage and processing from access through shared resources.

A hybrid cloud offers a combination of a private cloud on site and a public cloud provided by a third party. An increasing number of financial institutions have been selecting this option. In addition, various service models include software as a service (SaaS), platform as a service (PaaS), and infrastructure as a service (IaaS). SaaS offer various types of applications, whereas PaaS allows users to build and deploy applications. IaaS may provide storage, networking, or computing servers to users.

The bank cloud IT architecture makes use of SaaS, PaaS, and IaaS. Services are deployed using private cloud and public ownership. Large banks can build their own cloud, whereas smaller banks must depend on large banks or third-party cloud providers. Bank cloud providers in China include Tianyiyun, Ucloud, and Qingyun. Tencent Cloud is the most comprehensive cloud platform in China, providing cloud services for a range of industries and functions.

In China, the public cloud model reached a market value of $4 billion in 2017, and the private cloud model reached about $5.28 billion. In the public cloud market, IaaS has the largest market share.[6] Alicloud is the biggest cloud service provider, and most of its largest users are internet firms. China Telecom and China Unicom are the second- and third-largest cloud service providers, respectively. Most of their users are government institutions and firms. Traditional IT firms have been setting up cloud computing enterprises to keep up with the trend.

China's regulators support cloud computing. The most important policy in this field is the Opinions of the State Council Concerning the Promoting Innovation and Development of Cloud Computing and Cultivating New Format of Information Industry laid out in January 2015, which seeks to enhance cloud computing services and innovation, including cloud infrastructure capabilities and security. The Opinions Concerning Enhancing Cloud Computing Service Network Safety Management of the Party and Government Department issued in May 2015 centered on cloud computing security issues. In addition, the *Action Outlines of Promoting Big Data Development* issued in August 2015 committed to promoting the healthy development of the big data industry.

Furthermore, the Ministry of Industry and Information Technology's Three-Year Action Plan for Development of Cloud Computing promised that the government would provide fiscal and policy support for cloud computing companies.

Biometric Technology

Biometrics can greatly enhance the security of bank customers and increasingly is being used. This technology can be applied to identify customers at the counter or to identify customers using a camera at a bank branch or teller. In addition, the teller's registration and login can be verified. Biometric confirmation can minimize the possibility of security breaches through the authentication process.

Biometric technology also enhances financial inclusion for individuals lacking formal identification. Individuals living in poverty, particularly in developing countries, may not have identification (ID). For individuals who lack ID or who are illiterate, biometrics may provide a way to identify people without using written information.

In China, use of biometrics to pay bills, apply for social security qualification, and repay loans is on the rise. This has resulted in increased concerns about data privacy. To address this concern, Chinese legislators are working on a data privacy law that would protect citizens' personal and biometric information.[7]

Blockchain

Blockchain is a distributed, decentralized public ledger that stores transaction data. The network can be permission-less, meaning that it does not require a central authority to confirm or deny transactions, although it is also possible to set up the network as permissioned. Blocks store the data and are given a hash (or a unique code) to identify one from another. Entries are kept on a network of computers, rather than on a single computer. Blockchain can eliminate the need for third-party verification because of its ability to monitor fraudulent activity. The technology can be used in many areas of fintech, such as fund remittance, P2P payments, auditing, digital identity, and credit scoring.

Blockchain can have many applications, including providing proof of existence, which can show that a document existed at a particular time using a cryptographic function. The transformation of the document is called a digest. Blockchain also can be used to prove ownership of assets to create smart property. This proof can generate trust between two unknown parties. Blockchain can be applied to smart contracts, which use a computer code to execute actions as agreed on in a contract. The participants in the contract can communicate through the blockchain. Decentralized autonomous organization uses blockchain technology to associate smart contracts. The decentralized autonomous organization can act when transactions are added to the blockchain. Blockchain also has been used for digital currencies, such as Bitcoin, which use encryption techniques to verify their value.

The blockchain consists of a data layer, a network layer, a consensus layer, an incentive layer, a contract layer, and an application layer. The data layer contains technology to hold the underlying data blocks and associated data encryption and timestamps. The network layer contains the P2P participants in the distributed ledger using some type of core protocol. The consensus layer includes the consensus proof of work algorithm. The incentive layer keeps track of economic incentives, such as tokens, given in exchange for maintaining the ledger. The contract layer holds smart contracts. The application layer stores applications and allows access to those files.

The use of blockchain poses several challenges. These can include difficulties in achieving consensus, which requires approval of all participants; lack of standardization among blockchain network designs; lack of interoperability among blockchain platforms; challenges in increasing scalability, as new transactions must be confirmed by solving a computer problem; and problems associated with immutability, which means that once trades are carried out, they can be changed only by submitting an equal trade. Additional challenges include potential issues with security, as more participants are involved in the network; the increased importance of liquidity, which requires that assets are ready to be settled quickly; privacy concerns arising from possibility of information leakage; and lawsuits related to intellectual property, as blockchain technology may face legal challenges.[8]

Despite the challenges, blockchain is especially potentially useful in fintech, as it can reduce risks and lower the costs of verification. This technology also improves auditability of financial services. Generally, the two uses of blockchain include (1) the process efficiency rationale, which can create efficiencies in existing business models in developed markets; and (2) the new market creation rationale, which allows new market players to create value in emerging markets.[9] At present, twenty-four countries are investing in the technology and ninety banks are discussing its use worldwide.

Blockchain can be used for remittances. To go through this process, customers are added onto the blockchain, their documents and other data are added to the blockchain, customers' biometric data are set up to secure the transactions, and transactions are recorded and validated on the decentralized ledger. Last, financial institutions can access the customers' records with customer authorization.

As noted earlier, China is already involved in several blockchain ventures. The Postal Savings Bank of China has tested a blockchain-based asset custody system in collaboration with IBM and Hyperledger. Ant Financial is introducing a Bitcoin mobile wallet, and Tencent will use blockchain to offer digital asset management and authentication through a new platform. Baidu has invested in U.S. Bitcoin payment company Circle, and additional Chinese blockchain, and Huiyin Blockchain Ventures has invested in U.S.-based Purse.io and Indian UniCoin.

Blockchain also has been used for asset-backed securities platforms, with Bank of Communications launching full-process blockchain asset securitization platform and Ping An's financial account book issuing the ALFA (Alpha) Intelligence ABS platform.[10]

Artificial Intelligence

AI allows machines to learn from experience and carry out tasks that humans once performed. AI can perform high-volume tasks repeatedly, adding intelligence to existing products. AI can be applied to fintech in areas like digital assistance, transaction searches, credit risk assessment, and automated claims processing.

AI can be cultivated through machine learning, such as supervised learning, in which training data that contain labels are fed into an algorithm for the algorithm to learn a general classification scheme; unsupervised learning, in which data that is fed into an algorithm does not contain labels for the algorithm to detect patterns and identify clusters of data; reinforcement learning, in which an algorithm is given an unlabeled data set, chooses an action, and receives feedback to aid in the learning process; and deep learning, in which algorithms work in layers or artificial neural networks for supervised, unsupervised, or reinforcement learning.[11]

AI technically consists of a base layer, a technology layer, and an application layer. The base layer holds data resources, software facilities, and hardware facilities. The technology layer contains hardware, software, and data resources of the base layer. The application layer includes industry-oriented applications, such as smart finance, smart education, and smart health care.[12] Innovations for each layer are rapidly emerging.

AI is increasingly used in fintech and has become invaluable in credit-scoring applications. Traditionally, banks have relied on transaction and payment history to determine creditworthiness, but at present, banks and fintech companies have turned to less traditional data, including social media or phone use and text activity, to determine credit scores. This is particularly true in China, where smaller borrowers often lack a traditional credit history.

AI can be used in the insurance underwriting process. Highly detailed data, such as online shopping behavior or telemetrics, can be used to improve the price of insurance. This technology also can be used in insurance claims processing to determine the cost of repairs. In the future, it is possible that AI will be used to prevent accidents by connecting to the Internet of Things.

Chatbots are another application of AI that use natural language processing and machine learning outcomes to interact with customers and improve over time. Chatbots are used increasingly to advise customers and prompt them to act.

AI also may be used in the operations process to improve capital allocation by fintech firms, enhance risk management, and conduct market impact analysis. The benefit of using AI is that it has far greater processing power than do humans and can retrieve and analyze data much faster. As more and more data are fed into the system, the algorithm improves.

AI can be applied to trading and portfolio management as well as to regulatory compliance and supervision. AI allows potentially millions of trades to be carried out at their optimal prices and reduces the likelihood of mistakes.

China is leading the science of AI, and this has translated into business terms. Businesses assist financial firms in analyzing data to improve efficiency, reduce risks, and lower costs. For example, 100credit provides firms with risk management solutions using big data and AI. The firm assists fintech companies in knowing their customers when clients lack sufficient credit history. The company uses AI to understand which customers are fraudulent and applies different tasks at every stage of the lending process. Robots can make calls to follow up on transactions with clients.

Other firms integrate AI into their core businesses. Lexin uses proprietary technology to trace back bad credit and identify risks. This allows the firm to provide small and microcredit loans. AI helps firm managers assess risks properly using location information and social network activity as fraudulent users tend to congregate.

China's government has been a big supporter of AI, and the New Generation Artificial Intelligence Development Plan, mentioned earlier, coupled with the Made in China 2025 strategy, are core elements of China's AI strategy. The emphasis on investment in AI technologies has pushed China to a competitive position in the AI field. President Xi Jinping held a Politburo Study Session on the topic in October 2018, underscoring the fact that making strides in this area is a top policy goal.

China also faces some core weaknesses in the development of AI. The case has been made that China's AI success rests on its access to global technologies.[13] It lacks top talent and is weak in the areas of hardware and algorithm development. The top machine learning software environments were developed outside of China. China also tends to rely on foreign-designed chips, which play a central role in the implementation of AI. China is doing its best to catch up in these areas through government policy and investment.

Internet of Things

The Internet of Things is a network of computing devices, machines, objects, and people with specific identifiers within a system that can move data without human intervention. This creates advantages for data collection and processing through the ability to gather information on user behavior and preferences. The Internet of Things can improve customer service as well as decision making and risk management for a fintech company.

The Internet of Things can be applied to fintech in several ways. For example, it can improve usage of automated teller machines through smart devices, reduce insurance risks by communicating with devices in the home or car, and make payments easier by working with wearable gadgets. The Internet of Things is expected to receive a big boost from the upgrade from 4G to 5G telecommunications technology and the development of AI, which will further allow smart objects to communicate with computers and one another in a more seamless fashion.

Smart Machines

Smart machines include virtual customer assistants and smart advisors. Such machines use machine-to-machine or cognitive computing technologies like AI or machine learning in the processes of dynamic pricing models or fraud detection.

Many fintech firms have launched virtual customer assistants. These assistants use AI to improve customer satisfaction and loyalty, even tracking customer emotions in some uses. Virtual assistants can help fintech companies to defend their core business and enhance their competitiveness.

To reduce costs, China Construction Bank has set up 1,600 smart machines in its 360 branches throughout Beijing. The bank also has a branch that is entirely manned by robots, as described earlier. Live help from client relationship managers is available in a private room designated for remote chats through a video link.

Augmented and Virtual Reality

Augmented reality combines interactive digital elements with the real-world environment. Virtual reality creates an immersive environment to simulate an experience. These technologies can be applied in data visualization in wealth management, for example, virtual reality payments and biometric security.

Augmented and virtual reality have many potential applications in the fintech world. The technology could be used for virtual branch banking, biometric authentication, virtual or contactless credit cards, new payment methods, marketing, reporting presentation, and streamlining of business processes.[14] Augmented reality can help to reduce customer service costs and increase customer recruitment and retention. At present, mobile-based augmented reality is attracting significant attention, because it allows users to employ their phones as a virtual display.

Leading banks are already exploring this technology. For example, FNB's eBucks Partner locator uses augmented reality to locate nearby eBucks retail partners. In addition, BNP Paribas has rolled out a virtual reality–based app for retail banking customers in France. The program allows users to virtually access account activity and transaction records.[15] Ant Financial also has a virtual reality payment system for use of Alipay.

API Platforms

API platforms allow third-party firms to build applications using a fintech firm's data in a secure fashion. The API platforms create an environment in which firms can design and build APIs to securely share their services. Third-party APIs also may be better, as they are built externally and may provide more flexibility.

APIs have been used in the fintech industry for P2P lending networks, investment management, improving access to data, payments, regtech, and smart contracts.

Banking as a service (BaaS) banks can also allow fintechs to form partnerships with them. Through this process, fintech companies can use the bank's license to comply with bank-related regulations. Banking as a platform (BaaP) uses an API model to allow banks to connect with new services offered by fintech firms. Essentially, this means that banks can safely provide access to their internal systems for third-party developers to create new apps. Some partners may be specialized in particular services, such as crowdfunding or payment splitting apps.

The Hong Kong Monetary Authority (HKMA) created its own version of an API framework in July 2018. In 2019, the HKMA began to help banks use the framework, starting with sharing product and services information and then adopting other API functions, such as applications for new products and services. Mainland China does not have open banking rules, but fintech companies like Ant Financial and Tencent use open APIs to provide a means for third-party firms to offer services to their customers. Ping An Insurance has introduced a Smart Insurance Cloud, which is an API platform that Ping An offers to its partners.[16]

Quantum Computing

Quantum computing can allow several potential outputs to be produced at the same time, speeding up the time for processing an outcome. A normal computer stores data in binary states of zeros and ones in a bit. A storage unit qubit of a quantum computer, in addition to zeros and ones, can implement a plurality of states. This technology may be considered a substitute for improvements in chip processing speed, which has been slowing. This technology may soon be widely applied in fintech. For example, quantum computing could be applied to determining the risk of fraudulent payments or high-frequency trading.

Prescriptive security can transform human experiences and analytical capabilities into machine intelligence to improve security against attacks. This system uses a combination of big data, AI, machine learning, advanced analytics, and enhanced threat intelligence.

China is currently aiming to implement quantum computing to secure its sensitive networks. China's Quantum Beijing-Shanghai Trunk runs between Shanghai and Beijing and includes thirty-two stations.[17] Researchers at the Chinese Academy of Sciences are in the process of building a "national wide-area quantum confidential communications backbone network."[18] This network will support financial, government, power, telecommunications, and other private network applications. The researchers plan to localize core quantum communication devices, formulate national technology standards for the industry, and create international technical standards. Chinese firms like Baidu and Alibaba are attempting to stay in the lead in the field of quantum computing, and as a result of research from the University of Science and Technology of China, firms such as Quantum CTek, whose business is in quantum communications, are emerging.

Quantum computing's improved processing speed will boost the development of AI. China's New Generation Artificial Intelligence Development Plan of July 2017 lays out plans for advances in theoretical research in quantum intelligent computing.

Robotic Process Automation

Robotic process automation can automate a variety of processes, including, for example, carrying out a set of rules across a data set. The system can learn from decisions and data patterns to reduce the costs of administrative and regulatory processes. It can carry out tasks such as removing duplicates, reproducing tasks, and performing regular tasks, thus simplifying user interactions and accelerating enterprise-level processes.

Intelligent process automation combines robotic process automation with machine learning, intelligent workflow, natural language generation, and cognitive agents. Machine learning allows machines to identify patterns, while intelligent workflow integrates tasks carried out by humans and machines. Natural language generation is a software engine that converts observations from data into prose and, finally, a cognitive agent integrates machine learning and natural language generation to build a virtual workforce (or agent) that can perform tasks and communicate.

In China, robotic process automation is already being used in fintech. In 2016, for example, Cobos and China Postal Savings Bank began to cooperate, and the bank employed robots to improve marketing and customer service. Robots were embedded with customer reception guidelines, business consulting solutions, and financial product promotions. The robot's "new automatic reception module" allowed it to accurately identify high-market-value customers. The Postal Savings Bank also purchased remote video teller machines to run its bank counters in a more efficient manner.[19]

Instant Payments

Instant payments are payments that can be made at any time and that have immediate or close-to-immediate interbank transaction clearing. Instant payments are becoming more widely used in different formats, with banks offering smaller companies the infrastructure for instant payments, and companies that already have the payment infrastructure offering their services to end users.

Instant payments increase liquidity among merchants, because funds can be transferred immediately. Instant payments can reduce the incidence of fraud, because they are associated with high levels of security. These electronic payments improve transaction tracking capabilities, especially compared with a cash-based system.

China uses the Internet Banking Payment System (IBPS), which is a part of a second-generation payment system introduced by the PBC. This connects the online banking system of Chinese banks, transferring payments in real time in a process called Super Online Banking. IBPS is part of the China National Advanced Payment Systems. IBPS also allows individuals and firms to use the interbank account inquiry functionality to view account information from different banks.

E-Commerce and Social Media Platforms

Major e-commerce and social media platforms provide platforms or infrastructure to fintech firms. These include Alibaba, for which Alipay was initially created, and WeChat, which includes WeChat Wallet. E-commerce and social media platforms have the advantage of possessing both the audience that demands the use of fintech services as well as the data needed to improve customer credit risk assessment.

Alipay was launched in 2004 by Alibaba to service the e-commerce platform Taobao, allowing users to safely make payments on the website.

WeChat Wallet includes WeChat Pay, and from the Wallet, users can make bill payments, recharge their mobile phones, make online purchases, and make QR payments. The Wallet also allows users to purchase wealth management products and virtual currency. WeChat Pay has "gamified" fintech by allowing users to send red packets, which can include cash or games that allow users to compete to snatch a red packet, and WeChat allows uses to connect with friends to make purchases on platforms like Pinduoduo, a group purchasing app. Tencent owns WeChat as well as the QQ messaging service and QQ Wallet, a mobile payment service provider.

Baidu Wallet, now called Du Xiaoman Pay, is used on the Chinese search engine Baidu and can be used to make payments. Baidu Wallet allows users to make interbank transfers for free and to pay for online purchases and utility fees. Users and merchants are linked through the Baidu app, Baidu Map, and iQIYI. Baidu customers can purchase wealth management products online.

Interestingly, some fintech companies also use social media and e-commerce platforms to assess consumer creditworthiness using the large-scale data available on these platforms. The connection between social media and fintech is even further extended by the interaction between customers and fintech firms through the social media chat functions for customer service and through interaction between the consumer and advertisers.

Conclusion

Chinese fintech firms are using new and innovative technologies and reaching customers through online and offline channels. Technologies are rapidly changing, and the emergence of AI and 5G networks will boost the speed and ubiquity of these fintech products. In the next chapter, we describe the outlook for China's fintech industry and provide concluding remarks.

CHAPTER TEN

Outlook and Summing Up

CHINA'S FINTECH INDUSTRY has changed rapidly in the past decade. Fintech companies have greatly improved their ability to assess credit risks, which has meant that companies not able to do so have become obsolete. Fintech firms have accustomed users to managing many aspects of their finances online. This trend is particularly evident in the area of digital payments, but also in terms of lending and borrowing. Financial customers can now interact less often with bank employees and conduct a greater proportion of their financial lives online.

Three primary challenges remain. The first is the lack of skilled workers in this field. The second is the uncertainty about the regulatory regime, and the third is heavy competition. We discuss each of these challenges in turn, review information security and consumers' rights, and then examine the future of China's fintech industry.

Challenges

Fintech firms face several major challenges in the current environment. How well these firms address these issues will determine whether they succeed at the top or languish at the bottom of the sector.

First, the fintech industry is facing a shortage of experienced professionals who have a deep knowledge of finance and technology. Finding employees who fit a specific position is a major challenge. Small and medium-size cities in particular face a shortage of talent at all levels.[1] Even when talented individuals are hired, the fintech job market is highly fluid, and those employees may move to another firm in search of a better position.

Li and Lu recommend teaching students in the field of fintech. The authors recommend that the curriculum focus on science and technology, including internet finance, computer knowledge and network technology, and data mining, credit evaluation, and risk assessment.[2] This recommended curriculum should be divided into the areas of professional basic knowledge and professional operation ability, with courses in economics, computer science, and finance. Training should be given in the areas of internet wealth management, internet financial risk and management courses, and other practical areas.

At the same time, many traditional jobs in the financial industry are expected to be replaced by the use of artificial intelligence (AI), declining by about 23 percent by 2027.[3] The insurance and banking industries may be affected most significantly. Specifically, jobs in customer service, risk analysis, trading, and back-end finance are likely to be cut. New technology-oriented roles, including in the fintech industry, are expected to arise in their stead.

Second, another major challenge faced by fintech companies is uncertainty regarding regulations. Although regulations are being implemented in a number of areas, some firms have found new regulations to be so stringent that they cannot continue to operate. This has been rampant in the peer-to-peer (P2P) lending industry, which encountered several new rules with which companies struggled to adapt. As China's fintech sector continues to develop, new innovations will result in unforeseen risks. Therefore, the implementation of new regulations will continue to create challenges for existing firms in a variety of fintech industries. Hopefully, the emergence of regtech will reduce volatility created by the implementation of new regulations, assisting firms in ensuring compliance.

Finally, heavy competition creates barriers to entry. Chinese respondents to a global fintech survey in 2017 viewed competition as the biggest challenge to entering and remaining in the industry.[4] Heavy competition results in lower prices and loss of market share as well as a rise in customer churn. China has faced a competitive landscape in which the best-performing fintech companies dominate, particularly in areas such as payments. One reason for this competition is that innovation and access to data is costly, so that companies with large fund reserves or built-in data access channels (such as Alibaba for Alipay) have an enormous advantage over companies that lack these resources.

Although risk control technology using big data is becoming more commonplace, it is no longer the case that just any company, no matter the resources, can enter and survive in China's complex fintech environment. This is only going to further divide those with resources and those without, as large technology strides are made and as the largest market shareholders seize even more market share. Overcoming barriers to entry and competition will remain a major challenge for Chinese fintech companies in the future.

Information Security and Consumers' Rights

Information security remains an ongoing issue for fintech companies. Even traditional banking, which has developed a system to protect consumer information and consumers' rights, is flawed in dealing with consumer protection. The existing financial regulatory system and industry self-discipline system have failed to address complaints of financial consumers, and financial consumers often are forced to directly appeal to judicial channels to safeguard their interests. As a result, fintech is a new industry that faces a number of challenges in these areas.

Network and system security must adapt to a constantly changing environment. Network boundaries become blurred by the increasing frequency of information. Traditional network security processes cannot meet these needs as big data grows even bigger. This growth of data as well as the need to analyze data and use encryption and other security measures have placed pressure on hardware performance as well. This is why cloud computing has become so essential—these systems have better computing and storage capacity as well as reliability and scalability.

With the development of cloud technology, especially the development of shared cloud technology, the traditional security boundary is disappearing, and the boundaries between the internal network and the external network are blurring. In particular for large financial companies that provide financial cloud security services, it is difficult to accurately define security boundaries. In the area of internet finance, the application of new technologies and new services is accompanied by various new types of attacks (such as ransomware). In response to these attacks, organizations have to increase various types of safety equipment and platforms at the technical protection level, which has resulted in a rapid increase in safety costs.[5]

Mobile phone payments alone face several security risks. Many mobile phones are based on the Android system, which has a unique structure. This has led to a lack of effective unified supervision of applications on mobile phones and to the proliferation of malware and rogue software. Applications can be downloaded just by scanning a QR code, which also has raised issues. Applications downloaded into users' stored data on their mobile phones can read their personal information. Some nonstandard applications can locate customer data and sell this information. Other applications insert malware into existing applications for users to download and use. Application security issues include activity component security and hijacking, which can allow for external control of the phone and malware that can use phishing activity to trick the user into providing additional information.[6]

Websites associated with mobile phone payments also have security issues. Mobile applications interact with the server through the internet, and they may be subject to network-level attacks, web application attacks, and content tampering, such as changing the web content to illegal content.

China has implemented regulations to safeguard personal information. These include the Regulations on the Management of Credit Information Industry, Notice on the Protection of Banking Financial Institutions for Personal Financial Information Protection, Notice on Financial Institutions to Further Improve Customer Personal Financial Information Protection, and the Guidelines for the Protection of Personal Information, among others.[7]

Information security remains a problem, even in industrial countries. For example, Equifax, a credit scoring company in the United States, was hacked and leaked the information of more than one hundred million customers. Gemalto's 2017 Breach Level Index report of global incidents found that the known number of data records compromised by data breaches was greater than two and a half billion, up 88 percent from 2016.[8] More than half of these breaches contained an unknown number of compromised records. Much of this was due to human error, stemming from poorly configured databases, accidental losses, and poor record disposal processing. Data breaches led to identity theft in 69 percent of the incidents. Industries that experienced the breaches included health care (27 percent), financial services (12 percent), education (11 percent), and government (11 percent). Sectors with the most records stolen included government (18 percent), financial services (9.1 percent), and technology (16 percent).

Internet financial consumers' rights and interests need to be better protected by clarifying the concept of who the consumers are. Internet finance businesses should follow the principles of good faith, fairness, and rationality. Consumers should be protected in the right to information security and fair trading as well in access to a full disclosure of information. The mechanism of supervision must be improved in this sector.

Consumers' rights also need to be protected both during fintech firms' operation and exit to ensure that consumers do not lose their funds. Jia Du recommends constructing a fintech consumer privacy protection system under a law similar to the U.S. Financial Privacy Bill of 1978 to safeguard consumers' personal information and creating a fintech risk warning system so that fintech firms can alert consumers of potential risks.[9] A multilevel fintech consumer protection system would be beneficial and would include an independent fintech consumer dispute resolution platform within the fintech institutions, develop an open and transparent petition system, and set up sound consumer complaint procedures.

Internet finance consumer education should be a key component of the internet financial consumer rights protection system. A full-time responsible agency for internet financial consumer education should be established, and industry associations should be encouraged to educate consumers and provide them with comprehensive and multi-perspective knowledge learning guides.[10]

The Future

Some of the innovations that fintech will bring in the future cannot be anticipated. Some fintech companies, however, have a vision, and as such, they likely will figure strongly in shaping that picture.

For example, Tencent aims to use fintech and related technology to create a smart city solution for Xiong'an New Area in Hebei province, located sixty miles southwest of Beijing. This area will incorporate fintech as well as cloud computing, blockchain, and big data. In addition,

Ant Financial and a Tencent subsidiary will establish a nonprofit institute to research smart city development. Companies with a new vision for the future, combined with enough funding and government backing, will succeed in China's environment of fintech innovation.

Blockchain technology will continue to become increasingly prominent. Its technical properties of decentralization and nontampering have great potential to change the basic financial service model. At present, a few financial institutions gradually have begun to apply blockchain technology in multiple business areas, such as supply chain finance, smart contracts, and cross-border payments. The current legal framework must be improved, however, for blockchain technology to develop. At present, the application of blockchain in the financial field is still based on exploration. The large-scale application of blockchain requires shared support of the technology, law, and business environments, but it will continue to evolve. New ventures in this area represent a strong future trend.

Regtech is at the cutting edge of the fintech industry. Although fintech has brought a series of innovative financial business models to promote the transformation of the financial industry into inclusive finance, microfinance, and smart finance, the application of fintech in promoting the transformation and development of the financial industry also has brought a series of new risks. These risks have put forward new requirements for financial supervision and need to be supported by regulatory innovation. From the perspective of future development trends, the mutual driving role of fintech and regtech will become increasingly apparent. The supervision of financial technology will gradually improve, especially at the level of user data protection.

Many experts believe that as 5G telecommunications develop, along with AI and communication between objects through the Internet of Things, the speed and response of technology will increase many times over. 5G technology is already being implemented in China, and AI applications are becoming increasingly better. We can expect to see, by 2025 and especially by 2030, a markedly different fintech landscape in China and around the world than we see today. It suffices to say that firms that are investing in new technologies have a far better chance of survival and profitability than firms that are not investing in new tech. Technology will separate the good from the great firms, and the divide will become only greater as time passes.

Notes

1. Overview of China's Fintech Industry

1. Cliff Sheng, Jasper Yip, and James Cheng, *Fintech in China: Hitting the Moving Target* (Oliver Wyman report, August 2017), 5.

2. At that time, credit cards were not common in China. They still are used less frequently in China than in the United States and elsewhere. They have been around for a long time, however, and thus we can view credit cards as a type of financial innovation that is not classified as fintech per se, as the technology used is decades old. Fintech generally refers to digital and online financial innovations.

3. Daniel Ren, "China Regulators Warn that 90 pc of Peer-to-Peer Lenders Could Fail in 2017," *South China Morning Post*, February 19, 2017.

4. Bloomberg News, "China Planning Major Purge of $176 Billion Loan Market," Bloomberg.com, November 29, 2018, https://www.bloomberg.com /news/articles/2018-11-29/china-is-said-to-plan-major-purge-of-176-billion -loan-market.

5. Yang Wei, China Financial Technology Enterprise Database, 2018, http:// www.fintechdb.cn/.

6. China Internet Network Information Center (CNNIC), *Statistical Report on Internet Development in China* (in Chinese), CNNIC.com, 2017, http://cnnic.com.cn/IDR/ReportDownloads/201706/P020170608523 740585924.pdf.

7. Wei Wang and David Dollar, *What's Happening with China's Fintech Industry?* (Brookings Institution, February 8, 2018), https://www.brookings .edu/blog/order-from-chaos/2018/02/08/whats-happening-with-chinas -fintech-industry/.

8. China Internet Information Center, China.org.cn, 2018.

9. Aleid Werker, "The Role of Alipay in Commerce in China" (master's thesis, Leiden University, Netherlands, 2017), 19, https://openaccess.leidenuniv.nl/bitstream/handle/1887/51299/Aleid%20Werker%2C%20MA%20THESIS.pdf?sequence=1.

10. Joe Zhang, *Chasing Subprime Credit: How China's Fintech Sector Is Thriving* (Hong Kong: Enrich Professional Publishing, 2017), 72.

11. BCG, *Global Digital Wealth Management Report 2018* (Boston, MA: Boston Consulting Group Report, May 2018), 26, http://media-publications.bcg.com/BCG_Global_Digital_Wealth_Management_Report_May_2018_ENG.PDF.

12. Liu Xiao, "Tencent Money-Market Fund Triples in Three Years," Caixin, May 22, 2018, https://www.caixinglobal.com/2018-03-22/tencent-money-market-fund-triples-in-three-years-101224888.html.

13. Bloomberg, "Tencent Sets Up an Online Trading Platform for Chinese Bonds," South China Morning Post, June 22, 2018, https://www.scmp.com/tech/enterprises/article/2152029/tencent-sets-online-trading-platform-chinese-bonds.

14. "Qudian Management Presentation," Qudian.com, May 2018, ir.qudian.com%2Fdownload%2FQD%2BMP_20180515.pdf.

15. "Cloud Computing Trends in China," Alibaba Cloud, 2016, http://alicloud-common.oss-ap-southeast-1.aliyuncs.com/Updated_Materials/Infopaper%20-%20Cloud%20Computing%20Trends%20in%20China%20-%20updated.pdf.

16. Philip Russom, *Big Data Analytics* (TDWI Best Practices Report, Seattle, WA: The Data Warehousing Institute, Fourth Quarter 2011), http://tdwi.org/research/2011/09/best-practices-report-q4-big-data-analytics.aspx.fourth quarter 2011), http://download.101com.com/pub/tdwi/Files/TDWI_BPReport_Q411_Big_Data_Analytics_Web.pdf.

17. Thomas H. Davenport, "China Is Catching Up to the US on Artificial Intelligence Research," The Conversation, February 27, 2019, http://theconversation.com/china-is-catching-up-to-the-us-on-artificial-intelligence-research-112119.

18. State Council, *Guiding Opinions on Advancing the Healthy Development of Internet Finance* (in Chinese) (China Ministry of Finance, People's Republic of China, 2015), http://www.mof.gov.cn/zhengwuxinxi/zhengcefabu/201507/t20150720_1332370.htm.

19. "Investment in Chinese FinTech Companies Surpassed $1bn in Q1 2018," Fintech Global, May 16, 2018, https://fintech.global/investment-in-chinese-fintech-companies-surpassed-1bn-in-q1-2018; David Meyer, "Jack Ma's Chinese Fintech Firm Just Raised So Much Money It's Now Worth More Than Goldman Sachs," *Fortune*, June 8, 2018, http://fortune.com/2018/06/08/ant-financial-alipay-14-billion-funding/.

20. "Global Venture Capital Investment in Fintech Industry Set Record in 2017, Driven by Surge in India, US and UK, Accenture Analysis Finds," Accenture Newsroom, February 28, 2018, https://newsroom.accenture .com/news/global-venture-capital-investment-in-fintech-industry-set-record -in-2017-driven-by-surge-in-india-us-and-uk-accenture-analysis-finds.htm.

21. Samantha Hurst, "Chinese Fintech Wecash Raises $160 Million During Series D Funding Round Led By ORIX Asia Capital & SEA Group," CrowdFund Insider, March 2, 2018, https://www.crowdfundinsider.com /2018/03/129067-chinese-fintech-wecash-raises-160-million-series-d-funding -round-led-orix-asia-capital-sea-group/.

22. Jiang Xueqing, "Pintec Raises $103m, Partners with Sina to Tap Fintech Sector," *China Daily*, June 6, 2018, http://www.chinadaily.com .cn/a/201806/06/WS5b177534a31001b82571e73d.html.

23. Sachin Mittal and James Lloyd, *The Rise of Fintech in China: Redefining Financial Services* (collaborative report, DBS and EY, 2016), https://www .ey.com/cn/en/industries/financial-services/ey-the-rise-of-fintech-in-china.

24. International Bank for Reconstruction and Development, World Bank, and the People's Bank of China, *Toward Universal Financial Inclusion in China: Models, Challenges, and Global Lessons* (Washington, DC: World Bank Group, February 2018), http://documents.worldbank.org/curated/en /281231518106429557/pdf/123323-FinancialInclusionChina-9Aug18 .pdf.

25. State Council, *China to Boost Inclusive Finance* (China Ministry of Finance, January 15, 2016).

26. Digital Finance Research Center of Peking University, "Digital Inclusive Financial Indicator System and Index Compilation" (working paper, Digital Finance Research Center of Peking University, 2016).

27. Wei Lu and Hongchang Li, "Research on the Development of Inclusive Finance under Internet Finance" (in Chinese), *Cooperative Economy and Technology* 9 (2018): 63.

28. Lin He, Shuo Cheng, Guan-yi tong Zhang, and Le Zhang, "Desire Demand of Internet Finance for Farmers and Expanding of Rural Financial Market," *Guangdong Agricultural Science* 45, no. 5 (2018): 142.

29. Chao Xu, "Analysis of the Ways of Internet Finance Promoting the Development of Rural Inclusive Finance" (in Chinese), *Times Finance* 3 (2018): 31.

30. Shaolan Chen, Hongjun Liu, and Wenhui Zheng, "The Role of Internet Finance in the Development of Rural Inclusive Finance" (in Chinese), *Jiangsu Agricultural Sciences* 46, no. 14 (2018): 340.

31. Wei Liu and Jie Wei, " 'Tiandong Model' to Solve the Problems of Rural Internet Financial Services: Background, Experience and Enlightenment" (in Chinese), *Guangxi Social Sciences* 28, no. 6 (2018): 116.

32. Jack Zhou and Xiuping Hua, "Digital Financial Inclusion Growing in China," *China Daily*, January 13, 2018, https://www.chinadaily.com .cn/a/201801/13/WS5a59b862a3102c394518f050.html.

33. Gang-zhen Wang and Xu Wu, "Research on the Model of Internet Financial Poverty Alleviation Based on E-commerce Platform—An Example of Jingdong," *Journal of UESTC* 20, no. 4 (2018): 1.

34. Tiecheng Wang, "Examining New Structural Economics: A Multidimensional Perspective," *Journal of Hubei University of Economics* 16, no. 1 (2018), 31.

35. Qifeng Pan and Mingmin Zhao, " 'The Strategy of Agricultural Banks' Layout Optimization under the Background of Internet Finance" (in Chinese), *National Chinese Core Journal Modern Finance* 10 (2017): 54.

36. Zhenggen He, "Promoting the Financial Benefits of the Village Area with Digital Financial Innovation" (in Chinese), *Tsinghua Financial Review*, April 2017: 100.

37. "Yilongdai Helps Farmers," Yilongdai, June 15, 2018, https://cj.eloancn .com/about/snNews-157.html.

38. CNNIC, *Statistical Report on Internet Development in China* (in Chinese).

39. Joseph A. Schumpeter, *Capitalism, Socialism and Democracy* (New York: Harper, 1950), 83.

40. Joseph Schumpeter, *The Theory of Economic Development: An Inquiry into Profits, Capital, Credit, Interest and the Business Cycle* (Cambridge, MA: Harvard University Press, 1934), 74.

41. World Bank, Global Financial Inclusion (Global Findex) Database, 2014, http://datatopics.worldbank.org/financialinclusion/.

42. J. Fred Weston, Susan E. Hoag, and Kwang S. Chung, *Mergers, Restructuring and Corporate Control* (New York: Prentice Hall, 1998).

43. Mancy Sun, Piyush Mubayi, Tian Lu, and Stanley Tian, *Future of Finance: The Rise of China Fintech* (Equity Research report, Goldman Sachs, August 7, 2017), 3, https://hybg.cebnet.com.cn/upload/gaoshengfintech.pdf.

44. Sun et al., *Future of Finance*.

45. Chris Anderson, *The Long Tail: Why the Future of Business Is Selling Less of More* (New York: Hachette Books, 2004).

46. George A. Akerlof, "The Market for 'Lemons': Quality Uncertainty and the Market Mechanism," *Quarterly Journal of Economics* 84, no. 3 (1970): 488–500; Michael Spence, "Job Market Signaling," *Quarterly Journal of Economics* 87, no. 3 (1973): 355.

47. Douglas W. Diamond and Philip H. Dybvig, "Bank Runs, Deposit Insurance, and Liquidity," *Journal of Political Economy* 91, no. 3 (1983): 401.

48. Hyman Minsky, *The Financial-Instability Hypothesis: Capitalist Processes and the Behavior of the Economy*, ed. Charles P., Kindleberger and Jean-Pierre

Laffargue (Cambridge: Cambridge University Press, 1982), 13–38; Jan A. Kregel, "Margins of Safety and Weight of the Argument in Generating Financial Fragility," *Journal of Economics Issues* 31 (1997): 543.

49. Joseph Bower and Clayton M. Christensen, "Disruptive Technologies: Catching the Wave," *Harvard Business Review* (January-February 1995).

50. Bower and Christensen, "Disruptive Technologies," 45.

51. Ronald I. McKinnon, *Money and Capital in Economics Development* (Washington, DC: Brookings Institution, 1973); Edward S. Shaw, *Financial Deepening in Economic Development* (New York: Oxford University Press, 1973).

52. Jianjun Li and Yongbin Lu, "Thoughts on the Construction of Internet Finance Courses and Talents Training Mode" (in Chinese), *Chinese University Teaching* 2018 (5): 64.

53. Zhuo Huang, Wang Haiming, Shen Yan, and Xie Lili, *The Chinese Era of Financial Technology: 12 Lectures on Digital Finance* (Beijing: People's University Press, 2017).

54. Huang et al., *The Chinese Era of Financial Technology*, 30.

55. Hong Kong Financial Services Development Council, "The Future of FinTech in Hong Kong" (FSDC paper 29, Fsdc.org.hk, 2017), 2, http://www.fsdc.org.hk/sites/default/files/FSDC%20Paper_FinTech_E.pdf.

56. Benita Yu and Jason Webber, *Hong Kong* (Slaughter and May, 2018), 43, https://www.slaughterandmay.com/media/2536387/fintech-in-hong-kong-2018.pdf.

57. PwC, *PwC Hong Kong Fintech Survey* (PwC, 2017a), 1, https://www.pwchk.com/en/financial-services/publications/fintech/hong-kong-fintech-survey-2017.pdf.

58. Carla Stamegna and Cemal Karakas, *Fintech (Financial Technology) and the European Union: State of Play and Outlook* (European Parliamentary Research Service, February 2019), 1, https://www.fintech2019.eu/wp-content/uploads/2019/03/EPRS_BRI2019635513_EN.pdf.

59. Maria Demertzis, Silvia Merler, and Guntram B. Wolff, "Capital Markets Union and the Fintech Opportunity," *Policy Contribution* no. 22 (September 2017), 8, http://bruegel.org/wp-content/uploads/2017/09/PC-22-2017.pdf.

60. Steven Mnuchin and Craig Phillips, *A Financial System That Creates Economic Opportunities: Nonbank Financials, Fintech, and Innovation* (Washington, DC: U.S. Department of the Treasury, August 2018), 5, https://home.treasury.gov/sites/default/files/2018-07/A-Financial-System-that-Creates-Economic-Opportunities---Nonbank-Financi....pdf.

61. Gerald Tsai, "Fintech and the U.S. Regulatory Response," remarks at the 4th Bund Summit on Fintech, Federal Reserve Bank of San Francisco, July 9, 2017, San Francisco, CA.

62. H. Q. Han, "Fintech in China: An Introduction," Wharton Fintech, April 1, 2018, https://medium.com/wharton-fintech/fintech-in-china-an -introduction-6b11abd9cb64.

2. Digital Payment Systems

1. Consultative Group to Assist the Poor (CGAP), "China's Alipay and WeChat Pay: Reaching Rural Users," *CGAP Brief* (December 2017), 1, http://www.cgap.org/sites/default/files/Brief-Chinas-Alipay-and-WeChat -Pay-Dec-2017.pdf.

2. Wei Tang. "Development Research and Innovation Path of Third Party Payment Platform under 'Internet +,' " *Business Economics* 8 (2018): 171.

3. Eric Duflos and Leora Klapper, "New Accounts in China Drive Global Financial Inclusion Figures," *World Bank* (blog), June 18, 2015, http://blogs.worldbank.org/eastasiapacific/new-accounts-china-drive -global-financial-inclusion-figures.

4. Ipsos, *2017 Mobile Payment Usage in China Report* (Ipsos, August 2017), 10, https://www.ipsos.com/sites/default/files/ct/publication/documents /2017-08/Mobile_payments_in_China-2017.pdf.

5. China Internet Information Center, China Internet Information Center website, 2018 www.china.org.cn.

6. CGAP, "China's Alipay and WeChat Pay," 3.

7. Ai Media Consulting, *2017–2018 China Third Party Mobile Payment Market Research Report* (in Chinese) (Ai Media Report, April 23, 2018), http://www.iimedia.cn/61209.html.

8. National Bureau of Statistics of China, "Annual Data," National Bureau of Statistics, 2017, http://www.stats.gov.cn/english/Statisticaldata/AnnualData/.

9. Mobile Payments Today. "PayPal's TIO Networks Says Data Breach Affected 1.6M Users," Mobile Payments Today, December 4, 2017.

10. Haifeng Gu and Lixiang Yang, "Research on Risk Evaluation of Third Party Mobile Payment in China under Internet Finance" (in Chinese), *Journal of Financial Management Research* 5 (2017): 1.

11. "Payment Code Scams are Rampant" (in Chinese), Payone, December 27, 2017. https://zhuanlan.zhihu.com/p/32383607.

12. Pei Yu and Jiayi Xu, *Internet Finance Industry In-depth Research* (in Chinese) (Sinolink Securities Report, March 2018), 12, http://pg.jrj.com .cn/acc/Res/CN_RES/INDUS/2018/3/6/ceb73bb1-be3c-44bf-8690 -766f16bca0f6.pdf.

13. CreditEase and Yirendai, "China Payment Industry Research Report" (in Chinese) (research presentation, Qichacha, February 2018), 7, http://co-image .qichacha.com/upload/chacha/att/20180206/1517896169579837.pdf.

14. Jonathan Woetzel, Jeongmin Seong, Kevin Wei Wang, James Manyika, Michael Chui, and Wendy Wong, *China's Digital Economy: A Leading Global Force* (McKinsey Global Institute, August 2017), 2, https://www.mckinsey.com/featured-insights/china/chinas-digital-economy-a-leading-global-force.

15. Zen Soo, "China's Mobile Payment Giants Forcing Incumbents to Innovate," *South China Morning Post*, December 16, 2017. https://www.scmp.com/tech/china-tech/article/2124512/chinas-mobile-payment-giants-forcing-incumbents-innovate.

16. Celia Chen and Iris Deng, "WeChat Pay to Keep Overseas Focus on Outbound Tourism Instead of Offering More Local Wallets," *South China Morning Post*, July 11, 2018. https://www.scmp.com/tech/article/2154828/wechat-pay-keep-overseas-focus-outbound-tourism-instead-offering-more-local.

17. S. Y. Lau, *Measuring the Digital Economy: Higher Education Forum Malaysia* (Tencent, 2017), 31, http://www.bnm.gov.my/documents/conference_vol/2017_PaymentSystem/The%20Growth%20of%20Digital%20Payment%20Ecosystem%20in%20China.pdf.

18. Lau, *Measuring the Digital Economy*, 24.

19. Tang, "Development Research and Innovation Path of Third Party Payment Platform," 171.

20. CreditEase and Yirendai, "China Payment Industry Research Report," 5.

21. Dashan Guo, "Research on Cross-Border RMB Settlement Business of Third-Party Payment Institutions" (in Chinese), *Hainan Finance* 7 (2018): 82.

22. Guo, "Research on Cross-Border RMB Settlement Business," 83.

23. IYiou Intelligence, "Ant Financial Service Development Turning Event," Ant Financial Case Study, April 25, 2019. https://www.iyiou.com/intelligence/report625.html.

24. David (Kuo Chuen) Lee and Ernie G. S. Teo, "Emergence of Fintech and the LASIC Principles," *Journal of Financial Perspectives: FinTech* Winter (2015): 24.

25. Lee and Teo, "Emergence of Fintech and the LASIC Principles."

26. Capgemini and BNP Paribas, *World Payments Report 2017* (Capgemini, 2017), https://www.worldpaymentsreport.com.

27. Chen and Deng, "WeChat Pay to Keep Overseas Focus on Outbound Tourism."

3. Peer-to-Peer Lending and Crowdfunding

1. Yan Shen and Cangshu Li, *Research on Network Borrowing Risk Relief Mechanism* (in Chinese) (Research Group of Digital Finance Research Center of Peking University, May 20, 2018), 8, http://osscdn.wdzj.com/upload/fengxianhuanshi.pdf.

2. Prospective Industry Research Institute, "2016 P2P Online Loan Market Volume and Platform Statistics" (in Chinese), Qianzhan, 2018, https://bg.qianzhan.com/report/detail/459/170116-76b6eb15.html.

3. Lufax, "P2P Lending Market in China," Lendit Commissioned Paper, April 2015, 20, https://blog.lendit.com/a-closer-look-at-chinas-p2p-lending -market/.

4. ACCA Global, *The Rise of Peer-to-Peer Lending in China: An Overview and Survey Case Study* (London, UK: Association of Chartered Certified Accountants, October 2015), 5, https://www.accaglobal.com/content /dam/ACCA_Global/Technical/manage/ea-china-p2p-lending.pdf.

5. Report Hall, "P2P Online Loan Industry Status and 2017 Development Trend Analysis: The Number of Platforms Shrinks" (in Chinese), Report Hall, July 31, 2018. http://www.chinabgao.com/freereport/76214.html; First Online Loan, "2017 National P2P Online Loan Industry Big Data Report" (in Chinese), Jianshu.com, January 9, 2018, https://www.jianshu.com/p /dc7a3c48354f.

6. Caroline Stern, Mikko Mäkinen, and Zongxin Qian, "FinTechs in China—With a Special Focus on Peer to Peer Lending," *Journal of Chinese Economic and Foreign Trade Studies* 10, no. 3 (2017): 215.

7. Xugang Yu, "Comparative Analysis of China's Banking Business Performance Based on SCP Perspective in Internet Financial Environment— Taking China Merchants Bank and Minsheng Bank as Examples" (in Chinese), *Financial Observation* 2 (2018): 137–138.

8. Online Loan Home. "P2P Active Investment and Borrowings" (in Chinese), Online Loan Home, 2018, https://www.wdzj.com/wdzj/front/search /index?type=12&referer=//www.wdzj.com/front/search/index&key=%25 E6%259C%2588%25E6%258A%25A5.

9. Sara Hsu, "Chinese P2P Players Yirendai and Hexindai On Making It in China's Lending Industry," *Forbes*, April 17, 2018. https://www.forbes.com /sites/sarahsu/2018/04/17/chinese-p2p-players-yirendai-and-hexindai-on -making-it-in-chinas-lending-industry/#1e1463383ed2.

10. Qizhi Tao, Dong Yizhe, and Ziming Lin, "Who Can Get Money? Evidence from the Chinese Peer-to-Peer Lending Platform," *Information Systems Frontiers* 19, no. 3 (2017): 425.

11. Zhihong Li, Lanteng Wu, and Hongting Tang, "Optimizing the Borrowing Limit and Interest Rate in P2P System: From Borrowers' Perspective," *Hindawi Scientific Programming* (2018): 2.

12. WIND, Wind Data, 2018, www.wind.com.cn.

13. Lei Xue. "Discussion of the Risks and Risk Control of P2P in China," *Modern Economy* 7 (2016): 399.

14. Ying-fei Zheng and Xiao-Jing Chen, "The Principal and Interest Guarantee of P2P Online Lending and Investors' Reaction" (in Chinese), *Financial Forum* 1 (2018): 66.

15. Zhongyan Yun, "Online Creditors Personally Remember How: 8 Loan Companies Let Me Accumulate Liabilities" (in Chinese), *Securities Times*, June 14, 2018, http://news.stcn.com/2018/0614/14315669.shtml.

16. Yun, "Online Creditors Personally Remember How."

17. Hang Yin, "P2P Lending Industry in China," *International Journal of Industrial and Business Management* 1, no. 4 (2017): 2.

18. Tianxiang Gu, "Nature and Regulation of P2P Network Lending Performance Guarantee Insurance" (in Chinese), *People's Justice* 4 (2018): 17.

19. Shen and Li, *Research on Network Borrowing Risk Relief Mechanism*, 22.

20. Robin Hui Huang, "Online P2P Lending and Regulatory Responses in China: Opportunities and Challenges," *European Business Organization Law Review* 19, no. 1 (2018): 71.

21. Reuters, "Leader of China's $9 billion Ezubao Online Scam Gets Life; 26 Jailed," Reuters, September 12, 2017, https://www.reuters.com/article/us-china-fraud/leader-of-chinas-9-billion-ezubao-online-scam-gets-life-26-jailed-idUSKCN1BN0J6.

22. Chuntian Hao and Lijuan Xu, "P2P Network Lending Risk and Response Research-Taking 'Ezubao' as an Example" (in Chinese), *Shandong Economy* 28, no. 7 (2018): 30.

23. Hao and Xu, "P2P Network Lending Risk and Response," 30.

24. Lingjian Yan, "Online Investment Wants to Double the Income but Can't Withdraw Cash" (in Chinese), *Modern Express Special Feature* (2018): 26.

25. China Banking Regulatory Commission (CBRC), "China Banking Regulatory Commission Ministry of Industry and Information Technology of the People's Republic of China Ministry of Public Security of the People's Republic of China National Internet Information Office Order" (in Chinese), CBRC, 2016, http://www.cbrc.gov.cn/chinese/home/docDOC_ReadView/D934AAE7E05849D185CD497936D767CF.html.

26. National Internet Finance Association of China (NIFAC), "NIFAC Rule on Self-Regulation of Information Disclosure," wdzj.com, October 28, 2016, https://www.wdzj.com/zhuanti/xpbz/.

27. CBRC, "Guideline on the Custodian Business for Online Lending," cbrc.gov.cn, February 22, 2017.

28. Ken Shih, *China Fintech Sector* (DBS Group Research, January 22, 2018), 2, https://www.dbs.com.sg/corporate/aics/pdfController.page?pdfpath=/content/article/pdf/ AIO/092018/180924_insights_bargain_hunting_opportunity.pdf.

29. Chenxi Jin, "P2P Network Lending Legal Risk Prevention" (in Chinese), *Economy and Law* 8 (2018): 73.

30. Yuejin Zhang, Haifeng Li, Mo Hai, Jiaxuan Li, and Aihua Li. "Information Technology and Quantitative Management: Determinants of Loan Funded Successful in Online P2P," *Procedia Computer Science* 122 (2017): 896.

31. Yan Feng, Xinlu Fan, and Yeujun Yoon. "Lenders and Borrowers' Strategies in Online Peer-to-Peer Lending Market: An Empirical Analysis of PPDAI.com," *Journal of Electronic Commerce Research* 16, no. 3 (2015): 242.

32. Dongyu Chen, Fujun Lai, and Zhangxi Lin. "A Trust Model for Online Peer-to-Peer Lending: A Lender's Perspective" (in Chinese), *Information Technology Management* 15 (2014): 239.

33. Tao, Dong, and Lin, "A Trust Model for Online Peer-to-Peer Lending," 42.

34. Hongfeng Peng and Ruifeng Xu, "Is the Interest Rate Pricing of the P2P Online Lending Platform Reasonable?—Based on Empirical Evidence of Renrendai" (in Chinese), *Financial Forum* 9, no. 273 (2018): 61.

35. Liao Li, Li Mengran, and Wang Zhengwei, "Smart Investors: Incomplete Market-Based Interest Rate and Risk Identification—Evidence from P2P Network Lending" (in Chinese), *Economic Research* 7 (2014): 125.

36. Wujun Sun, and Fan Xiaoying, "Borrowing Quota, Financier Heterogeneity and Success Rate of Lending—Experience Evidence from the P2P Platform 'Renrendai'" (in Chinese), *Journal of Beijing Institute of Technology* 32, no. 4 (2017): 97.

37. Weishi Song, "The Risk Preference of Investor Group in P2P Lending Pattern," *Financial Forum* 6 (2017): 21.

38. Cuiqing Jiang, Ruiya Wang, and Ding Yong, "P2P Network Lending Default Prediction Method Incorporating Soft Information" (in Chinese), *Chinese Journal of Management Science* 25, 11 (2017): 10.

39. Jinxi Hu and Xiaoxiao Zhang, "P2P Platform under the Influence of Shareholder Background, Default Risk and Business Risk" (in Chinese), *Journal of Shandong University* 4 (2018): 120.

40. Yu Gao, Shih-Heng Yu, and Yih-Chearng Shiue, "The Performance of the P2P Finance Industry in China," *Electronic Commerce Research and Applications* 30 (2018): 142.

41. Dongyu Chen, Xiaolin Li, and Fujun Lai, "Gender Discrimination in Online Peer-to-Peer Credit Lending: Evidence from Lending Platform in China," in *Proceedings of Pacific Asia Conference on Information* (2014), https://pdfs.semanticscholar.org/0e98/92cf8a085f194f3de43fe68da7d22b6bd10e.pdf.

42. Xinhua Dou, Xinbo Meng, and Fang-zhao Zhou, "Gender Discrimination in P2P Network Lending—Empirical Study on the Data from Renrendai," *Accounting Science* 32, no. 8 (2018): 121.

43. Nanfei Zhang, "Rationality of Investors in P2P Online Lending Platform with Guarantee Mechanism: Evidence in China," *Journal of Applied Finance and Banking* 7, no. 3 (2017): 1.

44. Jinxi Hu and Weishi Song, "The Rational Awareness and Trade-off Behavior of Investors in P2P Lending—An Empirical Analysis Based on the

Data of Renrendai" (in Chinese), *Journal of Financial Research* 445, no. 7 (2017): 86.

45. Xiao Lei, "Improving China's P2P Lending Regulatory System: An Examination of International Regulatory Experience," *US-China Law Review* 13 (2016): 460.

46. Xudong Wang, "The Establishment of College Students' Credit Evaluation System under the Background of Internet Finance" (in Chinese), *Fiscal Taxation* 9 (2018): 81.

47. Wei Li, "Analysis of the Status Quo of Internet Financial Loan in University Campus and Risk Prevention Measures" (in Chinese), *Financial Sight* 8 (2018): 39.

48. Ping and Sun, "Study on the Risk of P2P Lending for College Students and Preventive Measure" (in Chinese), *Management and Technology of SMEs* 2 (2018): 100.

49. Ronggang Zhang and Jingping Xu, "Path Selection and Risk Screening of Small Micro Enterprise Network Crowdfunding," *Science Research Management* 39, no. 8 (2018): 219.

50. Jian Feng, "Financing Research SME Financing Model and Implementation Path under the Internet Financial Environment" (in Chinese), *Financing Research* 23 (2018): 13.

51. Jiaxin Wang and Wang Juan, "A Review of Public Welfare Crowd Research on Social Media Text" (in Chinese), *E-Finance* 8 (2018): 47.

52. Yixin Su, "Legal Regulation and Improvement of Equity Crowdfunding in the Perspective of Internet Finance—Taking Xiamen Ximing District Equity Crowdfunding Platform 'Xiaxue Credit' as an Example" (in Chinese), *Journal of Anhui Vocational College of Police Officers* 4 (2017): 68.

53. Xianyin Zhu, "Analysis of the Connotation of Equity Crowdfunding and Its Legal Value," *Economic Law* 2018: 144.

54. Huasheng Zhu and Zach Zhizhong Zhou, "Analysis and Outlook of Applications of Blockchain Technology to Equity Crowdfunding in China," *Financial Innovation* 2 (2016): 29.

55. "Internet Equity Crowdfunding Platform Development Report" (in Chinese), *Beijing Time*, April 3, 2018, https://item.btime.com/m _93dd3311b06c07ce6?page=1.

4. Online Consumer Credit, Online Supply Chain Finance, and Internet Banks

1. Jianguo Shen and Jiakun Shen, "Research on the Development of Internet Finance" (in Chinese), *Digital Economy* 22 (2018): 188.

2. International Bank for Reconstruction and Development, World Bank, and People's Republic of China, *Toward Universal Financial Inclusion in China: Models, Challenges, and Global Lessons* (Washington, DC: World Bank Group, February 2018), https://openknowledge.worldbank.org/bitstream /handle/10986/29336/FinancialInclusion ChinaP158554.pdf?sequence=9.

3. Prospective Industry Research Institute, "2018 China's Internet Consumer Finance Development Status and Market Trends Analysis of the Explosive Growth of Lending Scale" (in Chinese), Qianzhan, February 8, 2019, https://www.qianzhan.com/analyst/detail/220/190201-20f83e47.html.

4. Sara Hsu, "This Chinese Credit Card Company Plans On Outsmarting Tencent and Alipay with a More Secure Product," *Forbes*, April 17, 2018, https://www.forbes.com/sites/sarahsu/2018/04/17/chinese-p2p -players-yirendai-and-hexindai-on-making-it-in-chinas-lending-industry /#1e1463383ed2.

5. People's Bank of China (in Chinese), 2018, www.pbc.gov.cn.

6. Prospective Industry Research Institute, "China's supply chain financial industry market status and trend analysis in 2019," Qianzhan, March 8, 2019, https://bg.qianzhan.com/report/detail/459/190308-db6b8559.html.

7. Jun Du and Li Jiaxin, "Research on Online Cooperation between E-commerce and Bank under Internet Environment" (in Chinese), *Journal of Gansu Sciences* 30, no. 1 (2018): 130.

8. Yuefei Hu, "Digital Supply Chain Finance in the 'Double Light' Era" (in Chinese), *Commercial Bank* (2018): 44.

9. Qishang Bank Co., Ltd., "Analysis of Six Specific Innovation Models of Bank Supply Chain Finance from the Perspective of Internet" (in Chinese), *China Banking Industry* 3, no. 81 (2018): 78.

10. Wen Zhang, "Research on the Innovation of Supply Chain Financial Model in Commercial Banks" (in Chinese), *National Chinese Core Journal Modern Finance* 7, (2018): 23.

11. Ministry of Industry and Information Technology, *2018 China Blockchain Industry White Paper* (in Chinese) (Beijing, China: Ministry of Industry and Information Technology Information Center, May 2018), http://www .miit.gov.cn/n1146290/n1146402/n1146445/c6180238/part/6180297 .pdf.

12. WeBank, *Annual Report of WeBank 2017* (WeBank, 2018), https:// www.webankcdn.net/s/hjupload/app/pdf/annual_report_2017.pdf.

5. Online Investment and Insurance

1. BCG, *Global Digital Wealth Management Report 2018* (Boston, MA: Boston Consulting Group Report, May 2018), 25, http://media-publications

.bcg.com/BCG_Global_Digital_Wealth_Management_Report_May_2018
_ENG.PDF.

2. JD Finance and CAICT, *Blockchain Solutions for Financial Services* (in Chinese) (JD Finance and CAICT, April 2018), 72, https://www.gwkjbc
.com/Uploads/2018-08-15/5b73d5f5b6636.pdf.

3. Annamaria Lusardi and Olivia S. Mitchell, "The Economic Importance of Financial Literacy: Theory and Evidence," *Journal of Economic Literature* 52, no. 1 (2014): 5.

4. Mingrui Xiao, "Virtual Speculation, Hundreds of Millions of Investment Funds Online Evaporation" (in Chinese), *Rule of Law Online* (2018): 47.

5. Xiao, "Virtual Speculation," 47.

6. Gordon Watts, "Fears Grow Over Chinese Investors Snared in $11 Billion Fraud Probe," *AI Times*, 2018, http://www.atimes.com/article/fears
-grow-chinese-investors-snared-11-billion-fraud-probe/.

7. Jingjing Yang, "Risk and Regulation of Chinese Online Investment Products," *Chinese Business Review* 16, no. 5 (2017): 234.

8. "Ant Financial Development Report" (in Chinese), *Beijing Time*, 2018, https://item.btime.com/40kea81aacr9d1bsrm0hnscgpfe?page=1.

9. "Ant Financial Development Report."

10. Jonathan Rogers, "Digital China: New Wealth Gets Wise," *Global Finance*, February 15, 2018, https://www.gfmag.com/magazine/february
-2018/digital-china-new-wealth-gets-wise.

11. Accenture, *The Rise of Robo-Advice* (Accenture, 2015), https://www
.accenture.com/_acnmedia/PDF-2/Accenture-Wealth-Management-Rise
-of-Robo-Advice.pdf.

12. Gewei Wu, "Analysis of the Influence of Internet Finance on the Development of Real Estate Industry" (in Chinese), *Technology and Economic Guide* 26 (2018): 180.

13. Jiaqi Jian and Wu Fan, "Analysis of the Innovative Development of Personal Banking Business of Commercial Banks in the Internet Finance Era under the New Normal" (in Chinese), *Financial Forum* 5 (2018): 161.

14. Ping An Finance, *2017 Internet Wealth Management White Paper* (Ping An Finance, January 22, 2018), https://www.wdzj.com/hjzs/ptsj
/20180122/505353-1.html.

15. Hao Wen, "Yirendai APP Heavy Upgrade: Wealth Management Begins with the Promotion of 'Financial Business' " (in Chinese), Sohu, May 25, 2019, http://www.sohu.com/a/316378365_115931.

16. Chuanming Zhang, "Everbright Bank's New On-line 'Wealth Check' Features Eye Science Hedge" (in Chinese), Zhongxin Net Jiangsu, May 29, 2019, http://www.js.chinanews.com/75/2019/0529/59604.html.

17. China Banking News, "Tencent's Surging Fintech Growth Driven by Online Wealth Management," China Banking News, February 2019,

http://www.chinabankingnews.com/2019/02/19/tencents-fintech
-growth-driven-by-online-wealth-management/.

18. Oliver Wyman, *China Credit-Tech Market Report* (Oliver Wyman, April 2019), https://www.oliverwyman.com/content/dam/oliver-wyman /v2/publications/2019/apr/china-credit-tech-market-report-4.pdf.

19. Oliver Wyman, *China Insuretech: Industry Report* (Oliver Wyman, October 2016), 9, https://www.oliverwyman.com/content/dam/oliver -wyman/global/en/2016/oct/OliverWyman_ChinaInsuretech.pdf.

20. Xu Meng, "Third Party Network Platform Engaged in Insurance Business Legal Regulation" (in Chinese), *Insurance Law* (2018): 58.

21. Xiaodong Liu, "Application Research and Development Strategies of Insurance E-commerce in China" (in Chinese), *Management Science, Education Science and Human Development* 72 (2017): 246.

22. JD Finance and CAICT, *Blockchain Solutions for Financial Services.*

23. International Bank for Reconstruction and Development, World Bank, and People's Republic of China, *Toward Universal Financial Inclusion in China Models, Challenges, and Global Lessons* (Washington, DC: World Bank Group, February 2018), https://openknowledge.worldbank.org/bitstream /handle/10986/29336/FinancialInclusion ChinaP158554.pdf?sequence=9.

24. Ken Shih and Keith Tsang, *China Insurance Sector* (DBS Research, November 1, 2017), 34.

25. Gang Hu, "Research on Information Security Management Strategy of P Insurance Company Network Mall" (in Chinese), *Modern Information Technology*, 2017, 1, http://kns.cnki.net/kcms/detail/44.1736.TN.20180212 .1021.108.html.

26. International Bank for Reconstruction and Development, World Bank, and People's Republic of China, *Toward Universal Financial Inclusion in China.*

27. Yang Xiao, "Internet Insurance Market Analysis Report for the First Half of 2017" (in Chinese), csai.cn, August 25, 2017, https://www.csai.cn /baoxian/1247123.html.

28. Xiao, "Internet Insurance Market Analysis."

29. Xiao, "Internet Insurance Market Analysis."

30. Liu, "Application Research and Development Strategies," 246.

31. Jianmin Zhang, "Is Network Security Insurance Ready?" *Insurance*, July 1, 2017, 58.

32. Xu, "Third Party Network Platform," 58.

33. Yiyi Yi, "On the Impact of China's Internet Insurance Development on Traditional Insurance—Taking 'Zhongan Insurance' as an Example" (in Chinese), *Inner Mongolia Science Technology and Economy* 2 (2018): 36.

34. Shuang Shuang, "Research on the Status Quo of Internet Insurance Development and Business Management Model in China—Taking Zhongan

Online as an Example" (in Chinese), ems86.com, 2018, http://www.ems86
.com/fuwu/html/?69229.html.

35. Hajime Minamimoto, "What Zhong An Group Knows About Efficient
Insurance System Development?" *Nomura Research Institute* 277 (February 13,
2018), 3, https://www.nri.com/~/media/PDF/global/opinion/lakyara/2018
/lkr2018277.pdf.

36. Sabine L. B. VanderLinden, Shan M. Millie, Nicole Anderson, and
Susanne Chishti, *The Insuretech Book* (Chichester, UK: Wiley, 2018).

37. Emma Lee, "Online Insurance Company Zhong An Rolled Out First
Product Zhonglebao," Technode, December 6, 2013, http://technode.com
/2013/12/06/online-insurance-company-zhong-an-rolled-out-first-product
-zhonglebao/.

38. Laura He, "Zhong An Generates 70pc of 2017 Car Insurance Premiums
in Just One Month," *South China Morning Post*, February 4, 2018, https://
www.scmp.com/business/companies/article/2131449/zhongan-generates
-70pc-2017-car-insurance-premiums-just-one-month.

39. Shih and Tsang, *China Insurance Sector*, 32.

40. Investor Education Center, *Retail Investor Study Research Report*
(Hong Kong: Investor Education Center, December 2017).

41. "Top FinTech Startups in Wealthtech," Fintechnews.hk, August 2017.
http://fintechnews.hk/top-20-fintech-startups-hong-kong/.

42. Shih and Tsang, *China Insurance Sector*, 38.

6. Blockchain Finance and Virtual Currencies

1. Ministry of Industry and Information Technology, *2018 China Blockchain Industry White Paper* (in Chinese) (Beijing, China: Ministry of Industry
and Information Technology Information Center, May 2018).

2. China Industry Information Network, "Analysis of the Development
Status and Industry Development Trend of China's Blockchain Industry in
2018," China Industry Information Network, June 14, 2018, http://www
.chyxx.com/industry/201806/649549.html.

3. Xingnan Wang and Rui Huang, *Fintech in China's Capital Market* (Nomura,
September 2017), 11, https://www.nomurafoundation.or.jp/wordpress/wp
-content/uploads/2017/09/NJACM2-1AU17-03_CHINA.pdf.

4. PricewaterhouseCoopers (PwC), *2018 Market Survey Report for (Non-
financial) Application of Blockchain in China* (PwC, 2018), 8, https://www
.pwccn.com/en/risk-assurance/2018-china-blockchain-survery-report-en.pdf.

5. Wolfie Zhao, "Chinese Bank Issues Securities Worth $66 Million on a
Blockchain," Coindesk, August 21, 2018, https://www.coindesk.com/china
-zheshang-bank-issues-securities-worth-66-million-on-blockchain/.

6. Lili Wang and Hong Wang, "Analysis on the Innovation Practice of the Bill Market under the Background of Internet Finance" (in Chinese), *Journal of Wuhu Vocational and Technical College* 20, no. 2 (2018): 37.

7. Xinhua, "Xi Jinping: Speech at the Nineteenth Academician Conference of the Chinese Academy of Sciences and the Fourteenth Academician Conference of the Chinese Academy of Engineering," Xinhuanet, May 28, 2018, http://www.xinhuanet.com/politics/2018-05/28/c_1122901308.htm.

8. Investment Research Institute, *2018 Blockchain Investment and Financing Report* (in Chinese) (Investment Research Institute, 2018), https://www.chinaventure.com.cn/cmsmodel/report/detail/1422.shtml.

9. China Blockchain Technology and Industry Development Forum, *China Blockchain Technology and Application Development White Paper* (in Chinese), Chainb.com, 2016, http://chainb.com/download/工信部-中国区块链技术和应用发展白皮书1014.pdf.

10. Heng Hou, "The Application of Blockchain Technology in E-Government in China," 2017 Twenty-Sixth International Conference on Computer Communication and Networks (ICCCN), July 31–August 3, 2017.

11. Miryam Amsili, "Blockchain In China: Local Is Everything," Supchina, August 28, 2018, https://supchina.com/2018/08/28/blockchain-in-china-local-is-everything/.

12. China Industry Information Network, "Analysis of the Development Status and Industry Development Trend."

13. Stan Schroeder, "Cryptocurrency Verge Gets Hacked with a Dangerous New Attack," Mashable, April 5, 2018, https://mashable.com/2018/04/05/verge-crypto-hack/#w6a63u5U0iqJ.

14. Jimmy Aki, "Police Launch Investigation Into $3.6 Million Cryptopia Hack," Blockonomi, January 17, 2019, https://blockonomi.com/police-investigation-cryptopia-hack/.

15. "The Attitude of the Regulatory Authorities to the Tolerance and Support of the Blockchain" (in Chinese), *China News Weekly*, February 2, 2018, http://www.chinanews.com/cj/2018/02-02/8439739.shtml.

16. MTS Staff, "China Emerges as Global Blockchain Leader," Martech Series, June 26, 2019, https://martechseries.com/technology/china-emerges-global-blockchain-leader/.

17. Garrick Hileman and Michel Rauchs, *Global Blockchain Benchmarking Study* (Cambridge: Cambridge Centre for Alternative Finance, 2017), 33.

18. PricewaterhouseCoopers (PwC), *PWC's Global Blockchain Survey 2018* (PwC, 2018), 3, https://www.pwccn.com/en/research-and-insights/publications/global-blockchain-survey-2018/global-blockchain-survey-2018-report.pdf.

19. China Institute of Information and Communications (CAICT), *Internet Investment and Financing in the Second Quarter of 2018* (in Chinese)

(CAICT, 2018), 7, http://www.caict.ac.cn/kxyj/qwfb/qwsj/201807/P020 180720343745695019.pdf.

20. Yan Jiang, "Impact and Prospect of Digital Currency Based on the Perspective of Shared Finance" (in Chinese), *Finance and Economy* (2018): 65.

21. "ICO Is Characterized as Suspected of Illegal Fundraising for a Night of Rich Dreams" (in Chinese), Caixin, September 2, 2017, http://finance.caixin.com/2017-09-02/101139644.html.

22. Allen Scott, "China Celebrates Killing Its Bitcoin Exchanges as CNY Volume Falls Under 1 Percent," Bitcoinist, July 10, 2018, https://bitcoinist.com/china-bitcoin-exchanges-volume-falls-1/.

23. Yao Qian, "Technical Considerations of the Central Bank's Digital Currency," Yicai News, March 8, 2018, https://www.yicai.com/news/5404436.html.

24. Endong Xu, Xiao Liu, Jun Wu, and Xiaoyu Shi, "The Exploration of the Central Bank's Legal Digital Currency" (in Chinese), *Times Finance* 7 (2018): 14.

25. Yuwen Zhang, "Feasibility Analysis of China's Central Bank Digital Currency Based on the Change of Currency Form" (in Chinese), *Financial Forum* 1 (2018): 127.

26. Yining Zheng, "The Impact of the Central Bank's Plan to Issue Digital Currency on Monetary Policy" (in Chinese), *Financial View* 33 (2017): 89.

27. Blockchain Forum, "The Central Bank Applies for a Digital Wallet Patent or Will Open the ICO Again" (in Chinese), Jung Media, June 2018, http://www.jungmedia.cn/news/i-9079.html.

28. Jinfu Du, "Digital Currency Issuance Theory and Path Selection" (in Chinese), *Expert Forum* (2018): 35.

29. Xiangguang Chen and Huang Zeqing, "The Formation Mechanism of Currency Anchor and Its Maintenance of Currency Quality—Also on the Anchor of Digital Currency" (in Chinese), *Journal of Renmin University of China* 4 (2018): 86.

30. Ben Kaiser, Mireya Jurado, and Alex Ledger, "The Looming Threat of China: An Analysis of Chinese Influence on Bitcoin" (arXiv working paper, Cornell University, October 5, 2018), 5, https://arxiv.org/pdf/1810.02466.pdf.

31. "BTC/USD–Bitcoin US Dollar," Investing.com, 2019, https://www.investing.com/crypto/bitcoin/btc-usd-historical-data.

7. Disruption of Traditional Banking

1. Ying Wang, "How to Build Integrated Services for Commercial Banks in the Internet + Era" (in Chinese), *Time Finance* 7 (2018): 94.

2. Ruihua Wang, "Reinterpretation of Money Supply under the Internet Environment" (in Chinese), *Bank Management* 3 (2018): 55.

3. Yiou Think Tank, *Financial Technology Company Service Banking Research Report* (in Chinese) (Yiou Think Tank, September 6, 2018), 16, https://www.iyiou.com/intelligence/report576.

4. Wei Liao, Jiang Tuanbiao, and Yu Weifeng, "The Impact of Internet Finance on Bank Innovation Capability—An Empirical Study Based on Panel Data of 58 Commercial Banks" (in Chinese), *Finance and Economics* 9 (2018): 52.

5. Weifeng Yu and Yi Zhou, "Internet Finance, Commercial Bank Scale and Risk" (in Chinese), *Journal of Yunnan University of Finance and Economics* 189, no. 1 (2018).

6. Cheng Qian, "Exploration on the Transformation and Innovation of Local Small and Medium-sized Banks Under the Impact of Internet Finance" (in Chinese), *Hangzhou Science and Technology* 6 (2017): 57.

7. Yan Li, "The Influence of Internet Finance on Traditional Commercial Banks and Countermeasures—Taking Minsheng Bank as an Example," *National Circulation Economy* 22 (2017): 59.

8. Shengmin Zhao and Liu Xiaotian, "China's Macroprudential Policy Research on Coordination Issues," *Contemporary Finance and Economics* 2 (2018): 49.

9. Ying Chen, "Technology and Economic Guide, Analysis on the Innovation Strategy of Commercial Bank Business under the Background of Internet Finance," *Science and Technology Economics Guide* 26, no. 10 (2018): 225.

10. Asia Pacific Foundation of Canada, *Will Fintech Upend the Banking Sector? From China's Experience* (Vancouver, BC: Asia Pacific Foundation of Canada, 2016), 4, https://www.asiapacific.ca/sites/default/files/filefield/fintech-report-final.pdf.

11. Zhiding Cao, "The Impact of Internet Finance on Traditional Banks and Policy Suggestions" (in Chinese), *Times Finance* 1 (2018): 64.

12. Maggie Zhang, "China Construction Bank Opens a Branch Managed by Robots," *South China Morning Post*, April 11, 2018, https://www.scmp.com/business/companies/article/2141203/meet-new-face-branch-banking.

13. Yufeng Dong, "Thoughts and Suggestions on the Development of Postal Savings Bank in the Internet Financial Era" (in Chinese), *Finance and Economy* 6 (2018): 56.

14. Lipeng He, "Research on the Innovation Strategy of Commercial Banks Under the Impact of Internet Finance" (in Chinese), *Financial Forum* 1 (2018): 138.

15. Ying Wang, "How to Build Integrated Services for Commercial Banks," 94.

16. "China's Leaders in Fintech 2017," *Euromoney*, December 19, 2017, https://www.euromoney.com/article/b1634tc7d2p1t8/china39s-leaders-in -fintech-2017.

17. International Bank for Reconstruction and Development, World Bank, and People's Republic of China, *Toward Universal Financial Inclusion in China Models, Challenges, and Global Lessons* (Washington, DC: World Bank Group, February 2018), https://openknowledge.worldbank.org/bitstream /handle/10986/29336/FinancialInclusion ChinaP158554.pdf?sequence=9.

18. Xugang Yu, "Comparative Analysis of China's Banking Business Performance Based on SCP Perspective in Internet Financial Environment—Taking China Merchants Bank and Minsheng Bank as Examples" (in Chinese), *Financial Observation* 2 (2018): 137.

19. Reuters, "Chairman of Bank of Beijing: Banks Should Actively Embrace Financial Innovation and Change," May 16, 2019, http://finance.sina.com .cn/meeting/2018-05-16/doc-ihapkuvm6941135.shtml.

20. Wei Sun, "Analysis of the Impact of Internet Finance Development on China's Commercial Banks and Countermeasures" (in Chinese), *Modern Marketing* (2018): 98.

21. Jianwen Qin, Tao Wang, and Bangding Huang, "The Study of Chinese Listed Bank's Efficiency Growth Mode in Internet Finance Era—Based on Full-Combination DEA-PCA Model," *American Journal of Industrial and Business Management* 6, no. 11 (2016): 1032.

22. Bing Yang, "List of Direct Selling Banks in China in the First Half of 2018" (in Chinese), *Internet Weekly*, August 5, 2018, 38.

23. Mengyao Lin and Chen Xiding, "The Impact of Internet Finance on Domestic City Commercial Banks and Countermeasures" (in Chinese), *Time Financial* 11, no. 679 (2017): 78.

24. Guo-qing Bai and Zhou Hai-yang, "The Impact of Internet Finance on the Strategic Transformation of Rural Financial Institutions" (in Chinese), *Value Engineering* 14 (2018): 41.

25. Chunli Wang, "Auditing Problems and Countermeasures of Commercial Banks in the Age of Internet Finance" (in Chinese), *Financial Economy* 5 (2018): 53.

26. Georgina Lee, "Chinese Banks Boost Fintech Spending and Launch Services to Counter Competition from Internet Giants," *South China Morning Post*, April 5, 2019, https://www.scmp.com/business/banking-finance /article/3004877/chinese-banks-boost-fintech-spending-and-launch-services.

27. Yuyao Liu, "Research on the Impact of Internet Finance Development on Industrial and Commercial Bank Management" (in Chinese), *Journal of Heilongjiang University of Technology* 18, no. 3 (2018): 112.

28. Zhuming Chen, Yushan Li, Yawen Wu, and Junjun Luo, "The Transition from Traditional Banking to Mobile Internet Finance: An Organizational

Innovation Perspective—A Comparative Study of Citibank and ICBC," *Financial Innovation* 3, no. 12 (2017), https://jfin-swufe.springeropen .com/articles/10.1186/s40854-017-0062-0.

29. Jingjing Zhang, "The Problems and Countermeasures of ICBC Developing Internet Finance" (in Chinese), *Times Finance* 7 (2018): 135.

30. Nanjing Rural Finance Society Research Group, "Innovative Practice and Enlightenment of Commercial Bank Retail Transformation" (in Chinese), *National Chinese Core Journal Modern Finance* 7 (2018): 6.

31. Ning Jiang, "Analysis on the Transformation of Agricultural Banks Promoting Direct Banks Under Internet Finance" (in Chinese), *National Chinese Core Journal Modern Finance* 11, no. 417 (2017).

8. Risks of Fintech and Regulatory Technology

1. Min Li, "Research on the Choice of Supervision Mode and Optimization Path of Financial Technology: Rethinking on the Supervision Sandbox Model" (in Chinese), *Journal of Financial Management Research* (November 2017): 27.

2. Yaqin Yang, "Application Analysis of Big Data Anti-fraud in Bank Internet Finance Innovation Business" (in Chinese), *Modern Economic Information* (2018): 328.

3. Junxian Yao, "Research on New Threats and Protection Technologies Faced by Bank Internet Financial Platform" (in Chinese), *Technical Application* (September 2017): 76.

4. Yao, "Research on New Threats and Protection Technologies," 76.

5. Financial Conduct Authority, "RegTech," https://innovate.fca.org.uk /innovation-hub/regtech-programme.

6. Institute of International Finance, "RegTech 2019," https://www.iif .com/ topics/regtech.

7. iYiou.com, "Sun Guofeng, Director of the Bank of China Institute of Finance: In-depth Interpretation of Regulatory Technology," November 10, 2018, https://www.iyiou.com/p/85155.html.

8. Guofeng Sun, "Developing Regulatory Technology to Build a New Financial Ecology" (in Chinese), *Tsinghua Financial Review* 3 (2018): 16.

9. JD Digits Research Institute, *Suptech: The Use of Regulatory Technology in the Regulatory Side* (in Chinese) (JD Finance Report, August 2018).

10. BCG, *Global Risk 2017: Staying the Course in Banking* (Boston, MA: Boston Consulting Group Report, March 2017), 5, http://image-src.bcg.com/BCG _COM/BCG-Staying-the-Course-in-Banking-Mar-2017_tcm9-146794.pdf.

11. Financial Stability Board, "Financial Stability Implications from FinTech Supervisory and Regulatory Issues that Merit Authorities' Attention," June 27, 2017, https://www.fsb.org/wp-content/uploads/R270617.pdf.

12. China Institute of Information and Communications (CAICT), *Internet Investment and Financing in the Second Quarter of 2018* (in Chinese) (China Institute of Information and Communications, 2018), 7, http://www.caict.ac.cn/kxyj/qwfb/qwsj/201807/P020180720343745695019.pdf.

13. Dagong Credit Data Co., *Dagong Data Internet Finance Online Loan Platform Early Warning Watch List Report* (in Chinese) (Dagong Credit Data Co., 2015), 1, http://iof.hexun.com/upload/yjgc.pdf.

14. Liqiang Wang, "Financial Technology Protects Financial Security" (in Chinese), Ant Financial Service ATEC City Summit, The New Force of Digital Finance, February 24, 2019, https://www.jianshu.com/p/75af67e247b2.

15. Yihan Zhang, "Analysis on the Development Path of Commercial Bank's Financial Management Business Under the Internet Financial Environment," *China International Business* 7 (2018): 296.

9. Credit Reporting and Key Financial Technologies

1. Liaowang Institute and China Financial Weekly, *China Social Credit System Development Report 2017* (Liaowang Institute and China Financial Weekly, 2017).

2. Liaowang Institute and China Financial Weekly, *China Social Credit System.*

3. Yuzhe Zhang, Peng Qinqin, and Dong Tongjian, "China Gives Little Credit to Companies Handpicked to Develop Credit-Reporting Sector," Caixin, May 15, 2017, https://www.caixinglobal.com/2017-05-15/china-gives-little-credit-to-companies-handpicked-to-develop-credit-reporting-sector-101089851.html.

4. Slavka Eley, "FinTech and Cloud in Banking," keynote speech, EBF Cloud Banking Conference, July 12, 2017, Brussels, Belgium, 5, https://eba.europa.eu/documents/10180/2055539/Slavka+Eley+-+Keynote+speech+at+the+EBF+Cloud+banking+Conference.pdf.

5. Oracle, *Cloud Computing in Financial Services: A Banker's Guide* (Redwood Shores, CA: Oracle, November 2015), 2, http://www.oracle.com/us/industries/financial-services/cloud-compute-financial-services-wp-3124965.pdf.

6. Matthew Murphy and Fei Dang, "Cloud Computing in China," Lexology, March 21, 2019, https://www.lexology.com/library/detail.aspx?g=998fe1a0-6634-41e7-a670-19ca406709e5.

7. Echo Xie, "China Working on Data Privacy Law but Enforcement Is a Stumbling Block," *South China Morning Post*, May 5, 2019, https://www.scmp.com/news/china/politics/article/3008844/china-working-data-privacy-law-enforcement-stumbling-block.

8. Rebecca Lewis, John McPartland, and Rajeev Ranjan, "Blockchain and Financial Market Innovation," *Economic Perspectives* 41, no. (2017): 12, https://www.chicagofed.org/publications/economic-perspectives/2017/7.

9. International Finance Corporation (IFC), *Blockchain: Opportunities for Private Enterprises in Emerging Markets* (Washington, DC: IFC, 2019), 4.

10. Zhang Di, "Financial Technology 2019 Is Booming: Artificial Intelligence, Blockchain Applications Are Accelerating" (in Chinese), Asiaott, February 13, 2019, https://www.asiaott.com/2019/02/13-178850.html.

11. Financial Stability Board (FSB), *Artificial Intelligence and Machine Learning in Financial Services: Market Developments and Financial Stability Implications* (Basel, Switzerland: FSB, November 1, 2017), 4, http://www.fsb.org/wp-content/uploads/P011117.pdf.

12. Baohong He, Zhang Xueli, Han Han, He Yang, Zhao Bo, Zhang Xiaoye, and Xu Yijun, *China's Financial Technology Frontier Technology Development Trend and Application Scenario Research* (in Chinese) (China Institute of Information and Communications Cloud Computing and Big Data Research Institute, 2018), http://www.caict.ac.cn/kxyj/qwfb/ztbg/201804/P020180116491991162222.pdf.

13. Gregory C. Allen, *Understanding China's AI Strategy: Clues to Chinese Strategic Thinking on Artificial Intelligence and National Security* (Zurich, Germany: Center for Security Studies, February 20, 2019), 4, http://www.css.ethz.ch/en/services/digital-library/articles/article.html/f561ac7c-465b-4add-9619-7d047f71547a/pdf.

14. Debmalya Dasbarman, Chaitanya Tallam, and Karunesh Mohan, *Future of Consumer Banking: The Augmented Way* (Bengaluru, India: Infosys, 2018), 4, https://www.infosys.com/industries/financial-services/white-papers/Documents/future-consumer-banking.pdf.

15. Alan McIntyre, Kelley Conway, Peter Sidebottom, Schira Lillis, and Peter McElwaine-John, *Building the Future-Ready Bank: Banking Technology Vision 2018* (Dublin, Ireland: Accenture, 2018), 12, https://www.accenture.com/_acnmedia/PDF-75/Accenture-Banking-Technology-Vision-2018.pdf.

16. Sean Creehan and Cindy Li, "Asia's Open Banking Push," *Federal Reserve Bank of San Francisco* (Pacific Exchange blog), December 5, 2018, https://www.frbsf.org/banking/asia-program/pacific-exchange-blog/asias-open-banking-push/.

17. Elsa B. Kania and John K. Costello, *Quantum Hegemony? China's Ambitions and the Challenge to U.S. Innovation Leadership* (Washington, DC: Center for a New American Security, September 2018), 14, https://s3.amazonaws.com/files.cnas.org/documents/CNASReport-Quantum-Tech_FINAL.pdf?mtime=20180912133406.

18. Kania and Costello, *Quantum Hegemony*, 14.

19. Siyan Yan, "Robotic Process Automation Opportunities in the Financial Industry," Chinabyte, May 21, 2018, http://info.chinabyte.com/464/245964.shtml.

10. Outlook and Summing Up

1. Qian Xu, "Research on the Demand of Financial Talents in Small and Medium Cities Under the Background of Internet—Taking Lianyungang City, Jiangsu Province as an Example" (in Chinese), *Times Finance* 7 (2018): 113.

2. Jianjun Li and Yongbin Lu, "Thoughts on the Construction of Internet Finance Courses and Talents Training Mode" (in Chinese), *Chinese University Teaching* 5 (2018): 64.

3. JRJ, "23 percent of China's Financial Industry Will Be Disrupted by AI in the Next 10 Years" (in Chinese), JRJ.com, May 5, 2018, http://money.jrj.com.cn/2018/05/05091024496044.shtml.

4. PricewaterhouseCoopers (PwC), *Global Fintech Survey China Summary 2017* (PwC Report, 2017), 10, https://www.pwccn.com/en/financial-services/publications/fintech/global-fintech-survey-china-summary-jun2017.pdf.

5. Bingchun An, Zhang Jian, and Tao Rong, "The Big-Data-Based Construction Thinking for Internet Finance" (in Chinese), *Financial Information Security* 37, no. 8 (2018): 7.

6. Wenbi Huang and Jiayi Chen, "Analysis of Mobile Terminal Security in Internet Finance Age" (in Chinese), *Computer Knowledge and Technology* 14, no. 19 (2018): 22.

7. Lin He, Shuo Cheng, Guan-yi tong Zhang, and Le Zhang, "Desire Demand of Internet Finance for Farmers and Expanding of Rural Financial Market," *Guangdong Agricultural Science* 45, no. 5 (2018): 142.

8. Gemalto, "2017 Data Breach Level Index: Full Year Results Are In . . .," *Gemalto* (blog), April 13, 2018, https://blog.gemalto.com/security/2018/04/13/data-breach-stats-for-2017-full-year-results-are-in/.

9. Jia Du, "Legal Realization Mechanism of Financial Consumer Rights and Interests Protection in the Internet Age" (in Chinese), *Legal System Expo* 8 (2018): 179.

10. Xiling Zheng, "Research on the Identification and Inclination Protection of Internet Finance Consumers" (in Chinese), *Hainan Finance* 8 (2018): 51.

Bibliography

ACCA Global. *The Rise of Peer-to-Peer Lending in China: An Overview and Survey Case Study.* London: Association of Chartered Certified Accountants, October 2015. https://www.accaglobal.com/content/dam/ACCA_Global /Technical/manage/ea-china-p2p-lending.pdf.

Accenture. "Global Venture Capital Investment in Fintech Industry Set Record in 2017, Driven by Surge in India, US and UK, Accenture Analysis Finds." *Accenture Newsroom,* February 28, 2018. https://newsroom.accenture .com/news/global-venture-capital-investment-in-fintech-industry-set-record -in-2017-driven-by-surge-in-india-us-and-uk-accenture-analysis-finds.htm.

Accenture. "The Rise of Robo-Advice." Accenture, 2015. https://www.accenture .com/_acnmedia/PDF-2/Accenture-Wealth-Management-Rise-of-Robo -Advice.pdf.

Ai Media Consulting. "2017–2018 China Third Party Mobile Payment Market Research Report" (in Chinese). Ai Media Report, April 23, 2018. http:// www.iimedia.cn/61209.html.

Akerlof, George A. "The Market for 'Lemons.' Quality Uncertainty and the Market Mechanism." *Quarterly Journal of Economics* 84, no. 3 (1970): 488–500.

Aki, Jimmy. "Police Launch Investigation Into $3.6 Million Cryptopia Hack." Blockonomi, January 17, 2019. https://blockonomi.com/police -investigation-cryptopia-hack/.

Alibaba Cloud. "Cloud Computing Trends in China." Alibaba Cloud, 2016. http://alicloud-common.oss-ap-southeast-1.aliyuncs.com/Updated _Materials/Infopaper%20-%20Cloud%20Computing%20Trends%20in%20 China%20-%20updated.pdf.

Allen, Gregory C. *Understanding China's AI Strategy: Clues to Chinese Strategic Thinking on Artificial Intelligence and National Security.* Zurich, Germany: Center for Security Studies, February 20, 2019. http://www

.css.ethz.ch/en/services/digital-library/articles/article.html/f561ac7c
-465b-4add-9619-7d047f71547a/pdf.

Amsili, Miryam. "Blockchain in China: Local Is Everything." Supchina, August
28, 2018. https://supchina.com/2018/08/28/blockchain-in-china-local
-is-everything/.

An, Bingchun, Zhang Jian, and Tao Rong. "The Big-Data-Based Construction
Thinking for Internet Finance" (in Chinese). *Financial Information Security*
37, no. 8 (2018): 7–10.

Anderson, Chris. *The Long Tail: Why the Future of Business Is Selling Less of
More.* New York: Hachette Books, 2004.

"Ant Financial Development Report" (in Chinese). *Beijing Time*, 2018. https://
item.btime.com/40kea81aacr9d1bsrm0hnscgpfe?page=1.

Asia Pacific Foundation of Canada. *Will Fintech Upend the Banking Sector?
From China's Experience.* Vancouver, BC: Asia Pacific Foundation of Canada,
2016. https://www.asiapacific.ca/sites/default/files/filefield/fintech-report
-final.pdf.

"The Attitude of the Regulatory Authorities to the Tolerance and Support
of the Blockchain" (in Chinese). *China News Weekly*, February 2, 2018.
http://www.chinanews.com/cj/2018/02-02/8439739.shtml.

Bai, Guo-qing, and Zhou Hai-yang. "The Impact of Internet Finance on
the Strategic Transformation of Rural Financial Institutions" (in Chinese).
Value Engineering 14 (2018): 41–43.

BCG. *Global Digital Wealth Management Report 2018.* Boston, MA: Boston
Consulting Group Report, May 2018. http://media-publications.bcg.com
/BCG_Global_Digital_Wealth_Management_Report_May_2018_ENG
.PDF.

———. *Global Risk 2017: Staying the Course in Banking.* Boston, MA: Boston
Consulting Group Report, March 2017. http://image-src.bcg.com/BCG
_COM/BCG-Staying-the-Course-in-Banking-Mar-2017_tcm9-146794.pdf.

Blockchain Forum. "The Central Bank Applies for a Digital Wallet Patent or
Will Open the ICO Again" (in Chinese). Jung Media, June 2018. http://
www.jungmedia.cn/news/i-9079.html.

Bloomberg. "Tencent Sets Up an Online Trading Platform for Chinese Bonds."
Bloomberg, June 22, 2018. https://www.scmp.com/tech/enterprises/article
/2152029/tencent-sets-online-trading-platform-chinese-bonds.

———. "China Planning Major Purge of $176 Billion Loan Market." Bloomberg
.com, November 29, 2018. https://www.bloomberg.com/news/articles
/2018-11-29/china-is-said-to-plan-major-purge-of-176-billion-loan-market.

Bower, Joseph, and Clayton M. Christensen. "Disruptive Technologies:
Catching the Wave." *Harvard Business Review* (January-February 1995).

"BTC/USD–Bitcoin US Dollar." Investing.com, 2019. https://www.investing
.com/crypto/bitcoin/btc-usd-historical-data.

Cao, Zhiding. "The Impact of Internet Finance on Traditional Banks and Policy Suggestions" (in Chinese). *Times Finance* 1 (2018): 64–65.

Capgemini and BNP Paribas. *World Payments Report 2017.* Capgemini, 2017. https://www.worldpaymentsreport.com.

Chen, Celia, and Iris Deng. "WeChat Pay to Keep Overseas Focus on Outbound Tourism Instead of Offering More Local Wallets." *South China Morning Post,* July 11, 2018. https://www.scmp.com/tech/article/2154828/wechat-pay-keep-overseas-focus-outbound-tourism-instead-offering-more-local.

Chen, Dongyu, Fujun Lai, and Zhangxi Lin. "A Trust Model for Online Peer-to-Peer Lending: A Lender's Perspective" (in Chinese). *Information Technology Management* 15 (2014): 239–254.

Chen, Dongyu, Xiaolin Li, and Fujun Lai. "Gender Discrimination in Online Peer-to-Peer Credit Lending: Evidence from Lending Platform in China." *Proceedings of the Pacific Asia Conference on Information* (2014). https://pdfs.semanticscholar.org/0e98/92cf8a085f194f3de43fe68da7d22b6bd10e.pdf.

Chen, Xiangguang, and Huang Zeqing. "The Formation Mechanism of Currency Anchor and Its Maintenance of Currency Quality—Also on the Anchor of Digital Currency" (in Chinese). *Journal of Renmin University of China* 4 (2018): 86–94.

Chen, Ying. "Technology and Economic Guide, Analysis on the Innovation Strategy of Commercial Bank Business Under the Background of Internet Finance." *Science and Technology Economics Guide* 26, no. 10 (2018): 225.

Chen, Zhu, and Huagui Hong. "The Impact of Internet Finance on Systematic Risks in China's Banking Industry—An Empirical Study Based on SCCA Model and Stepwise Regression Method." *Financial Economics Research* 33, no. 2 (2018): 50–59.

Chen, Zhuming, Yushan Li, Yawen Wu, and Junjun Luo. "The Transition from Traditional Banking to Mobile Internet Finance: An Organizational Innovation Perspective—A Comparative Study of Citibank and ICBC." *Financial Innovation* 3, no. 12 (2017). https://jfin-swufe.springeropen.com/articles/10.1186/s40854-017-0062-0.

China Banking News. "Tencent's Surging Fintech Growth Driven by Online Wealth Management." China Banking News, February 2019. http://www.chinabankingnews.com/2019/02/19/tencents-fintech-growth-driven-by-online-wealth-management/.

China Banking Regulatory Commission (CBRC). "China Banking Regulatory Commission Ministry of Industry and Information Technology of the People's Republic of China Ministry of Public Security of the People's Republic of China National Internet Information Office Order" (in Chinese). cbrc.gov.cn, 2016. http://www.cbrc.gov.cn/chinese/home/docDOC_ReadView/D934AAE7E05849D185CD497936D767CF.html.

———. "Guideline on the Custodian Business for Online Lending." cbrc.gov. cn, February 22, 2017.

China Blockchain Technology and Industry Development Forum. *China Blockchain Technology and Application Development White Paper* (in Chinese). Chainb.com, 2016. http://chainb.com/download/工信部-中国区块链 技术和应用发展白皮书1014.pdf.

China Industry Information Network. "Analysis of the Development Status and Industry Development Trend of China's Blockchain Industry in 2018." China Industry Information Network, June 14, 2018. http:// www.chyxx.com/industry/201806/649549.html.

China Institute of Information and Communications (CAICT). *Internet Investment and Financing in the Second Quarter of 2018* (in Chinese). CAICT, 2018.http://www.caict.ac.cn/kxyj/qwfb/qwsj/201807/P020180720343 745695019.pdf.

China Internet Information Center. China Internet Information Center website. 2018. China.org.cn.

China Internet Network Information Center (CNNIC). *Statistical Report on Internet Development in China* (in Chinese). CNNIC.com, January 2017. http://cnnic.com.cn/IDR/ReportDownloads/201706/P020170608523 740585924.pdf.

"China's Leaders in Fintech 2017." *Euromoney*, December 19, 2017. https:// www.euromoney.com/article/b1634tc7d2p1t8/china39s-leaders-in -fintech-2017.

Consultative Group to Assist the Poor (CGAP). "China's Alipay and WeChat Pay: Reaching Rural Users." *CGAP Brief* (December 2017). http://www.cgap .org/sites/default/files/Brief-Chinas-Alipay-and-WeChat-Pay-Dec-2017.pdf.

CreditEase and Yirendai. *China Payment Industry Research Report* (in Chinese). Research presentation, Qichacha, February 2018. http://co-image .qichacha.com/upload/chacha/att/20180206/1517896169579837.pdf.

Creehan, Sean, and Cindy Li. "Asia's Open Banking Push." *Federal Reserve Bank of San Francisco* (Pacific Exchange blog), December 5, 2018. https:// www.frbsf.org/banking/asia-program/pacific-exchange-blog/asias-open -banking-push/.

CSRC. "Be Wary of the 'Illegal Recommendation' Risk of the Internet" (in Chinese). CSRC, July 10, 2018, http://www.csrc.gov.cn.

Dagong Credit Data Co. *Dagong Data Internet Finance Online Loan Platform Early Warning Watch List Report* (in Chinese). Dagong Credit Data Co., 2015. http://iof.hexun.com/upload/yjgc.pdf.

Dasbarman, Debmalya, Chaitanya Tallam, and Karunesh Mohan. *Future of Consumer Banking: The Augmented Way*. Bengaluru, India: Infosys, 2018. https://www.infosys.com/industries/financial-services/white-papers /Documents/future-consumer-banking.pdf.

Davenport, Thomas H. "China Is Catching up to the US on Artificial Intelligence Research." The Conversation, February 27, 2019. http://theconversation .com/china-is-catching-up-to-the-us-on-artificial-intelligence-research -112119.

Demertzis, Maria, Silvia Merler, and Guntram B. Wolff. "Capital Markets Union and the Fintech Opportunity." *Policy Contribution* 22 (September 2017). http://bruegel.org/wp-content/uploads/2017/09/PC-22-2017.pdf.

Diamond, Douglas W., and Philip H. Dybvig. "Bank Runs, Deposit Insurance, and Liquidity." *Journal of Political Economy* 91, no. 3 (1983): 401–419.

Digital Finance Research Center of Peking University. "Digital Inclusive Financial Indicator System and Index Compilation." Working Paper of Digital Finance Research Center of Peking University, 2016.

Dong, Yufeng. "Thoughts and Suggestions on the Development of Postal Savings Bank in the Internet Financial Era" (in Chinese). *Finance and Economy* 6 (2018): 56–58.

Dou, Xinhua, Xinbo Meng, and Fang-zhao Zhou. "Gender Discrimination in P2P Lending—Empirical Study on the Data from Renrendai." *Accounting Science* 32, no. 8 (2018): 121–124.

Du, Jia. "Legal Realization Mechanism of Financial Consumer Rights and Interests Protection in the Internet Age" (in Chinese). *Legal System Expo* 8 (2018): 179.

Du, Jinfu. "Digital Currency Issuance Theory and Path Selection" (in Chinese). *Expert Forum* (2018): 35–36.

Du, Jun, and Li Jiaxin. "Research on Online Cooperation Between E-commerce and Bank Under Internet Environment" (in Chinese). *Journal of Gansu Sciences* 30, no. 1 (2018): 130–138.

Duflos, Eric, and Leora Klapper. "New Accounts in China Drive Global Financial Inclusion Figures." *World Bank* (blog), June 18, 2015. http:// blogs.worldbank.org/eastasiapacific/new-accounts-china-drive-global -financial-inclusion-figures.

Eley, Slavka. "FinTech and Cloud in Banking." Keynote Speech, EBF Cloud Banking Conference, July 12, 2017, Brussels, Belgium. https://eba .europa.eu/documents/10180/2055539/Slavka+Eley+-+Keynote+speech +at+the+EBF+Cloud+banking+Conference.pdf.

Feng, Jian. "Financing Research SME Financing Model and Implementation Path Under the Internet Financial Environment" (in Chinese). *Financing Research* 23 (2018): 13.

Feng, Yan, Xinlu Fan, and Yeujun Yoon. "Lenders and Borrowers' Strategies in Online Peer-to-Peer Lending Market: An Empirical Analysis of PPDAI. com." *Journal of Electronic Commerce Research*, 16, no. 3 (2015). http:// web.csulb.edu/journals/jecr/issues/20153/Paper5.pdf.

Financial Stability Board (FSB). *Artificial Intelligence and Machine Learning in Financial Services: Market Developments and Financial Stability Implications*. Basel, Switzerland: FSB, November 1, 2017. http://www.fsb.org/wp -content/uploads/P011117.pdf.

Fintech Global. "Investment in Chinese FinTech Companies Surpassed $1bn in Q1 2018." Fintech Global, May 16, 2018. http://fintech.global/investment -in-chinese-fintech-companies-surpassed-1bn-in-q1-2018/.

First Online Loan. "2017 National P2P Online Loan Industry Big Data Report" (in Chinese). P2P001.com, January 9, 2018http://www.p2p001 .com/Netloan/shownews/id/16590.html.

Gao, Yu, Shih-Heng Yu, and Yih-Chearng Shiue. "The Performance of the P2P Finance Industry in China." *Electronic Commerce Research and Applications* 30 (2018): 138–148. https://doi.org/10.1016/j.elerap .2018.06.002.

Garvey, Kieran, Brian Zhang, Deborah Ralston, Kong Ying, Rodney Maddock, Hung-Yi Chen, Edward Buckingham, Yianni Katiforis, Luke Deer, Tania Ziegler, Ben Shenglin, Zheng Xinwei, Pawee Jenweeranon, Jingxuan Zhang, Wenwei Li, Rui Hao, and Eva Huang. *The Second Asia Pacific Region Alternative Finance Industry Report*. Cambridge Centre for Alternative Finance at University of Cambridge and Australian Centre for Financial Studies at Monash University. 2017. https://australiancentre.com.au/wp-content /uploads/2017/09/Cutivating-growth.pdf.

Gu, Haifeng, and Lixiang Yang. "Research on Risk Evaluation of Third Party Mobile Payment in China Under Internet Finance" (in Chinese). *Journal of Financial Management Research*, 5 (2017): 1–21.

Gu, Tianxiang. "Nature and Regulation of P2P Network Lending Performance Guarantee Insurance" (in Chinese). *People's Justice* 4 (2018): 17–21.

Guo, Dashan. "Research on Cross-Border RMB Settlement Business of Third-Party Payment Institutions" (in Chinese). *Hainan Finance* 8 (2018): 82–88.

Gemalto. "2017 Data Breach Level Index: Full Year Results Are In. . . ." *Gemalto* (blog), April 13, 2018. https://blog.gemalto.com/security/2018/04/13 /data-breach-stats-for-2017-full-year-results-are-in/.

Han, H. Q. "Fintech in China: An Introduction." Wharton Fintech, Medium, April 1, 2018. https://medium.com/wharton-fintech/fintech-in-china-an -introduction-6b11abd9cb64.

Hao, Chuntian, and Lijuan Xu. "P2P Network Lending Risk and Response Research-Taking 'Ezubao' as an Example" (in Chinese). *Shandong Economy* 28, no. 7 (2018): 28–30.

He, Baohong, Zhang Xueli, Han Han, He Yang, Zhao Bo, Zhang Xiaoye, and Xu Yijun. *China's Financial Technology Frontier Technology Development Trend and Application Scenario Research* (in Chinese). China Institute of Information and Communications Cloud Computing and Big Data Research Institute, 2018. http://www.caict.ac.cn/kxyj/qwfb/ztbg/201804 /P020180116491991162222.pdf.

He, Laura. "Zhong An Generates 70pc of 2017 Car Insurance Premiums in Just One Month." *South China Morning Post*, February 4, 2018. https:// www.scmp.com/business/companies/article/2131449/zhongan-generates -70pc-2017-car-insurance-premiums-just-one-month.

He, Lin, Shuo Cheng, Guan-yi tong Zhang, and Le Zhang. "Desire Demand of Internet Finance for Farmers and Expanding of Rural Financial Market." *Guangdong Agricultural Science* 45, no. 5 (2018): 142–150.

He, Lipeng. "Research on the Innovation Strategy of Commercial Banks Under the Impact of Internet Finance" (in Chinese). *Financial Forum* 1 (2018): 138–139.

He, Zhenggen. "Promoting the Financial Benefits of the Village Area with Digital Financial Innovation" (in Chinese). *Tsinghua Financial Review* (April 2017): 100–101.

Hileman, Garrick, and Michel Rauchs. *Global Blockchain Benchmarking Study*. Cambridge: Cambridge Centre for Alternative Finance, 2017.

Hong Kong Financial Services Development Council (FSDC). "The Future of FinTech in Hong Kong." FSDC Paper No. 29, 2017. http://www.fsdc .org.hk/sites/default/files/FSDC%20Paper_FinTech_E.pdf.

Hou, Heng. "The Application of Blockchain Technology in E-Government in China." 2017 Twenty-Sixth International Conference on Computer Communication and Networks (ICCCN), July 31–August 3, 2017.

Hsu, Sara. "This Chinese Credit Card Company Plans On Outsmarting Tencent and Alipay with a More Secure Product." *Forbes*, July 25, 2017. https:// www.forbes.com/sites/sarahsu/2017/07/25/this-chinese-credit-card -company-plans-on-outsmarting-tencent-and-alipay-with-a-more-secure -product/#5f950de433a0.

———. "Chinese P2P Players Yirendai and Hexindai On Making It in China's Lending Industry." *Forbes*, April 17, 2018. https://www.forbes.com /sites/sarahsu/2018/04/17/chinese-p2p-players-yirendai-and-hexindai -on-making-it-in-chinas-lending-industry/#1e1463383ed2.

Hu, Gang. "Research on Information Security Management Strategy of P Insurance Company Network Mall" (in Chinese). *Modern Information Technology* (2017): 1–7. http://kns.cnki.net/kcms/detail/44.1736.TN.20180212 .1021.108.html.

Hu, Jinxi, and Weishi Song. "The Rational Awareness and Trade-off Behavior of Investors in P2P Lending—An Empirical Analysis Based on the Data of Renrendai" (in Chinese). *Journal of Financial Research* 445, no. 7 (2017): 86–104.

Hu, Jinxi, and Xiaoxiao Zhang. "P2P Platform Under the Influence of Share-holder Background, Default Risk and Business Risk" (in Chinese). *Journal of Shandong University* 4 (2018): 120–129.

Hu, Yuefei. "Digital Supply Chain Finance in the 'Double Light' Era" (in Chinese). *Commercial Bank* (2018): 44–46.

Huang, Robin Hui. "Online P2P Lending and Regulatory Responses in China: Opportunities and Challenges." *European Business Organization Law Review* 19, no. 1 (2018): 63–92.

Huang, Wenbi, and Jiayi Chen. "Analysis of Mobile Terminal Security in Internet Finance Age" (in Chinese). *Computer Knowledge and Technology* 14, no. 19 (2018): 22–23.

Huang, Zhuo, Wang Haiming, Shen Yan, and Xie Lili. *The Chinese Era of Financial Technology: 12 Lectures on Digital Finance.* Beijing: People's University Press, 2017.

Hurst, Samantha. "Chinese Fintech Wecash Raises $160 Million During Series D Funding Round Led by ORIX Asia Capital and SEA Group." Crowd Fund Insider, March 2, 2018. https://www.crowdfundinsider.com/2018/03/129067-chinese-fintech-wecash-raises-160-million-series-d-funding-round-led-orix-asia-capital-sea-group/.

"ICO Is Characterized as Suspected of Illegal Fundraising for a Night of Rich Dreams" (in Chinese). Caixin, September 2, 2017. http://finance.caixin.com/2017-09-02/101139644.html.

International Bank for Reconstruction and Development, World Bank, and People's Republic of China. *Toward Universal Financial Inclusion in China Models, Challenges, and Global Lessons.* Washington, DC: World Bank Group, February 2018. https://openknowledge.worldbank.org/bitstream/handle/10986/29336/FinancialInclusion ChinaP158554.pdf?sequence=9.

International Finance Corporation (IFC). *Blockchain: Opportunities for Private Enterprises in Emerging Markets.* Washington, DC: IFC, 2019.

"Internet Equity Crowdfunding Platform Development Report" (in Chinese). *Beijing Time,* April 3, 2018. https://item.btime.com/m_93dd3311b06c07ce6?page=1.

Investment Research Institute. *2018 Blockchain Investment and Financing Report* (in Chinese). Investment Research Institute, 2018. https://www.chinaventure.com.cn/cmsmodel/report/detail/1422.shtml.

Investor Education Center. *Retail Investor Study Research Report.* Hong Kong: Investor Education Center, December 2017. https://www.thechinfamily.hk/web/common/pdf/about_iec/IEC-Retail-Investor-Study-report.pdf.

Ipsos. *2017 Mobile Payment Usage in China Report.* Ipsos, August 2017. https://www.ipsos.com/sites/default/files/ct/publication/documents/2017-08/Mobile_payments_in_China-2017.pdf.

IYiou Intelligence. "Ant Financial Service Development Turning Event." Ant Financial Case Study, April 25, 2019. https://www.iyiou.com/intelligence/report625.html.

JD Digits Research Institute. "Suptech: The Use of Regulatory Technology in the Regulatory Side" (in Chinese). *JD Finance Report*, August 2018.

JD Finance and CAICT. *Blockchain Solutions for Financial Services* (in Chinese). JD Finance and CAICT, April 2018. https://www.gwkjbc.com/Uploads/2018-08-15/5b73d5f5b6636.pdf.

Jian, Jiaqi, and Wu Fan. "Analysis of the Innovative Development of Personal Banking Business of Commercial Banks in the Internet Finance Era Under the New Normal" (in Chinese). *Financial Forum* 5 (2018): 161–162.

Jiang, Cuiqing, Ruiya Wang, and Ding Yong. "P2P Network Lending Default Prediction Method Incorporating Soft Information" (in Chinese). *Chinese Journal of Management Science* 25, no. 11 (2017): 10–21.

Jiang, Ning. "Analysis on the Transformation of Agricultural Banks Promoting Direct Banks Under Internet Finance" (in Chinese). *National Chinese Core Journal Modern Finance* 11, no. 417 (2017).

Jiang, Xueqing. "Pintec Raises $103m, Partners with Sina to Tap Fintech Sector." *China Daily*, June 6, 2018. http://www.chinadaily.com.cn/a/201806/06/WS5b177534a31001b82571e73d.html.

Jiang, Yan. "Impact and Prospect of Digital Currency Based on the Perspective of Shared Finance" (in Chinese). *Finance and Economy* (2018): 65–66.

Jin, Chenxi. "P2P Network Lending Legal Risk Prevention" (in Chinese). *Economy and Law* 8 (2018): 73–74.

JRJ. "23 percent of China's Financial Industry Will Be Disrupted by AI in the Next 10 Years" (in Chinese). JRJ.com, May 5, 2018. http://money.jrj.com.cn/2018/05/05091024496044.shtml.

Kaiser, Ben, Mireya Jurado, and Alex Ledger. "The Looming Threat of China: An Analysis of Chinese Influence on Bitcoin." arXiv Working Paper, Cornell University, October 5, 2018. https://arxiv.org/pdf/1810.02466.pdf.

Kania, Elsa B., and John K. Costello. *Quantum Hegemony? China's Ambitions and the Challenge to U.S. Innovation Leadership*. Washington, DC: Center for a New American Security, September 2018. https://s3.amazonaws.com/files.cnas.org/documents/CNASReport-Quantum-Tech_FINAL.pdf?mtime=20180912133406.

Kregel, Jan A. "Margins of Safety and Weight of the Argument in Generating Financial Fragility." *Journal of Economics Issues* 31 (1997): 543–548.

Lau, S. Y. *Measuring the Digital Economy. Higher Education Forum Malaysia*. Tencent, 2017. http://www.bnm.gov.my/documents/conference_vol/2017_PaymentSystem/The%20Growth%20of%20Digital%20Payment%20Ecosystem%20in%20China.pdf.

Lee, David (Kuo Chuen), and Ernie G. S. Teo. "Emergence of Fintech and the LASIC Principles." *Journal of Financial Perspectives: FinTech* (Winter 2015): 24–36.

Lee, Emma. "Online Insurance Company Zhong An Rolled Out First Product Zhonglebao." Technode, December 6, 2013. https://technode.com/2013/12/06/online-insurance-company-zhong-an-rolled-out-first-product-zhonglebao/.

Lee, Georgina. "Chinese Banks Boost Fintech Spending and Launch Services to Counter Competition from Internet Giants." *South China Morning Post*, April 5, 2019. https://www.scmp.com/business/banking-finance/article/3004877/chinese-banks-boost-fintech-spending-and-launch-services.

Lei, Xiao. "Improving China's P2P Lending Regulatory System: An Examination of International Regulatory Experience." *US-China Law Review* 13 (2016): 460–473.

Lewis, Rebecca, John McPartland, and Rajeev Ranjan. "Blockchain and Financial Market Innovation." *Economic Perspectives* 41, no. 7 (2017). https://www.chicagofed.org/publications/economic-perspectives/2017/7.

Li, Jianjun, and Yongbin Lu. "Thoughts on the Construction of Internet Finance Courses and Talents Training Mode" (in Chinese). *Chinese University Teaching* 5 (2018): 64–68.

Li, Liao, Li Mengran, and Wang Zhengwei. "Smart Investors: Incomplete Market-Based Interest Rate and Risk Identification—Evidence from P2P Network Lending" (in Chinese). *Economic Research* 7 (2014): 125–137.

Li, Min. "Research on the Choice of Supervision Mode and Optimization Path of Financial Technology: Rethinking on the Supervision Sandbox Model" (in Chinese). *Journal of Financial Management Research* (November 2017): 21–37.

Li, Wei. "Analysis of the Status Quo of Internet Financial Loan in University Campus and Risk Prevention Measures" (in Chinese). *Financial Sight* 8 (2018): 39–41.

Li, Xiaojin, and Wenli Hu. "Research on Supply Chain Financial Model and Practice Based on B2B Platform" (in Chinese). *Economy and Management* 31, no. 5 (2017): 35–38.

Li, Yan. "The Influence of Internet Finance on Traditional Commercial Banks and Countermeasures—Taking Minsheng Bank as an Example." *National Circulation Economy* 22 (2017): 59–60.

Li, Zhihong, Lanteng Wu, and Hongting Tang. "Optimizing the Borrowing Limit and Interest Rate in P2P System: From Borrowers' Perspective." *Hindawi Scientific Programming* (2018): 1–14.

Liao, Wei, Jiang Tuanbiao, and Yu Weifeng. "The Impact of Internet Finance on Bank Innovation Capability—An Empirical Study Based on Panel Data of 58 Commercial Banks" (in Chinese). *Finance and Economics* 9 (2018): 52–57.

Liaowang Institute and China Financial Weekly. "China Social Credit System Development Report 2017." *Liaowang Institute and China Financial Weekly*, 2017.

Lin, Mengyao, and Chen Xiding. "The Impact of Internet Finance on Domestic City Commercial Banks and Countermeasures" (in Chinese). *Time Financial* 11, no. 679 (2017): 78–79.

Liu, Wei, and Jie Wei. " 'Tiandong Model' to Solve the Problems of Rural Internet Financial Services: Background, Experience and Enlightenment (in Chinese). *Guangxi Social Sciences* 28, no. 6 (2018): 116–118.

Liu, Xiao. "Tencent Money-Market Fund Triples in Three Years." Caixin, March 22, 2018. https://www.caixinglobal.com/2018-03-22/tencent-money-market-fund-triples-in-three-years-101224888.html.

Liu, Xiaodong. "Application Research and Development Strategies of Insurance E-commerce in China" (in Chinese). *Management Science, Education Science and Human Development* 72 (20172): 246–251.

Liu, Yuyao. "Research on the Impact of Internet Finance Development on Industrial and Commercial Bank Management" (in Chinese). *Journal of Heilongjiang University of Technology* 18, no. 3 (2018): 112–116.

Lu, Wei, and Hongchang Li. "Research on the Development of Inclusive Finance Under Internet Finance" (in Chinese). *Cooperative Economy and Technology* 9 (2018): 63–65.

Lusardi, Annamaria, and Olivia S. Mitchell. "The Economic Importance of Financial Literacy: Theory and Evidence." *Journal of Economic Literature* 52, no. 1 (2014): 5–44.

McIntyre, Alan, Kelley Conway, Peter Sidebottom, Schira Lillis, and Peter McElwaine-John. *Building the Future-Ready Bank: Banking Technology Vision 2018*. Dublin, Ireland: Accenture, 2018. https://www.accenture.com/_acnmedia/PDF-75/Accenture-Banking-Technology-Vision-2018.pdf.

McKinnon, Ronald I. *Money and Capital in Economics Development*. Washington, DC: Brookings Institution, 1973.

Meyer, David. "Jack Ma's Chinese Fintech Firm Just Raised So Much Money It's Now Worth More Than Goldman Sachs." *Fortune*, June 8, 2018. http://fortune.com/2018/06/08/ant-financial-alipay-14-billion-funding/.

Minamimoto, Hajime. "What Zhong An Group Knows About Efficient Insurance System Development?" *Nomura Research Institute* 277 (February 13, 2018). https://www.nri.com/~/media/PDF/global/opinion/lakyara/2018/lkr2018277.pdf.

Ministry of Industry and Information Technology. *2018 China Blockchain Industry White Paper* (in Chinese). Beijing, China: Ministry of Industry and Information Technology Information Center, May 2018. http://www.miit.gov.cn/n1146290/n1146402/n1146445/c6180238/part/6180297.pdf.

Minsky, Hyman. *The Financial-Instability Hypothesis: Capitalist Processes and the Behavior of the Economy*, edited by Charles P., Kindlberger and Jean-Pierre Laffargue, 13–38. Cambridge: Cambridge University Press, 1982.

Mittal, Sachin, and James Lloyd. "The Rise of Fintech in China: Redefining Financial Services." DBS and EY, 2016. https://www.dbs.com/insights/uploads/20161202-03-Report-031-CHINA-FINTECH-LOWRES.pdf.

Mnuchin, Steven, and Craig Phillips. *A Financial System That Creates Economic Opportunities: Nonbank Financials, Fintech, and Innovation*. Washington, DC: U.S. Department of the Treasury, July 2018. https://home.treasury.gov/sites/default/files/2018-07/A-Financial-System-that-Creates-Economic-Opportunities---Nonbank-Financi....pdf.

Mobile Payments Today. "PayPal's TIO Networks Says Data Breach Affected 1.6M Users." Mobile Payments Today, December 4, 2017. https://www.mobilepaymentstoday.com/news/paypals-tio-networks-says-data-breach-affected-16m-users/.

Murphy, Matthew, and Fei Dang. "Cloud Computing in China." Lexology, March 21, 2019. https://www.lexology.com/library/detail.aspx?g=998fe1a0-6634-41e7-a670-19ca406709e5.

Nanjing Rural Finance Society Research Group. "Innovative Practice and Enlightenment of Commercial Bank Retail Transformation" (in Chinese). *National Chinese Core Journal Modern Finance* 7 (2018): 6–9.

National Bureau of Statistics of China. "Annual Data." National Bureau of Statistics, 2017. http://www.stats.gov.cn/english/Statisticaldata/AnnualData/.

National Internet Finance Association of China (NIFAC). "NIFAC Rule on Self-Regulation of Information Disclosure." wdzj.com, October 28, 2016. https://www.wdzj.com/zhuanti/xpbz/.

Oliver Wyman. *China Credit-Tech Market Report*. Oliver Wyman, April 2019. https://www.oliverwyman.com/content/dam/oliver-wyman/v2/publications/2019/apr/china-credit-tech-market-report-4.pdf.

———. *China Insuretech: Industry Report*. Oliver Wyman, October 2016. https://www.oliverwyman.com/content/dam/oliver-wyman/global/en/2016/oct/OliverWyman_ChinaInsuretech.pdf.

Online Loan Home. "P2P Active Investment and Borrowings" (in Chinese). Online Loan Home, 2018. https://www.wdzj.com/wdzj/front/search/index?type=12&referer=//www.wdzj.com/front/search/index&key=%25E6%259C%2588%25E6%258A%25A5.

Oracle. *Cloud Computing in Financial Services: A Banker's Guide*. Redwood Shores, CA: Oracle, November 2015. http://www.oracle.com/us/industries/financial-services/cloud-compute-financial-services-wp-3124965.pdf.

Pan, Qifeng, and Mingmin Zhao. "The Strategy of Agricultural Banks' Layout Optimization Under the Background of Internet Finance" (in Chinese). *National Chinese Core Journal Modern Finance* 10 (2017): 54–55.

Payone. "Payment Code Scams Are Rampant" (in Chinese). Payone, December 27, 2017. https://zhuanlan.zhihu.com/p/32383607.

Peng, Hongfeng, and Ruifeng Xu. "Is the Interest Rate Pricing of the P2P Online Lending Platform Reasonable? Based on Empirical Evidence of Renrendai" (in Chinese). *Financial Forum* 9, no. 273 (2018): 61–80.

People's Bank of China (in Chinese). 2018. www.pbc.gov.cn.

Ping An Finance. *2017 Internet Wealth Management White Paper.* Ping An Finance, January 22, 2018. https://www.wdzj.com/hjzs/ptsj/20180122/505353-1.html.

Ping, Na, and Yue-yue Sun. "Study on the Risk of P2P Lending for College Students and Preventive Measure" (in Chinese). *Management and Technology of SMEs* 2 (2018): 100–101.

PricewaterhouseCoopers (PwC). *Global Fintech Survey China Summary 2017.* PwC Report, 2017. https://www.pwccn.com/en/financial-services/publications/fintech/global-fintech-survey-china-summary-jun2017.pdf.

———. *PWC Hong Kong Fintech Survey.* PwC, 2017. https://www.pwchk.com/en/financial-services/publications/fintech/hong-kong-fintech-survey-2017.pdf.

———. *PWC's Global Blockchain Survey 2018.* PwC, 2018. https://www.pwccn.com/en/research-and-insights/publications/global-blockchain-survey-2018/global-blockchain-survey-2018-report.pdf.

———. *2018 Market Survey Report for (Non-financial) Application of Blockchain in China.* PwC, 2018. https://www.pwccn.com/en/risk-assurance/2018-china-blockchain-survery-report-en.pdf.

Prospective Industry Research Institute. "2016 P2P Online Loan Market Volume and Platform Statistics" (in Chinese). Qianzhan, 2018. https://bg.qianzhan.com/report/detail/459/170116-76b6eb15.html.

———. "2018 China's Internet Consumer Finance Development Status and Market Trends Analysis of the Explosive Growth of Lending Scale" (in Chinese). Qianzhan, February 8, 2019. https://www.qianzhan.com/analyst/detail/220/190201-20f83e47.html.

Pu, Yiyi. "Edition. Traffic Wars Slogan, Brokerage Network Finance Trend 2.0 Era" (in Chinese). *Shanghai Securities News* 002 (January 25, 2018): 1–3.

Qian, Cheng. "Exploration on the Transformation and Innovation of Local Small and Medium-sized Banks Under the Impact of Internet Finance" (in Chinese). *Hangzhou Science and Technology* 6 (2017): 57–60.

Qian, Yao. "Technical Considerations of the Central Bank's Digital Currency." Yicai News, March 8, 2018. https://www.yicai.com/news/5404436.html.

Qin, Jianwen, Tao Wang, and Bangding Huang. "The Study of Chinese Listed Bank's Efficiency Growth Mode in Internet Finance Era—Based on Full-Combination DEA-PCA Model." *American Journal of Industrial and Business Management* 6, no. 11 (2016): 1032–1052.

Qishang Bank Co., Ltd. "Analysis of Six Specific Innovation Models of Bank Supply Chain Finance from the Perspective of Internet" (in Chinese). *China Banking Industry* 3, no. 81 (2018): 78–81.

Qudian. "Qudian Management Presentation." Qudian.com, May 2018. ir.qudian.com%2Fdownload%2FQD%2BMP_20180515.pdf.

Ren, Daniel. "China Regulators Warn that 90 pc of Peer-to-Peer Lenders Could Fail in 2017." *South China Morning Post*, February 19, 2017. https://www.scmp.com/business/china-business/article/2072177 /china-regulators-warns-90-pc-peer-peer-lenders-could-fail.

Report Hall. "P2P Online Loan Industry Status and 2017 Development Trend Analysis: The Number of Platforms Shrinks" (in Chinese). Report Hall, July 31, 2018. http://www.chinabgao.com/freereport/76214.html.

Reuters. "Leader of China's $9 billion Ezubao Online Scam Gets Life; 26 Jailed." Reuters, September 12, 2017. https://www.reuters.com/article /us-china-fraud/leader-of-chinas-9-billion-ezubao-online-scam-gets-life -26-jailed-idUSKCN1BN0J6.

Rogers, Jonathan. "Digital China: New Wealth Gets Wise." *Global Finance*, February 15, 2018. https://www.gfmag.com/magazine/february-2018 /digital-china-new-wealth-gets-wise.

Russom, Philip. *Big Data Analytics.* TDWI Best Practices Report. Seattle, WA: The Data Warehousing Institute, Fourth Quarter 2011. http://tdwi .org/research/2011/09/best-practices-report-q4-big-data-analytics.aspx.

Schroeder, Stan. "Cryptocurrency Verge Gets Hacked with a Dangerous New Attack." Mashable, April 5, 2018. https://mashable.com/2018/04/05 /verge-crypto-hack/#w6a63u5U0iqJ.

Schumpeter, Joseph A. *Capitalism, Socialism and Democracy.* New York: Harper, 1950.

———. *The Theory of Economic Development: An Inquiry into Profits, Capital, Credit, Interest and the Business Cycle.* Cambridge, MA: Harvard University Press, 1934.

Scott, Allen. "China Celebrates Killing Its Bitcoin Exchanges as CNY Volume Falls Under 1 Percent." Bitcoinist, July 10, 2018. https://bitcoinist.com /china-bitcoin-exchanges-volume-falls-1/.

Shaw, Edward S. *Financial Deepening in Economic Development.* New York: Oxford University Press, 1973

Shen, Ciyou. "The Impact of the Development of Financial Technology on Securities Companies" (in Chinese). Jianshu.com.cn, March 30, 2017. https://www.jianshu.com/p/23527afc9bfb.

Shen, Jianguo, and Jiakun Shen. "Research on the Development of Internet Finance" (in Chinese). *Digital Economy* 22 (2018): 188–189.

Shen, Yan, and Cangshu Li. *Research on Network Borrowing Risk Relief Mechanism* (in Chinese). Research Group of Digital Finance Research Center of Peking University, May 20, 2018. http://osscdn.wdzj.com/upload /fengxianhuanshi.pdf.

Sheng, Cliff, Jasper Yip, and James Cheng. *Fintech in China: Hitting the Moving Target*. Oliver Wyman, August 2017. http://www.oliverwyman.com /content/dam/oliver-wyman/v2/publications/2017/aug/Fintech_In _China_Hitting_The_Moving_Target.pdf.

Shih, Ken. *China Fintech Sector*. DBS Group Research, January 22, 2018. https://www.dbs.com.sg/corporate/aics/pdfController.page?pdfpath =/content/article/pdf/AIO/092018/180924_insights_bargain_hunting _opportunity.pdf.

Shih, Ken, and Keith Tsang. *China Insurance Sector*. DBS Research, November 1, 2017.

Shuang, Shuang. "Research on the Status Quo of Internet Insurance Development and Business Management Model in China—Taking Zhongan Online as an Example" (in Chinese). ems86.com, 2018. http://www.ems86.com /fuwu/html/?69229.html.

Song, Weishi. "The Risk Preference of Investor Group in P2P Lending Pattern." *Financial Forum* 6 (2017): 21–37.

Soo, Zen. "China's Mobile Payment Giants Forcing Incumbents to Innovate." *South China Morning Post*, December 16, 2017. https://www.scmp .com/tech/china-tech/article/2124512/chinas-mobile-payment-giants -forcing-incumbents-innovate.

Spence, Michael. "Job Market Signaling." *Quarterly Journal of Economics* 87, no. 3 (1973): 355–374.

Stamegna, Carla, and Cemal Karakas. *Fintech (Financial Technology) and the European Union: State of Play and Outlook*. European Parliamentary Research Service, February 2019. https://www.fintech2019.eu/wp-content/uploads /2019/03/EPRS_BRI2019635513_EN.pdf.

State Council. *Guiding Opinions on Advancing the Healthy Development of Internet Finance* (in Chinese). Ministry of Finance, People's Republic of China, 2015. http://www.mof.gov.cn/zhengwuxinxi/zhengcefabu/201507 /t20150720_1332370.htm.

———. "China to Boost Inclusive Finance." State Council, People's Republic of China, January 15, 2016. http://english.gov.cn/policies/latest_releases /2016/01/15/content_281475272471306.htm.

Stern, Caroline, Mikko Mäkinen, and Zongxin Qian. "FinTechs in China— With a Special Focus on Peer to Peer Lending." *Journal of Chinese Economic and Foreign Trade Studies* 10, no. 3 (2017): 215–228.

Su, Yixin. "Legal Regulation and Improvement of Equity Crowdfunding in the Perspective Internet Finance—Taking Xiamen Ximing District Equity Crowdfunding Platform 'Xiaxue Credit' as an Example" (in Chinese). *Journal of Anhui Vocational College of Police Officers* 4 (2017): 68–70.

Sun, Guofeng. "Developing Regulatory Technology to Build a New Financial Ecology" (in Chinese). *Tsinghua Financial Review* 3 (2018): 16–19.

Sun, Mancy, Piyush Mubayi, Tian Lu, and Stanley Tian. *Future of Finance: The Rise of China Fintech.* Goldman Sachs, 2017. https://hybg.cebnet .com.cn/upload/gaoshengfintech.pdf.

Sun, Wei. "Analysis of the Impact of Internet Finance Development on China's Commercial Banks and Countermeasures" (in Chinese). *Modern Marketing* (2018): 97–98.

Sun, Wujun, and Fan Xiaoying. "Borrowing Quota, Financier Heterogeneity and Success Rate of Lending—Experience Evidence from the P2P Platform 'Renrendai'" (in Chinese). *Journal of Beijing Institute of Technology* 32, no. 4 (2017): 97–107.

Tang, Wei. "Development Research and Innovation Path of Third Party Payment Platform Under 'Internet + .'" *Business Economics* 8 (2018): 171–173.

Tao, Qizhi, Dong Yizhe, and Ziming Lin. "Who Can Get Money? Evidence from the Chinese Peer-to-Peer Lending Platform." *Information Systems Frontiers* 19, no. 3 (2017): 425–441.

"Top FinTech Startups in Wealthtech." Fintechnews.hk, August 2017. http:// fintechnews.hk/top-20-fintech-startups-hong-kong/.

Tsai, Gerald. "Fintech and the U.S. Regulatory Response." Remarks at the Fourth Bund Summit on Fintech, Federal Reserve Bank of San Francisco, July 9, 2017, San Francisco, CA.

VanderLinden, Sabine L. B., Shan M. Millie, Nicole Anderson, and Susanne Chishti. *The Insuretech Book.* Chichester, UK: Wiley, 2018.

Wang, Chunli. "Auditing Problems and Countermeasures of Commercial Banks in the Age of Internet Finance" (in Chinese). *Financial Economy* 5 (2018): 53–54.

Wang, Gang-zhen, and Xu Wu. "Research on the Model of Internet Financial Poverty Alleviation Based on E-commerce Platform—An Example of Jingdong." *Journal of UESTC* 20, no. 4 (2018): 1–6.

Wang, Jiaxin, and Wang Juan. "A Review of Public Welfare Crowd Research on Social Media Text" (in Chinese). *E-Finance* 8 (2018): 47–49.

Wang, Lili, and Hong Wang. "Analysis on the Innovation Practice of the Bill Market Under the Background of Internet Finance" (in Chinese). *Journal of Wuhu Vocational and Technical College* 20, no. 2 (2018): 37–40.

Wang, Liqiang. "Financial Technology Protects Financial Security" (in Chinese). Ant Financial Service ATEC City Summit, The New Force of Digital Finance, February 24, 2019. https://www.jianshu.com/p/ 75af67e247b2.

Wang, Ruihua. "Reinterpretation of Money Supply Under the Internet Environment" (in Chinese). *Bank Management* 3 (2018): 55–58.

Wang, Wei, and David Dollar. *What's Happening with China's Fintech Industry?* Brookings Institution, February 8, 2018. https://www.brookings.edu /blog/order-from-chaos/2018/02/08/whats-happening-with-chinas -fintech-industry/.

Wang, Xingnan, and Rui Huang. *Fintech in China's Capital Market.* Nomura, September 2017. https://www.nomurafoundation.or.jp/wordpress/wp -content/uploads/2017/09/NJACM2-1AU17-03_CHINA.pdf.

Wang, Xudong. "The Establishment of College Students' Credit Evaluation System Under the Background of Internet Finance" (in Chinese). *Fiscal Taxation* 9 (2018): 81–83.

Wang, Ying. "How to Build Integrated Services for Commercial Banks in the Internet + Era" (in Chinese). *Time Finance* 7 (2018): 94–95.

Watts, Gordon. "Fears Grow Over Chinese Investors Snared in $11 Billion Fraud Probe." *AI Times,* January 15, 2018. http://www.atimes.com/article /fears-grow-chinese-investors-snared-11-billion-fraud-probe/.

WeBank. *Annual Report of WeBank 2017.* WeBank, 2018. https://www .webankcdn.net/s/hjupload/app/pdf/annual_report_2017.pdf.

Wei, Yang. China Financial Technology Enterprise Database. Fintechdb.cn, 2018. http://www.fintechdb.cn/.

Wen, Hao. "Yirendai APP Heavy Upgrade: Wealth Management Begins with the Promotion of 'Financial Business'" (in Chinese). Sohu, May 25, 2019. http://www.sohu.com/a/316378365_115931.

Werker, Aleid. "The Role of Alipay in Commerce in China." Master's thesis, Leiden University, Netherlands, 2017. https://openaccess.leidenuniv.nl /bitstream/handle/1887/51299/Aleid%20Werker%2C%20MA%20THESIS .pdf?sequence=1.

Weston, J. Fred, Susan E. Hoag, and Kwang S. Chung. *Mergers, Restructuring and Corporate Control.* New York: Prentice Hall, 1998.

WIND. Wind Data, 2018. www.wind.com.cn.

Woetzel, Jonathan, Jeongmin Seong, Kevin Wei Wang, James Manyika, Michael Chui, and Wendy Wong. *China's Digital Economy: A Leading Global Force.* McKinsey Global Institute, August 2017. https://www.mckinsey.com /featured-insights/china/chinas-digital-economy-a-leading-global-force.

World Bank. Global Findex Database, 2014. http://datatopics.worldbank .org/financialinclusion/.

Wu, Gewei. "Analysis of the Influence of Internet Finance on the Development of Real Estate Industry" (in Chinese). *Technology and Economic Guide* 26 (2018): 180–181.

Xiao, Mingrui. "Virtual Speculation, Hundreds of Millions of Investment Funds Online Evaporation" (in Chinese). *Rule of Law Online* (2018): 46–47.

Xiao, Yang. "Internet Insurance Market Analysis Report for the First Half of 2017" (in Chinese). csai.cn, August 25, 2017. https://www.csai.cn /baoxian/1247123.html.

Xie, Echo. "China Working on Data Privacy Law but Enforcement Is a Stumbling Block." *South China Morning Post*, May 5, 2019. https://www.scmp.com/news/china/politics/article/3008844/china-working-data-privacy-law-enforcement-stumbling-block.

Xinhua. "Xi Jinping: Speech at the Nineteenth Academician Conference of the Chinese Academy of Sciences and the Fourteenth Academician Conference of the Chinese Academy of Engineering." Xinhuanet, May 28, 2018. http://www.xinhuanet.com/politics/2018-05/28/c_1122901308.htm.

Xu, Chao. "Analysis of the Ways of Internet Finance Promoting the Development of Rural Inclusive Finance" (in Chinese). *Times Finance* 3 (2018): 31–32.

Xu, Endong, Xiao Liu, Jun Wu, and Xiaoyu Shi. "The Exploration of the Central Bank's Legal Currency" (in Chinese). *Times Finance* 7 (2018): 14–15.

Xu, Meng. "Third Party Network Platform Engaged in Insurance Business Legal Regulation" (in Chinese). *Insurance Law* (2018): 58–70.

Xu, Qian. "Research on the Demand of Financial Talents in Small and Medium Cities Under the Background of Internet—Taking Lianyungang City, Jiangsu Province as an Example" (in Chinese). *Times Finance* 7 (2018): 113–114.

Xue, Lei. "Discussion of the Risks and Risk Control of P2P in China." *Modern Economy* 7 (2016): 399–403.

Yan, Lingjian. "Online Investment Wants to Double the Income but Can't Withdraw Cash" (in Chinese). *Modern Express Special Feature* (2018): 26–27.

Yan, Siyan. "Robotic Process Automation RC Opportunities in the Financial Industry." Chinabyte, May 21, 2018. http://info.chinabyte.com/464/245964.shtml.

Yang, Bing. "List of Direct Selling Banks in China in the First Half of 2018" (in Chinese). *Internet Weekly*, August 5, 2018, 38–39.

Yang, Jingjing. "Risk and Regulation of Chinese Online Investment Products." *Chinese Business Review* 16, no. 5 (2017): 234–244.

Yang, Yaqin. "Application Analysis of Big Data Anti-fraud in Bank Internet Finance Innovation Business" (in Chinese). *Modern Economic Information* (2018): 328.

Yao, Junxian. "Research on New Threats and Protection Technologies Faced by Bank Internet Financial Platform" (in Chinese). *Technical Application* (September 2017): 76–77.

Yi, Yiyi. "On the Impact of China's Internet Insurance Development on Traditional Insurance—Taking 'Zhongan Insurance' as an Example" (in Chinese). *Inner Mongolia Science Technology and Economy* 2 (2018): 36–38.

Yilongdai. "Yilongdai Helps Farmers." Yilongdai, June 15, 2018. https://cj.eloancn.com/about/snNews-157.html.

Yin, Hang. "P2P Lending Industry in China." *International Journal of Industrial and Business Management* 1, no. 4 (2017): 1–13.

Yiou Think Tank. *Financial Technology Company Service Banking Research Report* (in Chinese). Yiou Think Tank, September 6, 2018. https://www
.iyiou.com/intelligence/report576.

Yu, Benita, and Jason Webber. "Hong Kong." *ICLG TO: FINTECH*, 2018.
https://www.slaughterandmay.com/media/2536387/fintech-in-hong
-kong-2018.pdf.

Yu, Pei, and Jiayi Xu. *Internet Finance Industry In-depth Research* (in Chinese).
Sinolink Securities Report, March 2018. http://pg.jrj.com.cn/acc/Res
/CN_RES/INDUS/2018/3/6/ceb73bb1-be3c-44bf-8690-766f16bca0f6
.pdf.

Yu, Weifeng, and Yi Zhou. "Internet Finance, Commercial Bank Scale and
Risk" (in Chinese). *Journal of Yunnan University of Finance and Economics* 189, no. 1 (2018).

Yu, Xugang. "Comparative Analysis of China's Banking Business Performance
Based on SCP Perspective in Internet Financial Environment—Taking
China Merchants Bank and Minsheng Bank as Examples" (in Chinese).
Financial Observation 2 (2018): 137–138.

Yun, Zhongyan. "Online Creditors Personally Remember How: 8 Loan
Companies Let Me Accumulate Liabilities" (in Chinese). *Securities Times*,
June 14, 2018. http://news.stcn.com/2018/0614/14315669.shtml.

Zembrowski, Piotr. "China's Mutual Funds: Two Charts." Fund Selector Asia,
February 8, 2018. https://fundselectorasia.com/chinas-mutual-funds-two
-charts/.

Zhang, Chuanming. "Everbright Bank's New On-line 'Wealth Check' Features Eye Science Hedge" (in Chinese). Zhongxin Net Jiangsu, May 29,
2019. http://www.js.chinanews.com/75/2019/0529/59604.html.

Zhang, Di. "Financial Technology 2019 Is Booming: Artificial Intelligence,
Blockchain Applications Are Accelerating" (in Chinese). Asiaott, February
13, 2019. https://www.asiaott.com/2019/02/13-178850.html.

Zhang, Jianmin. "Is Network Security Insurance Ready?" *Insurance*, July 1,
2017, 58–59.

Zhang, Jingjing. "The Problems and Countermeasures of ICBC Developing
Internet Finance" (in Chinese). *Times Finance* 7 (2018): 135.

Zhang, Joe. *Chasing Subprime Credit: How China's Fintech Sector Is Thriving.*
Hong Kong: Enrich Professional, 2017.

Zhang, Maggie. "China Construction Bank Opens a Branch Managed
by Robots." *South China Morning Post*, April 11, 2018. https://www
.scmp.com/business/companies/article/2141203/meet-new-face-branch
-banking.

Zhang, Nanfei. "Rationality of Investors in P2P Online Lending Platform
with Guarantee Mechanism: Evidence in China." *Journal of Applied
Finance and Banking* 7, no. 3 (2017): 1–8.

Zhang, Ronggang, and Jingping Xu. "Path Selection and Risk Screening of Small Micro Enterprise Network Crowdfunding." *Science Research Management* 39, no. 8 (2018): 219–225.

Zhang, Wen. "Research on the Innovation of Supply Chain Financial Model in Commercial Banks" (in Chinese). *National Chinese Core Journal Modern Finance* 7 (2018): 23–27.

Zhang, Yan. "UPS and JD.com's Distinctive Supply Chain Financial Services" (in Chinese). *Case and Practice* 4, (2017): 65–67.

Zhang, Yihan. "Analysis on the Development Path of Commercial Bank's Financial Management Business Under the Internet Financial Environment." *China International Business* 7 (2018): 296.

Zhang, Yuejin, Haifeng Li, Mo Hai, Jiaxuan Li, and Aihua Li. "Information Technology and Quantitative Management: Determinants of Loan Funded Successful in Online P2P." *Procedia Computer Science* 122 (2017): 896–901.

Zhang, Yuwen. "Feasibility Analysis of China's Central Bank Digital Currency Based on the Change of Currency Form" (in Chinese). *Financial Forum* 1 (2018): 127–129.

Zhang, Yuzhe, Peng Qinqin, and Dong Tongjian. "China Gives Little Credit to Companies Handpicked to Develop Credit-Reporting Sector." Caixin, May 15, 2017. https://www.caixinglobal.com/2017-05-15/china-gives -little-credit-to-companies-handpicked-to-develop-credit-reporting-sector -101089851.html.

Zhao, Shengmin, and Liu Xiaotian. "China's Macroprudential Policy Research on Coordination Issues." *Contemporary Finance and Economics* 2 (2018): 49–61.

Zhao, Wolfie. "Chinese Bank Issues Securities Worth $66 Million on a Blockchain." Coindesk, August 21, 2018. https://www.coindesk.com /china-zheshang-bank-issues-securities-worth-66-million-on-blockchain/.

Zheng, Xiling. "Research on the Identification and Inclination Protection of Internet Finance Consumers" (in Chinese). *Hainan Finance* 8 (2018): 51–57.

Zheng, Ying-Fei, and Xiao-Jing Chen. "The Principal and Interest Guarantee of P2P Online Lending and Investors' Reaction" (in Chinese). *Financial Forum* 1 (2018): 66–80.

Zheng, Yining. "The Impact of the Central Bank's Plan to Issue Digital Currency on Monetary Policy" (in Chinese). *Financial View* 33 (2017): 89–90.

Zhou, Jack. "Digital Financial Inclusion Growing in China." *China Daily*, January 13, 2018. http://www.chinadaily.com.cn/a/201801/13/WS5a59b 862a3102c394518f050.html.

Zhu, Huasheng, and Zach Zhizhong Zhou. "Analysis and Outlook of Applications of Blockchain Technology to Equity Crowdfunding in China." *Financial Innovation* 2 (2016): 29.

Zhu, Xianyin. "Analysis of the Connotation of Equity Crowdfunding and Its Legal Value." *Economic Law* (2018): 144–148.

Index